complete
perfect
recipes

complete perfect recipes

David Herbert

photography by Andre Martin

LANTERN

an imprint of
PENGUIN BOOKS

LANTERN

Published by the Penguin Group
Penguin Group (Australia)
250 Camberwell Road, Camberwell, Victoria 3124, Australia
(a division of Pearson Australia Group Pty Ltd)
Penguin Group (USA) Inc.
375 Hudson Street, New York, New York 10014, USA
Penguin Group (Canada)
90 Eglinton Avenue East, Suite 700, Toronto, Canada ON M4P 2Y3
(a division of Pearson Penguin Canada Inc.)
Penguin Books Ltd
80 Strand, London WC2R 0RL England
Penguin Ireland
25 St Stephen's Green, Dublin 2, Ireland
(a division of Penguin Books Ltd)
Penguin Books India Pvt Ltd
11 Community Centre, Panchsheel Park, New Delhi – 110 017, India
Penguin Group (NZ)
67 Apollo Drive, Rosedale, North Shore 0632, New Zealand
(a division of Pearson New Zealand Ltd)
Penguin Books (South Africa) (Pty) Ltd
24 Sturdee Avenue, Rosebank, Johannesburg 2196, South Africa

Penguin Books Ltd, Registered Offices: 80 Strand, London, WC2R 0RL, England

First published as *The Perfect Cookbook* (Penguin Books Australia Ltd, 2003)
and *More Perfect Recipes* (Penguin Group (Australia), 2005)
This edition, with additional recipes, published by Penguin Group (Australia), 2007

10 9 8 7 6 5 4 3 2

Text copyright © David Herbert 2003, 2005, 2007
Photographs copyright © Andre Martin 2003, 2005

'Slow-roasted Pork' from *Nigella Bites* by Nigella Lawson published by Chatto & Windus.
Used by permission of Random House Group Limited.
Extracted from *Nigella Bites* by Nigella Lawson. Copyright Text © Nigella Lawson 2001.
Reprinted by permission of Knopf Canada.

Cover design by Daniel New © Penguin Group (Australia)
Text design by Louise Leffler and Brad Maxwell © Penguin Group (Australia)
Photographs by Andre Martin
Typeset in Meta and Bembo by Post Pre-press Group, Brisbane, Queensland
Printed and bound in Singapore through Imago Productions

National Library of Australia
Cataloguing-in-Publication data:

    Herbert, David.
    Complete perfect recipes.

    Includes index.
    ISBN 978 1 920 98980 4 (pbk).

    1. Cookery. I. Title

    641.5

www.penguin.com.au

For Freya, Rosie, Ella and Rory.
And to Frankie, with love.

an a-z of perfect recipes

introduction.

Complete Perfect Recipes has grown out of a series of articles originally written for *The Weekend Australian* newspaper. Each recipe included a method and a few helpful tips. The catch was that I only had 150 words for the whole lot!

Undaunted, I worked away at choosing classic recipes that were interesting and approachable and that would work every time. So began the 'perfect' recipes. The first one I wrote was the 'perfect roast chicken', which is still one of my most requested recipes by readers of the newspaper. I tested the recipe over and over again to make sure it was just right – it took me nearly a week to reduce the method to the required length. For me, writing the 'perfect' column has been a wonderful exercise in researching, refining, adapting and testing recipes to fit this straightforward format.

This book is a collection of my very favourites from the weekly column over the years (now expanded), along with a few new dishes. The recipes reflect my approach to cooking and eating – simple, nostalgic and eclectic, but never fussy or difficult. Anything that was too complicated, too demanding or lengthy did not make its way into the pages. The bottom line was that the recipes had to be foolproof and the dishes had to stand the test of time.

So cook them, taste them, change them to suit your individual taste. Use them as a base to expand your skills. Experiment! After all, it is only food. For the perfect mix, approach these recipes with a sense of fun, not with anxiety. Use good-quality seasonal ingredients and you can't go wrong.

affogato.

4 scoops good-quality vanilla ice-cream

50 ml (1¾ fl oz) Frangelico or amaretto liqueur

4 shots espresso coffee, freshly made

Place a scoop of ice-cream in each of four small glasses or demitasse (espresso cups). Drizzle an equal amount of the alcohol over each scoop of ice-cream and follow with the hot coffee. Serve immediately.

Serves 4

almond bread.

200 g (6½ oz) blanched almonds

5 egg whites

salt

200 g (6½ oz) caster (superfine) sugar

185 g (6 oz) plain (all-purpose) flour, sifted

Preheat the oven to 180°C (350°F, Gas Mark 4). Lightly grease a 23 × 11 × 8 cm (9 × 4½ × 3 in) loaf tin and line the base and two long sides with baking paper.

Spread the almonds on an oven tray and roast in the oven for 4–6 minutes, or until lightly toasted. Allow to cool.

Place the egg whites and a pinch of salt in a clean, dry bowl. Beat with an electric mixer on medium speed until stiff peaks form. (When you lift the mixer out of the bowl, the mixture should cling to the beaters, forming stiff and moist-looking peaks.) Add the sugar a little at a time, beating well after each addition. Beat until the mixture is stiff and glossy.

Gently fold the almonds and flour through the egg and sugar mixture with a large metal spoon. Spoon the mixture into the prepared tin and bake for 35–40 minutes, or until firm and lightly coloured. Remove from the oven and allow to cool in the tin.

Reduce the oven temperature to 140°C (275°F, Gas Mark 1).

Remove the almond bread from the tin and cut into 5 mm (¼ in) slices using a serrated knife. Place slices in a single layer on two baking sheets and 'dry' in the preheated oven, turning once, for 10–15 minutes, or until crisp and lightly golden. Cool on a wire rack.

Serve with coffee or as an accompaniment to ice-cream. This almond bread can be stored in an airtight container for up to 2 weeks.

Makes 35 slices

anzac biscuits.

These delicious oat and coconut biscuits were originally made to be sent in food parcels to Australian and New Zealand troops stationed in Europe during World War I. The recipe was created and named for the soldiers of the Australia and New Zealand Army Corps, hence the name Anzac.

1 cup plain (all-purpose) flour

1 cup rolled oats

1 cup desiccated (shredded) coconut

$^3/_4$ cup sugar

salt

$^1/_4$ cup golden syrup

125 g (4 oz) unsalted butter, cubed

1 teaspoon bicarbonate of soda
  (sodium bicarbonate)

2 tablespoons boiling water

Preheat the oven to 180°C (350°F, Gas Mark 4). Line two baking trays with baking paper.

Sift the flour into a mixing bowl and stir in the oats, coconut, sugar and a pinch of salt. Make a well in the centre.

Place the golden syrup and butter in a small saucepan. Stir over low heat until the butter has melted. In a cup, dissolve the bicarbonate of soda in the boiling water and add to the butter mixture. The mixture will foam a little.

Pour the butter mixture into the well in the centre of the dry ingredients and stir with a wooden spoon until combined. Add a little extra water if the mixture is dry.

Drop tablespoonfuls of the mixture onto the prepared trays, leaving 3 cm (1¼ in) between each to allow for spreading.

Bake for 12–15 minutes, or until golden. Allow to cool on the trays for a few minutes before transferring to wire racks to cool completely. Store in an airtight container for up to 2 weeks.

Makes 30

apple and cinnamon teacake.

This is a great cake – the sliced apples, sugar and cinnamon cook together to create a delicious topping.

1⅓ cups plain (all-purpose) flour

1 teaspoon baking powder

½ teaspoon salt

150 g (5 oz) unsalted butter, at room temperature

⅔ cup caster (superfine) sugar

finely grated zest of 1 lemon

3 eggs

¼ cup milk

2 Granny Smith apples

2 tablespoons demerara sugar or raw sugar

2 teaspoons ground cinnamon

Preheat the oven to 180°C (350°F, Gas Mark 4). Lightly grease a 23 cm (9 in) spring-form cake tin and line the base with baking paper.

Sift the flour, baking powder and salt into a bowl.

In a separate bowl, beat the butter, caster sugar and lemon zest with an electric mixer until fluffy, pale and well combined. Beat in the eggs one at a time, alternating with a little flour mixture, until all the eggs have been added. Fold in the remaining flour, then stir in the milk until the mixture is smooth. Spoon the batter into the prepared tin.

Peel, halve, core and thinly slice the apples and arrange on top of the cake, pressing down slightly. Combine the demerara sugar and cinnamon and sprinkle it over the apple.

Bake for 55–60 minutes, or until the cake feels firms to the touch and a skewer inserted into the centre comes out clean. Allow to cool in the tin for 10 minutes before removing and cooling on a wire rack.

apple pie.

1 quantity homemade regular shortcrust
　　pastry (see page 290), or 1 × 380 g
　　(12 oz) packet bought frozen shortcrust
　　pastry, thawed
5 large Granny Smith apples or cooking
　　apples
20 g (³/₄ oz) butter

½ cup caster (superfine) sugar
1 tablespoon lemon juice
2 tablespoons cornflour (cornstarch)
1 teaspoon ground cinnamon
pinch of ground cloves
1 egg, beaten
caster sugar, extra, to sprinkle

Prepare the pastry according to the instructions on page 290 and refrigerate for at least 30 minutes.

Peel, core and cut the apples into chunks.

Melt the butter in a large saucepan and add the apple, sugar, lemon juice and 1 tablespoon of water. Cook over medium heat for 5–7 minutes, or until the apple has softened. Taste and add extra sugar if needed.

Sprinkle over the cornflour and spices and cook, stirring well, for a further 1 minute. Set aside to cool.

Preheat the oven to 190°C (375°F, Gas Mark 5). Grease a 23 cm (9 in) pie tin or dish.

Roll out two-thirds of the dough between two sheets of baking paper until large enough to line the base and sides of the tin. Line the tin with the pastry, allowing any excess to hang over the sides. Pile the apple mixture into the pastry case.

Roll out the remaining pastry until large enough to cover the pie. Place over the pie and press the edges together to seal. Make two incisions in the centre of the lid for the steam to escape. Trim any overhanging pastry and brush the top of the pie with the beaten egg. Sprinkle the top with the extra caster sugar.

Bake for 40 minutes, or until golden.

Serves 8

apple tart.

This is my favourite kind of food – fast and simple (especially when made using ready-rolled puff pastry).

3 tablespoons apricot jam

1 sheet frozen puff pastry, thawed

2 dessert apples

2 tablespoons sugar

10 g (¼ oz) butter

Preheat the oven to 200°C (400°F, Gas Mark 6). Add 2 tablespoons of hot water to the jam and stir until soft and spreadable.

Place the sheet of pastry on an oven tray lined with baking paper. Trim to make a 23 cm (9 in) circle. Brush half the jam mixture over the pastry, leaving a 2 cm (¾ in) border all around.

Peel, halve and core the apples and cut each half into thin slices. Lay the slices, slightly overlapping, over the pastry, again leaving a 2 cm (¾ in) border all around.

Sprinkle the apples with the sugar and dot with the butter. Bake for 15–20 minutes, or until the pastry border is golden and its edges have risen.

Glaze the tart by brushing it with the remaining jam. Cut into quarters and serve hot or warm with cream or ice-cream.

Two peeled and thinly sliced ripe pears may be substituted for the apple. Ripe nectarines or large plums also make a delicious variation when in season. There is no need to peel them.

Serves 4

asparagus.

The lovely, fresh flavour and vibrant colour of asparagus is a real treat during spring and early summer, when this vegetable is at its best and cheapest. I love it boiled, grilled or roasted.

The key to perfectly boiled asparagus is to cook it briefly. Bring a large saucepan of salted water to a rapid boil. Add 250 g (8 oz) – one large bunch – of fresh asparagus. Return to the boil (the stems will turn bright green) and cook for 2–3 minutes, or until tender when pierced with a skewer.

To grill asparagus, preheat a ribbed grill plate to very hot. Lightly brush the asparagus spears with olive oil and cook in a single layer for 4–6 minutes (this will depend on the thickness of the stalks), turning occasionally, or until tender and lightly browned.

To roast asparagus, arrange the stems in a single layer in a baking tin. Brush with a little olive oil and season with freshly ground black pepper. Roast in a preheated 200°C (400°F, Gas Mark 6) oven for 8–12 minutes, turning occasionally, or until tender. Serve hot or at room temperature.

When buying asparagus, look for stiff, bright-green stalks with smooth tips and freshly cut ends. Choose stems of similar thickness so that they will cook evenly.

To prepare asparagus, trim away any woody stems.

To store asparagus, wrap it in moist paper or cloth and keep it refrigerated. Eat it within 2 days.

Cooked asparagus is great dotted with a little lemon butter. It is also delicious simply dressed with olive oil, lemon juice, salt and freshly ground black pepper. Good matches for asparagus are eggs, butter, cheese, mayonnaise, lemon, pastry, goat's cheese, feta, mint, salmon and prawns. It also goes well with buttered brown bread.

apricot jam.

A Sunday afternoon jam session is a great way to preserve your favourite fruit. Homemade apricot jam is a delicious store-cupboard treat and is not difficult to make.

1 kg (2 lb) stoned and quartered apricots

2 tablespoons lemon juice

1 kg (2 lb) sugar

Preheat the oven to 140°C (275°F, Gas Mark 1).

Place the apricots, lemon juice and 1½ cups of water in a large saucepan and bring to the boil over medium heat. Reduce the heat and simmer, stirring occasionally, for 20–25 minutes, or until the fruit is tender and the skin is soft.

Meanwhile, place the sugar in an ovenproof dish and warm in the oven for 10 minutes. Place clean jam jars in the oven to warm also. Put two saucers into the freezer to chill.

Add the warmed sugar to the apricot mixture and stir over low heat until the sugar has dissolved. Increase the heat and simmer gently for 20 minutes, stirring frequently. Skim off any scum that rises to the surface.

Remove from the heat. Drop 1 teaspoon of jam on one of the chilled saucers and return to the freezer for 1 minute. If the jam forms a skin and wrinkles when pushed by your fingertip, it has reached setting point. If not, continue to cook the mixture, testing every 5 minutes, until the jam reaches setting point. Remove from the heat and allow to stand for 15 minutes before bottling.

Spoon the jam into the warmed jars and allow to cool. Seal, label and date the jars. Store in a cool, dark place for up to 12 months.

Makes 6 cups

apricot turnovers.

1 quantity flaky pastry (see page 120) or
   380 g (12 oz) packet frozen puff pastry,
   thawed
8 ripe apricots, halved, stoned and peeled
2 tablespoons demerara sugar or raw sugar,
   plus extra to decorate

1 teaspoon vanilla extract
25 g (1 oz) butter
1 egg, beaten

Prepare the pastry according to the instructions on page 120.

Divide the pastry into four equal portions. Roll each portion out to an 18 cm (7 in) square. Using a saucer as a guide, cut one 16 cm (6 in) diameter circle from each square.

Lightly grease an oven tray and transfer pastry circles to it.

Preheat the oven to 200°C (400°F, Gas Mark 6).

Roughly chop the apricots and place a quarter of the fruit on one half of each pastry circle, leaving a 1 cm border. Sprinkle the sugar and vanilla equally over the piles of apricots, and dot each pile with a quarter of the butter.

Brush the edge of the pastry circle with a little of the beaten egg. Fold the pastry over the fruit to make a semicircle and seal the edge with a fork. Repeat with the remaining pastries.

Brush the turnovers with the remaining beaten egg and make 2 small slashes in the top of each. Sprinkle with a little extra sugar. Bake for 20 minutes, or until crisp and golden. Allow to cool on a wire rack for 5 minutes before eating. Serve with cream, crème fraîche or ice-cream.

Makes 4

asparagus.

The lovely, fresh flavour and vibrant colour of asparagus is a real treat during spring and early summer, when this vegetable is at its best and cheapest.
I love it boiled, grilled or roasted.

The key to perfectly boiled asparagus is to cook it briefly. Bring a large saucepan of salted water to a rapid boil. Add 250 g (8 oz) – one large bunch – of fresh asparagus. Return to the boil (the stems will turn bright green) and cook for 2–3 minutes, or until tender when pierced with a skewer.

To grill asparagus, preheat a ribbed grill plate to very hot. Lightly brush the asparagus spears with olive oil and cook in a single layer for 4–6 minutes (this will depend on the thickness of the stalks), turning occasionally, or until tender and lightly browned.

To roast asparagus, arrange the stems in a single layer in a baking tin. Brush with a little olive oil and season with freshly ground black pepper. Roast in a preheated 200°C (400°F, Gas Mark 6) oven for 8–12 minutes, turning occasionally, or until tender. Serve hot or at room temperature.

When buying asparagus, look for stiff, bright-green stalks with smooth tips and freshly cut ends. Choose stems of similar thickness so that they will cook evenly.

To prepare asparagus, trim away any woody stems.

To store asparagus, wrap it in moist paper or cloth and keep it refrigerated. Eat it within 2 days.

Cooked asparagus is great dotted with a little lemon butter. It is also delicious simply dressed with olive oil, lemon juice, salt and freshly ground black pepper. Good matches for asparagus are eggs, butter, cheese, mayonnaise, lemon, pastry, goat's cheese, feta, mint, salmon and prawns. It also goes well with buttered brown bread.

asparagus risotto.

1.25 litres chicken stock (see page 68) or
　　vegetable stock
1 × 250 g bunch asparagus, trimmed and cut
　　into 3 cm (1¼ in) lengths
40 g (1½ oz) butter
1 onion, finely chopped

1 cup Carnaroli or Vialone Nano rice
grated zest of 1 lemon
½ cup dry white wine
¾ cup freshly grated parmesan
salt and freshly ground black pepper

Bring the stock to a simmer in a large saucepan. Add asparagus and cook for 2 minutes. Remove with a slotted spoon and set aside, leaving stock simmering.

Melt half the butter in a large saucepan over medium heat. Add the onion and sauté for 5 minutes, or until soft. Add the rice and lemon zest and cook, stirring gently, for 2 minutes. Add the wine. Stir and allow most of the liquid to evaporate.

Add enough of the simmering stock to just cover the rice. Stirring frequently, allow the rice to absorb most of the stock. Repeat the process, stirring well and adding stock as required. It will take 18–25 minutes to cook. Taste the rice for texture – it should be soft but still retain a little bite.

Remove from the heat and gently stir in the asparagus and parmesan. Season to taste with salt and freshly ground black pepper. Dot with the remaining butter, cover and rest for 5 minutes before serving.

Arborio rice can also be used to make risotto, but Carnaroli or Vialone Nano rice will produce a creamier result.

Serves 4

bacon, leek and barley soup.

1 tablespoon vegetable oil

125 g (4 oz) unsmoked bacon (about
   5 rashers), chopped

3 leeks, sliced into 1 cm (½ in) rounds

1 clove of garlic, chopped

2 carrots, sliced

2 sticks celery, sliced

1 teaspoon fresh thyme leaves

1 bay leaf

1.25 litres (40 fl oz) chicken stock
   (see page 68)

½ cup pearl barley

salt and freshly ground black pepper

2 tablespoons chopped flat-leaf parsley

Heat the oil in a large saucepan over medium heat. Add the chopped bacon and cook, stirring, for 3–4 minutes. Add the leek, garlic, carrot, celery, thyme and bay leaf and cook over medium heat, stirring occasionally, for 7–10 minutes, or until the leeks have softened. Pour in the chicken stock, 500 ml (16 fl oz) water and the pearl barley. Bring to the boil, reduce the heat and then simmer gently for about 60 minutes, or until the barley is soft, skimming off any scum that forms.

Season well with salt and freshly ground black pepper. Serve hot, sprinkled with the parsley.

As a variation (and to add some fresh greens to the soup), add a large handful of chopped English spinach or some frozen peas about 5 minutes before serving.

You can also add 2 diced skinless chicken breasts to the soup about 10 minutes before serving – just be sure to simmer the meat until cooked.

Serves 4

baked apples.

Cold winter nights are the times to revive this simple, old-fashioned treat.

6 Granny Smith or Jonathan apples

¼ cup lightly packed brown sugar

50 g (1¾ oz) unsalted butter, softened

2 tablespoons chopped hazelnuts

¾ cup coarsely chopped raisins

1 teaspoon finely grated orange zest

½ teaspoon ground cinnamon

2 tablespoons honey or golden syrup

Preheat the oven to 180°C (350°F, Gas Mark 4).

Core the apples, leaving a slightly wider opening at the top than the bottom.

Combine the sugar, butter, hazelnuts, raisins, orange zest and cinnamon in a mixing bowl. Stuff the apples firmly with the mixture and pile any leftover filling on the top. Place the stuffed apples in a baking dish that holds them snugly.

Spoon about 1 teaspoon of honey over each apple. Gently pour ⅓ cup of water into the bottom of the dish and bake for 30–40 minutes, or until the apples are soft.

Serve drizzled with any syrup from the bottom of the dish. Accompany with a jug of thick cream.

Vary the filling by using different dried fruits or nuts. Sultanas and almonds, or dried figs and walnuts, are good combinations.

Serves 6

baked custard.

2 cups milk

1 cup cream

3 eggs

2 egg yolks

1 teaspoon vanilla essence

½ cup caster (superfine) sugar

¾ teaspoon ground nutmeg

Preheat the oven to 150°C (300°F, Gas Mark 2).

Combine the milk and cream in a medium-sized saucepan and heat gently until the mixture reaches boiling point.

Meanwhile, lightly beat the whole eggs, egg yolks, vanilla and sugar in a bowl. Pour the hot cream mixture into the egg mixture, and whisk well. Transfer to a 6-cup-capacity ovenproof dish and sprinkle with the nutmeg.

Stand the dish in a large baking tin and fill the tin with enough boiling water to come halfway up the sides of the dish. Carefully transfer to the oven and bake for 35–45 minutes, or until the custard has just set – it should still wobble a little. To test, insert a knife about 5 cm (2 in) from the side of the dish; if it comes out clean, the custard is ready.

Serve with fresh or poached fruit.

To make ginger-infused custard, add 1 teaspoon of grated fresh ginger to the cream mixture. Heat and allow the ginger to infuse for 10 minutes. Strain and make the custard as above.

Make individual custards by pouring the mixture into six small ramekins. Bake as above, but for 20–25 minutes only.

Serves 4–6

baked eggs.

This is good as a breakfast dish, or delicious served as a light lunch with a green salad.

½ cup cream

1 tablespoon chopped chives

4 large free-range eggs

salt and freshly ground black pepper

Preheat the oven to 180°C (350°F, Gas Mark 4). Lightly grease 4 × 200 ml (6½ fl oz) ramekins, soufflé dishes or ovenproof cups.

In a small bowl, combine the cream and the chives. Pour equal quantities of the mixture into the four ramekins. Break an egg into each ramekin. Season with salt and freshly ground black pepper.

Place the ramekins in a baking tin and fill the tin with enough boiling water to come one-third up the sides of the ramekins. Carefully transfer to the oven and bake for 8–10 minutes, or until the eggs are set to your liking. These eggs are delicious served with fingers of toasted Turkish bread or brioche.

Baked eggs lend themselves to all sorts of variations. Fresh crabmeat added to the cream mixture is good, as is chopped smoked salmon.

Tarragon, chervil or parsley can be substituted for the chives, if you prefer.

Serves 4

baked ricotta.

3 cups fresh ricotta

1 clove garlic, finely chopped

2 tablespoons chopped fresh herbs (chives, flat-leaf parsley and thyme are a good combination)

1 teaspoon grated lemon zest

1 teaspoon paprika, plus a little extra

salt and freshly ground black pepper

2 egg whites

extra-virgin olive oil, to drizzle

Place the ricotta in a fine sieve set over a bowl, and leave in a cool place to drain for 1–2 hours.

Preheat the oven to 180°C (350°F, Gas Mark 4). Grease a small loaf tin or 4-cup-capacity ovenproof dish with vegetable oil and line the base with baking paper.

Place the drained ricotta in a bowl and stir in the garlic, herbs, lemon zest and the 1 teaspoon of paprika. Season to taste with salt and freshly ground black pepper.

Beat the egg whites in a clean, dry bowl until soft peaks just form. Gently fold a little of the egg whites through the ricotta mixture to slacken it, then carefully fold through the remaining whites.

Spoon the mixture into the prepared tin or dish and smooth the top. Sprinkle with a few extra pinches of paprika and drizzle with a little extra-virgin olive oil. Bake for 55–65 minutes, or until set, risen slightly and golden. Allow to cool in the tin before turning out to serve.

Baked ricotta is delicious spread on crusty bread or cut into pieces and served with roasted vegetables or with a tomato salad.

Serves 10 as part of antipasto or meze plate

banana bread.

1½ cups plain (all-purpose) flour

1 teaspoon baking powder

1 teaspoon bicarbonate of soda
   (sodium bicarbonate)

¼ teaspoon salt

125 g (4 oz) unsalted butter, softened

1 cup sugar

2 eggs, lightly beaten

2 large very ripe bananas

½ cup buttermilk

icing (confectioners') sugar, to serve

Preheat the oven to 170°C (325°F, Gas Mark 3). Grease a 23 × 12 cm (9 × 5 in) loaf tin and line the base and sides with baking paper.

Sift together the flour, baking powder, bicarbonate of soda and salt.

In a separate bowl, use an electric mixer to beat the butter and sugar for 3–4 minutes, or until pale and fluffy. Gradually add the beaten eggs, mixing well after each addition.

Mash the bananas with a fork and add to the butter mixture. Stir well to combine. Add the combined dry ingredients alternately with the buttermilk, beating well after each addition.

Spoon the mixture into the prepared loaf tin and bake for 55–60 minutes, or until the top of the bread is firm and is a deep brown colour. A skewer inserted into the centre should come out clean. Allow to cool in the tin for 10 minutes before turning out onto a wire rack.

Serve dusted with icing sugar. The flavour improves on keeping. Store for up to 3 days covered in plastic wrap.

Day-old banana bread is delicious cut into slices and toasted.

Substitute a mixture of ¼ cup plain yoghurt and ¼ cup milk if you can't find buttermilk.

banana smoothie.

1 ripe banana, roughly chopped

¾ cup milk

½ cup plain natural yoghurt

1 tablespoon honey

4 ice cubes

pinch of grated nutmeg

Place the banana, milk, yoghurt, honey and ice cubes into a blender and pulse until smooth.

Divide the mixture between 2 large glasses. Garnish each smoothie with a pinch of nutmeg.

A few strawberries make a nice addition to a banana smoothie. And the milk can be replaced with freshly squeezed orange juice.

For a different flavour altogether, substitute the banana for a ripe mango or peach.

Makes 2

bang bang chicken.

4 cm (1½ in) piece fresh ginger, roughly
    chopped
2 shallots, peeled and quartered
1/2 lime
4 skinless chicken breast fillets
300 g (9½ oz) rice vermicelli noodles, cut
    with scissors into 10 cm (4 in) lengths
1 Lebanese cucumber, peeled and diced
salt and freshly ground black pepper
3 spring onions (scallions), sliced
1 red chilli, chopped
1–2 teaspoons sesame seeds

SAUCE
3 spring onions (scallions), sliced
1 tablespoon grated fresh ginger
1 long red chilli, sliced
125 g (4 oz) smooth peanut butter
1 tablespoon caster (superfine) sugar
2 tablespoons dry sherry
1 teaspoon soy sauce
juice of 1 lime

Place ginger, shallots and lime in a large saucepan. Add the chicken breasts and cover with water. Bring to the boil, reduce heat, cover and simmer gently for about 10 minutes. Remove from the heat, keep covered and set aside until cool. Remove the poached chicken from the pan, then strain and keep the liquid.

Make the sauce by placing all the ingredients in a food processor. With the motor running, gradually pour in enough of the reserved poaching liquid to form a smooth, thinnish paste with the consistency of double cream.

Soak the noodles in a large bowl of boiling water for about 10 minutes. Meanwhile, using your fingers, shred the chicken into another bowl, stir through the cucumber and season with a little salt and pepper. Drain the noodles then dress them with some of the sauce, tossing well until lightly coated.

Place the noodles in a large serving bowl and top with the chicken. Drizzle with the remaining sauce and garnish with the spring onions, chilli and sesame seeds.

Serves 4–6

barbecue sauce.

1 tablespoon vegetable oil

1 onion, finely chopped

2 cloves garlic, crushed

1 teaspoon grated fresh ginger

1 cup tomato sauce (ketchup)

100 ml (3½ fl oz) red-wine vinegar

½ cup lightly packed brown sugar

2 teaspoons French-style mustard

2 tablespoons Worcestershire sauce

2 tablespoons lemon juice

1 teaspoon crushed chilli

½ teaspoon cayenne pepper

½ teaspoon salt

salt, extra, and freshly ground black pepper

Heat the oil in a frying pan over medium heat and cook the onion, garlic and ginger for 4–5 minutes, or until the onion is soft. Add all the remaining ingredients except the extra salt and freshly ground black pepper, and bring to the boil. Reduce the heat and simmer gently for 30 minutes, stirring occasionally, until the sauce has thickened. Season to taste with salt and freshly ground black pepper.

This sauce will keep for several weeks in an airtight jar in the refrigerator.

Makes 2 cups

beef and mushroom pie.

100 ml (3½ fl oz) olive oil

2 onions, sliced

2 cloves garlic, crushed

150 g (5 oz) button mushrooms, halved

1 kg (2 lb) rump or chuck steak, cut into

    5 cm (2 in) cubes

⅓ cup plain (all-purpose) flour

300 ml (9½ fl oz) beef stock or water

300 ml (9½ fl oz) red wine

4 sprigs thyme

2 bay leaves

2 teaspoons Worcestershire sauce

salt and freshly ground black pepper

1 quantity flaky pastry (see page 120)

    or 1 × 380 g (12 oz) packet frozen puff

    pastry, thawed

1 egg, beaten, to glaze

Preheat the oven to 180°C (350°F, Gas Mark 4). Heat 2 tablespoons of the oil in a large frying pan over medium heat. Add the onion, garlic and mushrooms and cook, stirring occasionally, for 7 minutes, or until tender. Transfer to a large ovenproof saucepan or casserole dish.

Lightly dust the meat with the flour. Reserve 2 tablespoons of the flour.

Heat 2 tablespoons of the oil in the frying pan and cook the meat in batches over high heat, adding a little extra oil if needed, until browned. Transfer to the saucepan.

Sprinkle the frying pan with the reserved flour and cook, stirring, for 1 minute. Stir in the stock and wine and bring to the boil, then pour over the meat. Return the saucepan to the heat, add the thyme and bay leaves and bring to the boil. Cover, transfer to the oven and cook for 1½ hours, stirring occasionally. Stir in the Worcestershire sauce and season well with salt and pepper. Allow to cool – preferably chill overnight.

Preheat the oven to 190°C (375°F, Gas Mark 5).

Spoon the mixture into a large pie dish. Roll out the pastry to the size of the dish. Cover the pie, pressing down on the edges to seal. Trim away any excess pastry, brush with the beaten egg and bake for 40–45 minutes, or until the pastry is golden.

Serves 4

beef casserole.

¼ cup plain (all-purpose) flour

1.75 kg (3½ lb) rump or chuck steak,
   cut into 2 cm (¾ in) cubes

½ cup olive oil

3 rashers bacon, roughly chopped

8 small brown onions, peeled and quartered

2 cloves garlic, crushed

3 carrots, sliced

2 cups beef stock

2 cups red wine

1 × 400 g (13 oz) can chopped tomatoes

1 teaspoon finely grated orange zest

4 sprigs thyme

1 bay leaf

2 tablespoons chopped flat-leaf parsley

salt and freshly ground black pepper

Preheat the oven to 160°C (315°F, Gas Mark 2–3).

Place the flour in a clean plastic bag. Shake a few pieces of meat in the bag until lightly dusted. Repeat with the remaining pieces of meat.

Heat 2 tablespoons of the oil in a large frying pan over medium heat. Cook the steak in batches, adding a little extra oil if needed, until browned. Transfer to a large casserole dish.

Heat the remaining 2 tablespoons of oil in the frying pan over medium heat. Add the bacon and cook for 2 minutes. Add the onion, garlic and carrot, and cook, stirring occasionally, for 5 minutes, or until the onion is tender. Transfer to the casserole dish.

Drain any fat from the frying pan, add the stock and bring to the boil for 1 minute. Stir to incorporate any bits stuck to the bottom. Transfer to the casserole dish and stir in the wine, tomatoes, orange zest, thyme, bay leaf and parsley. Cover, transfer to the oven and cook for 3 hours. Stir the meat occasionally as it cooks.

Remove from the oven and check the sauce. Add a little extra water if it appears dry. Alternatively, if the sauce is a little watery, uncover and return to the oven to allow the sauce to reduce. Season well with salt and freshly ground black pepper. Serve with mashed potatoes or buttered noodles and plenty of crusty bread.

Serves 6

beer batter.

Batter provides a protective coating that keeps the tender flesh of fish and shellfish succulent and moist. The beer gives the batter a unique flavour and makes it crisp, providing the perfect contrast to the seafood.

1 cup self-raising (self-rising) flour
salt and freshly ground black pepper

1 cup chilled beer

Sift the flour into a bowl and season well with salt and freshly ground black pepper.

Gradually whisk in the beer and 2 tablespoons of water to form a smooth batter. Too much liquid added at the beginning makes it difficult to work out the lumps. If lumps occur, pour the batter through a sieve. The batter should be the consistency of cream and can be diluted with a little extra water or chilled beer if needed.

To apply the batter, dry the fish with kitchen paper and completely dip the fish into the batter for a few seconds. Allow any excess batter to run off.

Deep-fry in fresh oil at a temperature of 180°C (350°F) until golden. Do not overcrowd the pan or deep-fryer, or the oil will cool down.

Oysters and peeled and deveined prawns are delicious coated with batter and fried.
Try adding a little chilli or curry powder to the flour for a spicier version.

bircher muesli.

This will make a batch of muesli base that can be stored in a large jar in the cupboard. Simply add the fruit juice the night before you want this for breakfast and refrigerate until ready to serve.

500 g (1 lb) rolled oats

100 g (3½ oz) dried fruit (sultanas and chopped dried apricot or apple)

50 g (1¾ oz) sunflower seeds

100 g (3½ oz) slivered almonds

100 g (3½ oz) toasted hazelnuts, chopped

100 g (3½ oz) brown sugar

orange or apple juice, to serve

fresh fruit (blueberries, raspberries, sliced apple), to serve

plain yoghurt, to serve

honey, to serve (optional)

Combine the oats, dried fruit, seeds, nuts and sugar in a large bowl then transfer to a large jar or airtight container. Store in cupboard until needed.

To make up the Bircher muesli, pour your preferred amount of muesli base per person into a bowl and add just enough fresh fruit juice to cover. Place in the fridge to soak for at least 3 hours or overnight.

To serve, top with fresh fruit and a large dollop of yoghurt. Add a drizzle of honey, if desired.

You can vary this basic recipe to suit your own tastes by using seasonal fruit and juices. Try fresh peaches, mangoes, plums or a variety of berries.

Serves 8

biscotti.

100 g (3½ oz) blanched almonds

250 g (8 oz) plain (all-purpose) flour

1 teaspoon baking powder

250 g (8 oz) caster (superfine) sugar

2 teaspoons finely grated orange zest

1 teaspoon finely chopped rosemary

2 eggs, beaten

1 egg yolk

1 teaspoon vanilla essence

Preheat the oven to 180°C (350°F, Gas Mark 4).

Spread the almonds in a single layer on an oven tray and bake for 7–10 minutes, tossing occasionally, until fragrant and lightly toasted. Cool and roughly chop.

Sift the flour and baking powder into a mixing bowl. Stir in the sugar, orange zest, rosemary and chopped almonds. Add the beaten eggs, egg yolk and vanilla and mix to form a firm dough. If the dough is very sticky, add extra flour.

Knead the dough on a lightly floured surface for 5 minutes, or until smooth. Form into a slightly flattened log about 30 cm (12 in) in length. Place on an oven tray lined with baking paper and bake for 40 minutes, or until firm and golden. Allow to cool on a wire rack.

Reduce the oven temperature to 140°C (275°F, Gas Mark 1). Line two oven trays with baking paper.

With a long serrated knife, carefully cut the log diagonally into 5–10 mm (¼–½ in) thick slices. The slices will be crumbly on the edges, so work slowly.

Arrange the biscotti in a single layer on the prepared oven trays and return them to the oven for 20–25 minutes, turning occasionally, until dry and crisp. Store in an airtight container for 2–3 weeks.

Try substituting pistachios or hazelnuts for the almonds, dry-roasting them as above.

Makes 25–30

boiled eggs.

A boiled egg with toast 'soldiers' is the perfect breakfast. Not only is it compact and nutritious, it's also a great excuse to get the egg cups out of the cupboard. A boiled egg is also a great dish to have for supper if you have had a little too much to eat for Sunday lunch. The cooking time is crucial here – an extra minute on the boil can make a big difference.

4 eggs
salt and freshly ground black pepper

toast, buttered and cut into fingers, to serve

Place the eggs in a small saucepan and cover with cold water. Bring to the boil over medium heat. Reduce the heat and simmer for 3 minutes for soft, runny eggs, 4 minutes for a firmer set, or 5 minutes for hard-boiled.

Remove the eggs with a slotted spoon and transfer to egg cups. Use a knife to slice off the tops.

Serve with salt and freshly ground black pepper and buttered fingers of freshly toasted bread. Boiled eggs are also delicious served with seasoned salt or zaatar, a Middle Eastern herb mix, on the side.

To make seasoned salt, combine 2 teaspoons of sea salt, ½ teaspoon of freshly ground black pepper, ¼ teaspoon of ground coriander and a pinch of chilli powder.

To make zaatar, combine 2 teaspoons of sea salt, 1 teaspoon of sesame seeds, ¼ teaspoon of ground cumin and ½ teaspoon of dried thyme.

Serves 2

bolognese sauce.

Serve this versatile sauce with spaghetti, polenta, jacket potatoes,
or simply enjoy it hot on toast.

2 tablespoons olive oil

1 onion, finely chopped

1 carrot, chopped

1 clove garlic, crushed

500 g (1 lb) minced (ground) beef

$\frac{1}{2}$ cup red wine

2 × 400 g (13 oz) cans crushed tomatoes

1 cup beef stock

2 tablespoons tomato paste

$\frac{1}{2}$ teaspoon dried oregano

pinch of ground nutmeg

salt and freshly ground black pepper

Heat the olive oil in a large saucepan and gently sauté the onion and carrot for 5 minutes, or until tender and slightly coloured.

Add the garlic and minced beef to the vegetable mixture. Cook until the meat starts to brown. Break up any lumps of meat with a fork.

Add the red wine and cook, stirring frequently, until almost evaporated. Add the remaining ingredients except the salt and pepper. Cook, stirring occasionally, over low heat for 1½ hours.

Season with salt and freshly ground black pepper, and serve.

For a more robust flavour, add 125 g (4 oz) of finely chopped pancetta to the vegetable mixture at the beginning.

Bolognese sauce can be made in large quantities and frozen in small portions for up to 3 months.

Serves 4–6

braised pork chops with apple.

4 pork loin chops

$\frac{1}{3}$ cup plain (all-purpose) flour

$\frac{1}{3}$ cup olive oil

4 rashers streaky bacon, diced

1 large shallot, sliced

2 leeks, sliced

2 cloves garlic, crushed

1 cup dry cider or apple juice

about 2 cups chicken stock (see page 68)

1 large cooking apple, peeled and
    coarsely grated

4 sprigs thyme

1 bay leaf

salt and freshly ground black pepper

Preheat the oven to 200°C (400°F, Gas Mark 6). Lightly dust the chops with the flour.

Heat 2 tablespoons of the oil in a large frying pan over medium heat and cook two chops at a time, until brown on both sides. Transfer to a large casserole dish. Repeat with the remaining chops, adding a little extra oil if needed.

Heat the remaining 2 tablespoons of oil in the frying pan over medium heat. Add the bacon and cook for 2 minutes. Add the shallot, leek and garlic and cook, stirring occasionally, for 6–7 minutes, or until the vegetables are tender but not coloured. Transfer to the casserole dish. Deglaze the pan with cider and pour over the pork.

Stir into the casserole the stock (add enough to just cover the meat), apple, thyme and bay leaf and bring to the boil over medium heat. Cover, transfer to the oven and cook for 30 minutes. Reduce the heat to 170°C (330°F, Gas Mark 3) and cook for a further 45 minutes, or until tender. Turn the chops occasionally during cooking. Remove the lid about 30 minutes before the end of the cooking time.

Remove from the oven, skim off any fat and take out the bay leaf. Season well with salt and pepper and serve with boiled new potatoes and steamed green beans.

Serves 4

brandy butter.

Brandy butter, or 'hard sauce', is the traditional sauce that accompanies plum pudding. It can be made up to a week ahead and stored, covered, in the refrigerator. Served cold, it is a delicious contrast to any hot pudding.

250 g (8 oz) unsalted butter, softened	¼ cup brandy
1½ cups icing (confectioners') sugar, sifted	½ teaspoon vanilla essence

Place the butter and icing sugar in a mixing bowl and beat with an electric mixer until the mixture is pale and fluffy. Gradually add the brandy and vanilla, beating thoroughly after each addition.

Transfer to a serving dish and refrigerate for 1–2 hours until firm. Refrigerate until required.

A teaspoon of finely grated orange zest added to the sugar makes a nice addition.

A good but less traditional variation is to replace the brandy with a citrus-flavoured liqueur such as Grand Marnier or Cointreau.

Another way to serve brandy butter is to fill a piping bag fitted with a star-shaped or other decorative nozzle and pipe rosettes onto a plate or tray lined with baking paper. Refrigerate and serve with pudding.

Any leftover brandy butter is delicious on pancakes or spread onto hot raisin toast.

Serves 8–10

bread.

1 × 7 g (¼ oz) sachet (2 teaspoons) dry yeast	4 cups bread flour
1 teaspoon sugar	½ teaspoon salt
	1 tablespoon olive oil

Dissolve the yeast and sugar in a small jug with ½ cup of tepid water. Stir well and leave for 10 minutes, or until the mixture froths.

Place the flour and salt in a large mixing bowl. Make a well in the centre and add the yeast mixture, olive oil and 1 cup of tepid water. Mix until a firm dough forms. Add a little extra water if the dough is too dry.

Knead the dough on a lightly floured surface for 10–15 minutes, or until smooth and elastic. Place in a clean, lightly oiled bowl, cover with a cloth or plastic wrap and leave in a warm place for 1–1½ hours, or until the dough has doubled in size.

Punch down the dough with your fist to expel the air. Knead on a lightly floured surface for 2 minutes, or until smooth. Place in a large greased loaf tin.

Cover and leave for 45–60 minutes, or until the dough has doubled in size.

Preheat the oven to 200°C (400°F, Gas Mark 6).

Slash the top of the loaf a couple of times with a sharp knife. Bake for 40 minutes, or until the loaf has risen and is golden brown. Turn out the loaf, place on an oven tray and return it to the oven for 5 minutes. When cooked, the loaf should be golden and sound hollow when tapped on the bottom. Allow to cool on a wire rack.

Only use bread-making or strong flour, available from health-food shops or from the health-food section of supermarkets. Alternatively, look for bread flour at growers' markets or a local mill. Plain flour does not contain enough gluten, which gives the dough its elasticity.

Instead of making a loaf, shape the dough into whatever shapes you like and bake directly on an oven tray.

Experiment by replacing some of the white flour with wholemeal or rye flour.

bread and butter pudding.

This perennial favourite dates back to the eighteenth century and
is perfect served after a Sunday roast.

30 g (1 oz) unsalted butter, softened

3–4 slices white bread, crusts removed

2 tablespoons orange marmalade

½ cup sultanas or raisins

3 eggs

¼ cup caster (superfine) sugar

1 teaspoon vanilla essence

1 cup milk

1 cup cream

2 teaspoons demerara sugar or raw sugar

Butter the slices of bread. Brush with the marmalade and cut diagonally into quarters. Arrange the bread in two layers in a deep 5-cup-capacity ovenproof dish and sprinkle with the sultanas or raisins.

Whisk together the eggs, caster sugar, vanilla, milk and cream. Pour the mixture over the bread and sprinkle with the demerara sugar. Make sure there is enough liquid to cover the bread – add a little extra milk if necessary. Set aside for 30 minutes to allow the bread to soak up the liquid and to absorb the flavours.

Preheat the oven to 180°C (350°F, Gas Mark 4). Place the dish in a large baking tin and fill the tin with enough boiling water to come halfway up the sides of the dish. Carefully transfer to the oven and bake for 45–50 minutes, or until the custard is set and the bread is slightly puffed and golden on top.

Add a little ground ginger, freshly grated nutmeg, ground cinnamon or allspice to the cream mixture as a variation.

Substitute chopped dried apricots or figs for the sultanas or raisins.

Use brioche, panettone or light fruit bread for a more sophisticated pudding.

Serves 4

bread sauce.

Bread sauce is a traditional English sauce worthy of a revival. Made of spiced milk thickened with breadcrumbs, it's the perfect accompaniment to roast chicken (see page 268), turkey or game birds.

1 onion, halved

1 bay leaf

3 cloves

4 black peppercorns

1 cup milk

1 cup fresh breadcrumbs

¼ cup cream

pinch of cayenne pepper (optional)

salt and freshly ground black pepper

Place the onion, bay leaf, cloves, peppercorns and milk in a saucepan and bring to the boil over medium heat. Reduce the heat and simmer for 5 minutes. Remove from the heat, cover and allow the flavours to infuse for 20 minutes.

Strain the milk mixture and return the strained milk to the saucepan. Bring to the boil. Stir in the breadcrumbs and simmer, stirring frequently, for 5–7 minutes. Add the cream and cayenne pepper. The sauce should be quite thick. Add a little extra milk or cream if needed to thin the sauce. Taste and adjust the seasoning with salt and freshly ground black pepper.

I often stir in ¼ cup of the roasting pan juices as a substitute for the cream.

Makes 1½ cups

bruschetta.

Bruschetta are slices of toasted bread rubbed with garlic and drizzled with olive oil. They are classically (and best of all) served with lots of chopped ripe tomato, good-quality olive oil and freshly torn basil – a wonderfully simple and delicious snack.

4 × 1 cm (½ in) thick slices coarsely textured, crusty, Italian-style white bread
1 clove garlic, peeled

good-quality virgin olive oil
3 large ripe Roma (egg) tomatoes
fresh basil
sea salt and freshly ground black pepper

Toast the bread on both sides, or grill it on a ribbed chargrill pan. Rub the toasted slices lightly with the clove of garlic and drizzle each slice generously with olive oil.

Meanwhile, roughly chop the tomatoes and place in a bowl along with any juices. Add a few torn basil leaves and drizzle over a little olive oil. Season the tomato mixture well with sea salt and freshly ground black pepper.

Divide the tomato mixture between the slices of bread, spooning it generously over each slice. Serve immediately.

Use the best ripe tomatoes you can find – if possible, beg, borrow or steal some home-grown ones.
  As a variation, add some coarsely chopped rocket leaves to the tomato mix.
  Other interesting bruschetta toppings include cooked onions, sautéed sliced mushrooms mixed with herbs and garlic, or fried diced eggplant (aubergine) dressed with oil, lemon juice and sprinkled with mint.

Serves 2

caesar salad.

5 rashers bacon, chopped

4 thick slices white bread

1 tablespoon vegetable oil

2 baby cos (Romaine) lettuce

½ cup freshly shaved parmesan

DRESSING

4 anchovy fillets

1 clove garlic, crushed

2 tablespoons lemon juice

1 egg yolk

½ teaspoon Dijon mustard

¼ cup olive oil

salt and freshly ground black pepper

Cook the bacon in a large frying pan over medium heat for 5 minutes, or until crisp. Drain on kitchen paper.

Remove the crusts from the bread and cut the bread into 2 cm (¾ in) cubes. Add the oil to the frying pan and fry the bread over medium heat, tossing constantly, until golden brown. Drain the croutons on kitchen paper.

To make the dressing, place all the ingredients except the salt and pepper in a blender and pulse until combined. Season to taste with salt and freshly ground black pepper.

Separate the lettuce leaves, rinse well and dry with a clean tea towel. Place the leaves in a serving bowl, sprinkle over the bacon and croutons, and drizzle over the dressing. Finish with a sprinkle of shaved parmesan.

You can make chicken caesar salad by adding two cooked and roughly chopped chicken breasts to this salad.

Serves 4

carrot cake.

4 eggs, lightly beaten

1½ cups lightly packed brown sugar

¾ cup vegetable oil

⅓ cup golden syrup

1 cup plain (all-purpose) flour

1 cup self-raising (self-rising) flour

1 teaspoon bicarbonate of soda
    (sodium bicarbonate)

½ teaspoon ground cinnamon

2½ cups firmly packed grated carrot

½ cup drained crushed canned pineapple

½ cup chopped pecans or walnuts

Preheat the oven to 160°C (315°F, Gas Mark 2–3). Lightly grease a 23 cm (9 in) round cake tin and line the base with baking paper.

In a large mixing bowl, lightly whisk together the eggs and sugar until the sugar has dissolved and the mixture is frothy. Stir in the oil and golden syrup and mix with a wooden spoon until smooth.

Sift both flours, the bicarbonate of soda and the cinnamon into the egg mixture and mix until smooth. Stir in the carrot, pineapple and pecans or walnuts.

Spoon the mixture into the prepared cake tin and level the top. Bake for 1–1¼ hours, or until golden and firm to the touch. A skewer inserted into the centre should come out clean.

Allow to cool in the tin for 10 minutes before turning out onto a wire rack to cool completely. Serve dusted with icing (confectioners') sugar. Alternatively, spread with cream cheese icing.

To make cream cheese icing, beat 175 g (6 oz) of cream cheese with 60 g (2 oz) of softened unsalted butter until combined. Continue to beat while gradually adding 1½ cups of sifted icing (confectioners') sugar, 1 teaspoon of finely grated lemon zest and 2 tablespoons of lemon juice. Spread evenly over the top of the cooled cake.

carrot salad.

¼ cup olive oil

1 tablespoon lemon juice

1 clove garlic, crushed

salt and freshly ground black pepper

⅓ cup pine nuts

4 large carrots, scrubbed

2 tablespoons chopped mint

2 tablespoons chopped flat-leaf parsley

Combine the oil, lemon juice and garlic in a small screw-top jar. Season with salt and freshly ground black pepper.

Place the pine nuts in a dry frying pan over medium heat and toss for 5 minutes, or until toasted and golden. Set aside.

Finely grate the carrots into a bowl. Stir in the chopped herbs.

Shake the dressing until combined. Drizzle enough dressing over the carrots to just coat them. Sprinkle with the pine nuts.

Use only the best quality carrots, preferably organic, for this dish.

I sometimes replace one of the carrots with a finely grated apple.

Serves 4

cheese biscuits.

These crispy cheese-flavoured biscuits are perfect served with a glass of wine or beer. They also make an excellent accompaniment to vegetable soup.

175 g (6 oz) plain (all-purpose) flour
salt
100 g (3½ oz) unsalted butter, chilled and finely diced

125 g (4 oz) cheddar, finely grated
50 g (1¾ oz) parmesan, finely grated

Sift the flour and a pinch of salt into a mixing bowl. Add the butter and rub into the flour with your fingertips until the mixture resembles coarse breadcrumbs. Stir in the cheddar and parmesan. Mix well with your hands until the mixture forms a firm dough, then press into a ball. Alternatively, place in a food processor and pulse until the mixture comes together. You may need to add a little water to make the dough hold together, since cheeses and butters vary in their water content. The dough should be dry but smooth and just hold together without being sticky.

Divide the dough into two portions. With a rolling pin, roll each portion between two sheets of baking paper to a thickness of 5 mm (¼ in). Chill for 10–15 minutes.

Preheat the oven to 190°C (375°F, Gas Mark 5). Line an oven tray with baking paper.

Remove the top sheet of baking paper from each piece of dough and cut the dough into shapes with a cookie cutter. Carefully transfer the shapes to the prepared oven tray. Cook for 15–20 minutes, or until pale gold. Cool on a wire rack, then store in an airtight container.

These biscuits may be made without the parmesan. In this case, increase the amount of cheddar to 175 g (6 oz).

The parmesan may be replaced with gruyère or another firm tasty cheese.

Makes 24–30

cheese soufflés.

100 g (3½ oz) unsalted butter

½ cup plain (all-purpose) flour

300 ml (9½ fl oz) milk

1 cup grated cheddar

2 tablespoons freshly grated parmesan

½ teaspoon Dijon mustard

pinch of cayenne pepper

4 eggs, separated

Preheat the oven to 190°C (375°F, Gas Mark 5). Grease and lightly flour 6 × ½-cup-capacity soufflé dishes.

Melt the butter in a small saucepan over low heat. Add the flour and cook, stirring constantly, for 1 minute. Gradually add the milk and whisk continuously over medium heat until the mixture is smooth, thickens and comes to the boil. Allow to cool for 5 minutes.

Transfer the mixture to a bowl and stir in the cheddar, parmesan, mustard and cayenne pepper. Mix well.

Lightly beat the egg yolks and add these to the cheese mixture. Mix well.

With an electric mixer, whisk the egg whites in a clean bowl until firm peaks form. Fold a quarter of the whites through the cheese mixture to slacken it slightly, then gently fold through the remaining whites.

Spoon the mixture into the prepared dishes and bake for 20–25 minutes, or until risen and golden. Don't be tempted to open the oven until the soufflés have risen. Serve immediately.

The above mixture may also be cooked in a 6-cup-capacity soufflé dish. In this case it will take 30–35 minutes to cook.

Gruyère makes a good substitute for cheddar.

Vary the flavour by stirring 2 tablespoons of chopped chives, basil or chervil into the mixture before adding the egg whites.

Serves 6

cheesecake.

250 g (8 oz) plain sweet biscuits

¼ teaspoon ground ginger

125 g (4 oz) unsalted butter, melted

500 g (1 lb) cream cheese

¾ cup caster (superfine) sugar

3 eggs, separated

½ cup cream

2 teaspoons vanilla essence

1 teaspoon finely grated lemon zest

1 teaspoon lemon juice

icing (confectioners') sugar, to serve

Grease a 23 cm (9 in) springform cake tin and line the base with baking paper.

Place the biscuits and ginger in a food processor and pulse until crushed. Add the butter and process until the mixture comes together. Using your fingertips, press the crumb mixture into the base of the tin and two-thirds of the way up the sides. Refrigerate for 30 minutes.

Preheat the oven to 180°C (350°F, Gas Mark 4).

With an electric mixer, beat the cream cheese and caster sugar until creamy and well combined. Add the egg yolks, cream, vanilla, lemon zest and juice. Beat for 2–3 minutes, or until the mixture is light and fluffy.

Using clean beaters and a clean bowl, beat the egg whites for 3–4 minutes, or until stiff peaks form. Use a large metal spoon to gently fold the egg whites into the cream cheese mixture.

Spoon the mixture onto the prepared cheesecake base and smooth the top. Bake for 35–40 minutes, or until a pale golden colour and just set in the centre. Allow to cool, then refrigerate for 6–12 hours before serving.

To serve, cut into slices and dust with icing sugar.

Serves 8–12

chicken cacciatore.

4 chicken thighs

4 chicken legs

salt and freshly ground black pepper

¼ cup olive oil

150 g (5 oz) pancetta or bacon, roughly
    chopped

1 onion, chopped

2 sticks celery, thinly sliced

2 cloves garlic, crushed

100 ml (3½ fl oz) white wine

2 × 400 g (13 oz) cans crushed or chopped
    tomatoes

2 bay leaves

3 sprigs thyme

Season the chicken pieces with salt and freshly ground black pepper. Heat 2 tablespoons of the oil in a large frying pan over high heat and fry the chicken a few pieces at a time until golden on each side. Transfer the chicken to a large saucepan.

Heat the remaining oil in the frying pan over medium heat. Add the pancetta and cook, stirring occasionally, for 2 minutes. Add the onion, celery and garlic and cook, stirring from time to time, for 6–8 minutes, or until the onion is tender. Transfer to the saucepan with the chicken.

Return the frying pan to the heat and deglaze with the white wine. Transfer to the saucepan and add the tomatoes with their juice, bay leaves and thyme. Bring to the boil over medium heat. Reduce the heat, cover and leave to simmer, turning the chicken occasionally, for 25–30 minutes, or until the chicken is tender.

Check the sauce and add a little water if necessary. Alternatively, if the sauce is too thin, remove the chicken, increase the heat and cook until the sauce has reduced and thickened. Season to taste with salt and freshly ground black pepper and serve with boiled potatoes.

Serves 4

chicken casserole with peas and pancetta.

4 chicken breasts

4 chicken thighs with drumsticks attached

⅓ cup plain (all-purpose) flour

⅓ cup olive oil

150 g (5 oz) pancetta, cubed

12 very small onions (pickling onions),
    peeled

2 leeks, sliced

2 cloves garlic, crushed

2 cups white wine

2 cups chicken stock (see page 68)

1 bay leaf

250 g (8 oz) frozen peas, thawed

salt and freshly ground black pepper

2 tablespoons chopped flat-leaf parsley

Preheat the oven to 180°C (350°F, Gas Mark 4). Lightly dust chicken with the flour.

Heat half the oil in a large frying pan over medium heat. Season the chicken pieces and cook in batches, adding a little extra oil if needed, until browned. Be careful not to overcrowd the frying pan, as the meat will then steam rather than sear. Transfer to a large, heatproof casserole dish.

Heat the remaining oil in the frying pan over medium heat. Add the pancetta, onion, leek and garlic and cook, stirring occasionally, for 7–10 minutes, or until the vegetables are tender and the onion is lightly coloured. Transfer to the casserole dish.

Place the frying pan back over the heat and deglaze with the wine. Transfer to the casserole dish and stir in the stock and the bay leaf. Bring to the boil over medium heat. Cover, transfer to the oven and cook for 1 hour, stirring occasionally.

Stir in the peas, return to the oven and cook for a further 15 minutes. Season to taste with salt and freshly ground black pepper. Remove the bay leaf and stir in the parsley before serving.

Serves 4–6

chicken curry.

This is a mildly spiced, easy-to-prepare Thai-style green curry.

1 tablespoon vegetable oil

1 small brown onion, finely chopped

2 cloves garlic, chopped

1 teaspoon grated fresh ginger

2–3 tablespoons Thai green curry paste
(see page 331)

1 kg (2 lb) chicken breast or thigh fillets,
cut into 2 cm (³⁄₄ in) pieces

¹⁄₃ cup coconut milk

250 g (8 oz) snake beans or green beans,
chopped into 4 cm (1¹⁄₂ in) lengths

1 tablespoon chopped coriander
(cilantro)

salt

Heat the oil in a large saucepan and add the onion, garlic and ginger. Cook over medium heat, stirring occasionally, for 3 minutes. Add the curry paste and cook, stirring, for 1 minute. Add the chicken and cook, stirring occasionally, for 2 minutes.

Add the coconut milk and bring to the boil. Reduce the heat and simmer gently, stirring occasionally, for 30 minutes, or until the chicken is tender. The sauce should have reduced and thickened by this stage.

Add the beans, stir well, and cook for 10 minutes, or until tender. There should not be a lot of sauce – just enough to coat the pieces of meat. If the mixture is very liquid, increase the heat and simmer until reduced. Use a spoon to remove any oil that rises to the top.

Stir through the coriander and season to taste with salt. Serve with steamed rice.

Vary the amount of curry paste used to suit your taste.

Serves 4

chicken, lemon and rocket risotto.

1.25 litres (40 fl oz) chicken stock
(see page 68)
3 skinless chicken breasts
50 g (1¾ oz) butter
1 onion, finely chopped
1 cup arborio or Vialone Nano rice

grated zest of 1 lemon
⅓ cup dry white wine
75 g (2½ oz) parmesan, freshly grated
50 g (1¾ oz) rocket (arugula), shredded
salt and freshly ground black pepper

Bring the stock to a gentle simmer in a large saucepan. Add the chicken breasts, return to simmering point and cook for about 10 minutes, or until the chicken is cooked through. Remove the meat, allow it to cool a little, then shred or chop and set aside until the risotto is cooked.

Meanwhile, heat 30 g (1 oz) of the butter in a large, heavy-based saucepan over medium heat. Add the onion and cook, stirring, for 5 minutes, or until soft but not coloured. Add the rice and lemon zest to the onion and stir gently for 2 minutes. Add the wine, stir and allow most of the liquid to evaporate.

Add enough of the simmering stock to just cover the rice. Stir and allow the rice to absorb most of the stock. Repeat the process, stirring well and adding stock as required. It will take 18–25 minutes to cook. Taste the rice for texture – it should be soft but still retain a little bite.

Remove from the heat and stir in the chicken meat, parmesan and rocket. Add the remaining butter, cover and rest for 5 minutes before serving. Season to taste with salt and freshly ground black pepper.

Serves 4

chicken liver pâté.

Chicken liver pâté seems to have fallen out of fashion, and I can't understand why. It is easy to make, can be made ahead of time and is really delicious.

250 g (8 oz) chicken livers

225 g (7 oz) butter

1 clove garlic, finely chopped

2 small brown shallots or half an onion, finely chopped

½ teaspoon fresh thyme leaves

2 tablespoons brandy

pinch of grated nutmeg

salt and freshly ground black pepper

50 g (1¾ oz) butter, extra

Trim the chicken livers of any stringy or green bits. Rinse livers, then pat dry with kitchen paper.

Melt 20 g (¾ oz) of the butter in a large frying pan over medium heat. Add the garlic and shallots and cook, stirring, for about 5 minutes, or until softened. Add the livers and thyme and cook, stirring frequently, for about 3 minutes, or until the livers are coloured on the outside but pink in the centre. Pour in the brandy, cook for an extra 10 seconds, then transfer the mixture to an electric blender.

Meanwhile, dice the remaining butter and let it soften a little. Turn on the blender and add the diced butter bit by bit, until the mixture is really smooth. Add the nutmeg and season to taste with salt and freshly ground black pepper. Spoon the pâté into 4–6 × ¾-cup-capacity ramekins or one large terrine dish.

Melt the extra butter and pour a little over the pâté. Cover with plastic wrap and refrigerate for at least 12 hours before eating.

Remove the pâté from the fridge about 20 minutes prior to serving. Serve with crusty bread or hot toast with lashings of butter.

Serves 4–6

chicken noodle soup.

1 medium-sized chicken

2 carrots, roughly chopped

2 onions, quartered

2 sticks celery, roughly chopped

2 bay leaves

1 tablespoon vegetable oil

1 leek, sliced

1 clove garlic, chopped

2 carrots, extra, sliced

1 onion, extra, sliced

1 stick celery, extra, sliced

100 g (3½ oz) dried fine egg noodles

½ teaspoon grated fresh ginger

salt and freshly ground black pepper

2 tablespoons chopped flat-leaf parsley
or coriander (cilantro)

2 spring onions (scallions), finely sliced

Place the chicken, carrots, onions, celery and bay leaves in a large saucepan or stockpot. Add 2 litres (64 fl oz) of water, or enough to cover the chicken and vegetables. Bring to the boil, remove any scum and simmer for 1 hour, skimming occasionally.

Remove the chicken and set aside to cool slightly.

Strain the broth, discarding the solids.

Heat the oil in a large saucepan over medium heat. Add the leek, garlic and extra carrots, onion and celery, and cook, stirring occasionally, for 5 minutes, or until tender. Add the strained broth and bring to the boil. Reduce the heat and simmer for 10 minutes.

Meanwhile, strip the chicken meat from the bones and tear into bite-sized pieces. Add to the soup.

Add the noodles and ginger and simmer for 4–5 minutes, or until the noodles are tender. Season to taste with salt and freshly ground black pepper. Ladle into bowls and top with parsley and spring onions.

Serves 4

chicken pie.

1 medium-sized chicken

2 onions, quartered

2 carrots, chopped

1 bay leaf

1 tablespoon olive oil

2 leeks, sliced

50 g (1¾ oz) unsalted butter

2 tablespoons plain (all-purpose) flour

1 tablespoon chopped chives or parsley

salt and freshly ground black pepper

1 × 380 g (12 oz) block frozen
    puff pastry, thawed

1 egg, beaten

Place the chicken, onions, carrots and bay leaf in a large saucepan. Cover with cold water and bring to the boil. Skim off any fat, reduce the heat and simmer for 1 hour.

Remove the chicken from the broth and set aside to cool. Strain the broth, discard the solids and return the strained liquid to the saucepan. Boil rapidly until it has reduced to about 2 cups. Set this stock aside.

Remove the meat from the chicken, cut into bite-sized pieces and place in a bowl.

Heat the oil in a frying pan over medium heat. Add the leek and cook, stirring, for 4–5 minutes, or until tender. Transfer to the bowl containing the chicken meat.

Melt the butter in a small saucepan over medium heat. Stir in the flour and cook for 1 minute. Whisk in the reserved stock. Bring to the boil and continue to whisk until thickened and smooth. Stir in the chives and season well with salt and freshly ground black pepper.

Add enough of the sauce to the leek and chicken mixture to moisten it. Allow to cool.

Preheat the oven to 190°C (375°F, Gas Mark 5).

Spoon the mixture into a large pie dish or tin and insert a pie funnel (if using). Roll out the pastry to a size large enough to cover the pie. Place over the pie, pressing down on the edges to seal. Trim away any excess pastry and use to decorate the top of the pie. Brush the pastry with the beaten egg and bake for 40–45 minutes, or until the pastry is golden and has risen.

Serves 4–6

chicken pot roast.

This great all-in-one dish needs minimal attention once it's in the oven.

2 tablespoons vegetable oil

2 rashers bacon, chopped

2 onions, peeled and quartered

4–6 large carrots, peeled and cut into
5 cm (2 in) pieces

8–10 small potatoes, peeled and halved

1 leek, thickly sliced

salt and freshly ground black pepper

1 tablespoon plain (all-purpose) flour

1 cup white wine

1 large chicken

300 ml (9½ fl oz) chicken stock
(see page 68)

4 sprigs thyme

2 bay leaves

Preheat the oven to 180°C (350°F, Gas Mark 4).

Heat the oil in a large, heatproof casserole dish over medium heat. Add the bacon, onion, carrot, potato and leek. Cook over medium heat, stirring occasionally, for 5–10 minutes, or until slightly coloured. Season well with salt and freshly ground black pepper. Sprinkle over the flour and cook, stirring, for 1 minute. Pour in the wine and stir with a wooden spoon, scraping up any bits stuck to the bottom.

Add the chicken to the casserole and pour in the chicken stock. Tuck in the thyme and bay leaves. Cover tightly with foil or with a lid, place in the oven and roast for 1½ hours, basting occasionally with the pan juices. Remove the lid 20 minutes before the end of the cooking time to allow the chicken to brown.

Remove the chicken and vegetables to a warm dish and check the sauce. Skim off any fat, adjust the seasoning and, if the sauce is too thin, reduce it over high heat on the stove top. Pour the sauce over the chicken.

Serves 4

chicken stock.

Chicken stock is a great base for soups, risottos and sauces, and making your own is simple.

1.5 kg (3 lb) chicken bones (wings, necks
    and giblets are good)
2 unpeeled onions, quartered
2 carrots, chopped
2 sticks celery, roughly chopped

1 teaspoon black peppercorns
3 bay leaves
6–8 parsley stalks
4 sprigs thyme

Place the chicken bones in a large stockpot. Add the remainder of the ingredients and enough cold water to cover by 5 cm (2 in). Bring to the boil, reduce the heat to low and simmer gently for 3–4 hours. Be careful not to let the mixture boil, otherwise the stock will become cloudy. Skim the surface with a spoon to remove any scum.

Strain the stock and discard the solids. Allow the liquid to cool, then refrigerate overnight.

The next day, skim off any fat that has solidified on the top. Refrigerate for 2–3 days, or freeze in 2-cup containers for up to 3 months.

Use the bones left after your next roast chicken, boosted with a few wings or giblets, to make a perfectly good stock.

Try using other vegetables in the stock, such as mushroom trimmings and / or leeks.

Be careful not to add too many carrots, as they can make the stock very sweet.

Leaving the onion skins on gives the stock good colour. But if you want a paler broth, remove the skins.

Makes 2 litres (64 fl oz)

chilli oil.

Chilli oil is easy to make, and using it is a simple way to add a little spice to a dish. Use it in marinades or dressings, drizzle it on bread or a pizza or add a little when making a stir-fry.

2 cups olive oil or vegetable oil
4 large red chillies, roughly chopped
1 bay leaf

1 clove garlic, peeled
1 teaspoon cayenne pepper

Pour the oil into a saucepan and place over gentle heat. When the oil is hot but not simmering, add the chilli, bay leaf and garlic and stir in the cayenne pepper. Heat gently for 5 minutes.

Remove from the heat, cover the pan and set it aside to cool. Leave the oil to infuse for 4 hours.

Strain through a fine sieve (or through muslin if you have some) into a clean and sterilised bottle. Label and date the bottle.

I often add a large, fresh red chilli or two to the bottle before filling (pierce the chillies with a skewer to help them sink).

You can use either fresh or dried chillies for the oil. I use large, red, milder chillies, but add a few small hot ones if you like.

Use olive oil rather than vegetable oil if you want to give the chilli oil as a gift or use it for dressings.

Makes 2 cups

chilli sauce.

This recipe is an easy homemade version of sweet chilli sauce – great as an accompaniment to Asian-style chicken, fish or noodle dishes.

1 cup white-wine vinegar or rice vinegar

1 cup sugar

2 cloves garlic, finely chopped

3 large red chillies, finely chopped

1 × 1 cm (½ in) piece fresh ginger, grated

½ teaspoon salt

1 tablespoon fish sauce

Place the vinegar, sugar and ¾ cup of water in a saucepan. Bring to a boil over medium heat, stirring to dissolve the sugar. Add the garlic, chilli, ginger, salt and fish sauce. Reduce the heat and simmer for 25–30 minutes, or until the sauce has thickened and is syrupy.

Sterilise a 3-cup-capacity glass-lidded bottle or jar by filling it with boiling water. Drain on a clean tea towel.

Fill the jar with the hot sauce and seal. Store in the refrigerator for up to 1 month.

It's a good idea to always wear gloves when handling chillies.

Makes 2 cups

chinese-style braised chicken.

2 chicken breasts

4 chicken thighs with drumsticks attached

150 ml (4½ fl oz) soy sauce

200 ml (6½ fl oz) light soy sauce

⅓ cup dry sherry

2 whole star anise

2 cloves garlic, peeled

4 × 5 mm (¼ in) slices fresh ginger

1 tablespoon sea salt

salt, extra, and freshly ground black pepper

2 teaspoons sesame oil

Place the chicken pieces in a large saucepan and add the soy sauces, sherry, star anise, garlic, ginger and salt and enough water to just cover the chicken. Bring slowly to the boil over low heat. Cover and simmer gently for 15 minutes. Turn the chicken pieces, replace the lid and simmer very gently for a further 15 minutes. Remove from the heat and leave the chicken in the covered saucepan for 20 minutes.

Remove the chicken from the saucepan, reserving the sauce, and pat dry with kitchen paper. Cut the breasts in half. Bring the sauce back to the boil and season to taste with salt and freshly ground black pepper.

Meanwhile, lightly brush the chicken with the sesame oil and grill under medium–high heat for 5–10 minutes, or until heated and crisp.

Serve the chicken pieces in individual bowls and pour over a little of the sauce. Offer a bowl of sauce on the side, as a dipping sauce, and accompany the meat with spinach or steamed Asian greens.

Serves 4

chocolate brownies.

125 g (4 oz) dark chocolate,
    roughly chopped
125 g (4 oz) unsalted butter, cubed
4 eggs
1½ cups caster (superfine) sugar

1 teaspoon vanilla essence
1 cup plain (all-purpose) flour, sifted
100 g (3½ oz) pecans or walnuts, lightly
    toasted and roughly chopped

Preheat the oven to 160°C (315°F, Gas Mark 2–3). Grease a 20 × 30 cm (8 × 12 in) baking tin and line the base and sides with baking paper.

Melt the chocolate and butter in a heatproof bowl set over a saucepan of barely simmering water, stirring occasionally, until smooth. Allow to cool.

In an electric mixer, beat the eggs, sugar and vanilla for 3–4 minutes, or until pale and fluffy. Beat in the cooled chocolate mixture. Add the flour and beat until smooth. Stir in the nuts.

Spoon the mixture into the prepared baking tin and smooth the surface. Bake for 30 minutes, or until dark brown and the top has formed a crust. Allow to cool in the tin. Remove and cut into squares. Dust with icing (confectioners') sugar to serve.

To make orange and macadamia brownies, omit the pecans or walnuts and stir into the mixture 2 teaspoons of finely grated orange zest and 100 g (3½ oz) of roughly chopped macadamia nuts.

Brownies can be drizzled with melted chocolate or spread with chocolate icing, or frosting (see page 74).

Makes 24

chocolate cake.

This dark, fudgey and delicious chocolate cake is easy to make. It is perfect for afternoon tea or coffee, and packs well for lunch boxes or a picnic.

250 g (8 oz) dark chocolate,
    roughly chopped
250 g (8 oz) unsalted butter, cubed
1 teaspoon instant coffee powder

4 eggs, beaten
½ cup caster (superfine) sugar
1 cup self-raising (self-rising) flour, sifted
½ cup ground hazelnuts

Preheat the oven to 160°C (315°F, Gas Mark 2–3). Grease a 20 cm (8 in) springform cake tin and line the base with baking paper.

Melt the chocolate, butter and coffee powder in a heatproof bowl set over a saucepan of barely simmering water, stirring occasionally, until smooth. Allow to cool.

In an electric mixer, beat the eggs and sugar for 4–5 minutes, or until pale and fluffy. Beat in the cooled chocolate mixture until smooth. Gently fold in the flour and hazelnuts.

Pour the mixture into the prepared tin and bake for 50–55 minutes, or until a skewer inserted into the centre comes out clean. Leave to cool in the tin for 10 minutes before turning out. Allow to cool completely on a wire rack before serving lightly dusted with icing (confectioners') sugar.

The chocolate and butter can be melted in a microwave. Cook on medium for 1–2 minutes. Stir until smooth.

Replace the ground hazelnuts with ground almonds, if you prefer.

Make a simple icing (frosting) by melting 125 g (4 oz) of roughly chopped dark chocolate and 40 g (1¼ oz) of cubed unsalted butter. Stir until smooth. Allow to cool. Beat with a wooden spoon until fluffy, then spread over the cooled cake.

chocolate cake (flourless).

250 g (8 oz) dark chocolate,
   roughly chopped
²/₃ cup caster (superfine) sugar
150 g (5 oz) unsalted butter, cubed

1 tablespoon brandy
1 tablespoon strong black coffee
125 g (4 oz) ground almonds or hazelnuts
5 eggs, separated

Preheat the oven to 180°C (350°F, Gas Mark 4). Grease a 23 cm (9 in) springform cake tin and line the base with baking paper.

Melt the chocolate, sugar, butter, brandy and coffee in a heatproof bowl over a saucepan of barely simmering water, stirring occasionally until smooth.

Transfer to a large bowl and stir in the ground nuts. Add the egg yolks, one at a time, beating well after each addition.

In a separate clean bowl, whisk the egg whites until they form medium–firm peaks. Stir a third of the whites into the chocolate mixture to slacken it, then gently fold through the remaining whites with a large metal spoon or spatula.

Pour the mixture into the prepared tin and bake for 45–50 minutes, or until the cake is firm to the touch but still a little soft in the centre.

Allow to cool completely in the tin. The cake will sink a little as it cools. Carefully remove from the tin and serve lightly dusted with icing (confectioners') sugar.

chocolate chip cookies.

125 g (4 oz) plain (all-purpose) flour

$^1/_2$ teaspoon bicarbonate of soda
   (sodium bicarbonate)

salt

125 g (4 oz) butter, softened

$^1/_2$ cup caster (superfine) sugar

1 teaspoon vanilla essence

1 large egg, lightly beaten

125 g (4 oz) dark chocolate chips

Preheat the oven to 180°C (350°F, Gas Mark 4). Line two oven trays with baking paper.

Sift the flour, bicarbonate of soda and a pinch of salt into a bowl.

In a separate bowl, beat the butter, sugar and vanilla essence with an electric mixer until fluffy and pale. Beat in the egg, a little at a time, alternating with a little of the sifted flour mixture, until combined. Fold in the remaining flour, then stir in the chocolate chips until combined.

Using a tablespoon, scoop up walnut-sized pieces of dough and place them on the prepared oven trays, leaving room for each to spread a little. Bake for 8–10 minutes, or until the cookies are firm and coloured. You may need to bake a third tray if any mixture remains. Cool on a wire rack.

These cookies are also good with the addition of 50 g (1¼ oz) of chopped pecans.

Makes about 30

chocolate cookies.

With chocolate, as with everything else in cooking, the better the quality of the raw ingredient, the better the end result.

125 g (4 oz) dark chocolate,
    roughly chopped
125 g (4 oz) unsalted butter, chopped
1 egg

1 cup lightly packed brown sugar
1¼ cups self-raising (self-rising) flour,
    sifted

Preheat the oven to 180°C (350°F, Gas Mark 4). Line two oven trays with baking paper.

Melt the chocolate and butter in a heatproof bowl set over a saucepan of barely simmering water, stirring occasionally, until smooth.

In a separate bowl, beat the egg and sugar with a wooden spoon until combined.

Stir the chocolate mixture into the egg mixture. Add the flour and mix until smooth and thick. Refrigerate for 20 minutes.

Roll teaspoonfuls of the dough into balls and place on the oven trays, allowing 5 cm (2 in) between each for the biscuits to spread while cooking.

Bake for 7–10 minutes, or until the biscuits are firm to the touch and the tops have wrinkled slightly. Cool on a wire rack and store in an airtight container.

To decorate, these biscuits may be spread, dipped or drizzled with melted dark, milk or white chocolate.

Makes 24–30

chocolate fondant puddings.

200 g (6½ oz) good-quality dark chocolate, chopped (luxury Belgian dark chocolate is ideal)

100 g (3½ oz) butter, chopped

3 eggs

2 egg yolks

100 g (3½ oz) caster (superfine) sugar

¼ cup plain (all-purpose) flour

Thickly butter and flour 4 × 200 ml (6½ fl oz) metal pudding tins. Place the tins in the freezer to chill while you make the mixture.

Melt the chocolate and butter in a heatproof bowl set over a small saucepan of barely simmering water, stirring occasionally, until smooth.

In an electric mixer, beat the eggs, egg yolks and sugar on medium speed for 3–4 minutes, or until thick and pale. Gradually add the chocolate mixture, mixing until combined. Sift in the flour and fold through until smooth.

Spoon the mixture into the prepared pudding tins, filling them almost to the top. Transfer to the refrigerator and chill for at least 30 minutes – the puddings can be made ahead of time and stored in the refrigerator for up to 24 hours.

Preheat the oven to 200°C (400°F, Gas Mark 6).

Bake for 11 minutes (the cooking time is crucial) and remove from the oven. The puddings should be set on the top. Allow them to sit in their tins for 2 minutes, then loosen the puddings by running a knife around the inside edge of the tins. Invert each tin onto a serving plate and serve with scoops of vanilla ice-cream.

The mixture can also be frozen (uncooked) in pudding moulds for up to 4 weeks. Frozen puddings will need to be cooked for 25 minutes from frozen.

Makes 4

chocolate macaroons.

3 large egg whites
³/₄ cup caster (superfine) sugar
100 g (3¹/₂ oz) ground almonds
    (almond meal)

¹/₄ cup cocoa, sifted
salt
1 teaspoon vanilla extract

Preheat the oven to 170°C (340°F, Gas Mark 3). Line two oven trays with baking paper.

Using an electric mixer, whisk the egg whites until fluffy, then gradually beat in ¹/₃ cup of the sugar, until the mixture is glossy and firm peaks form.

Combine the remaining sugar and the ground almonds, cocoa and a pinch of salt, and gently fold into the egg whites with a large metal spoon, until thoroughly blended. Stir in the vanilla extract.

Drop tablespoonfuls of the mixture onto the prepared oven trays, leaving a little space between each for spreading. Bake for 15–20 minutes, or until the macaroons are firm but not dry. You may need to bake a third tray if any mixture remains. Allow to cool on the trays for 5 minutes before carefully transferring to a wire rack to cool completely. Store in an airtight container in a cool, dry place for up to 5 days.

Macaroons are wonderful sandwiched together with a little chocolate ganache. Melt 150 g (5 oz) of dark chocolate with 100 ml (3½ fl oz) of cream in a small saucepan over low heat, stirring until smooth. Chill, then beat well with a wooden spoon. Sandwich between macaroons and set aside for 2 hours before serving.

Makes about 36

chocolate mousse.

Universally adored and made with just three ingredients, chocolate mousse is equally at home at a dinner party or a simple supper.

3 eggs, separated
200 g (6½ oz) dark chocolate,
   roughly chopped

¾ cup cream

In a small bowl, lightly beat the egg yolks.

Melt the chocolate in a heatproof bowl set over a saucepan of barely simmering water, stirring occasionally, until smooth. Remove from the heat and gradually add the beaten yolks, mixing until smooth. Fold through the cream and stir until combined.

Whisk the egg whites with an electric mixer until soft peaks form. Fold a little of the whites into the mousse to slacken it, then gently fold through the remaining whites. Mix until there are no streaks or pockets of egg white.

Pour the mixture evenly into six small ramekins or cups, cover with plastic wrap and chill for at least 3 hours, or until firm.

Add to the mixture 2 tablespoons of strong espresso and a little brandy or liqueur for greater depth of flavour.

Chocolate mousse can be made ahead of time and kept covered in the fridge for 2–3 days.

Serves 6

chocolate muffins.

150 g (5 oz) dark chocolate, chopped

125 g (4 oz) butter, chopped

2 cups self-raising (self-rising) flour

1 teaspoon baking powder

4 tablespoons cocoa

salt

100 g (3½ oz) dark chocolate chips

1 cup caster (superfine) sugar

185 ml (6 fl oz) milk

1 teaspoon lemon juice

2 eggs

Preheat the oven to 180°C (350°F, Gas Mark 4). Grease a 12-cup muffin tin or line with paper patty cases.

Melt the chocolate and butter in a heatproof bowl set over a saucepan of barely simmering water, stirring occasionally, until smooth.

Sift the flour, baking powder, cocoa and a pinch of salt into a mixing bowl. Stir in the chocolate chips and sugar and make a well in the centre.

In a jug, combine the milk, lemon juice and eggs and pour into the well in the flour mixture. Pour in the melted chocolate and butter and stir until the ingredients are just combined. Do not over-mix – the batter should not be smooth.

Divide the mixture evenly between the muffin cups. Bake for 20 minutes, or until the muffins are firm to the touch. Allow to cool in the tin for 10 minutes, then turn out onto a wire rack to cool completely.

These muffins are good served warm and simply dusted with cocoa or icing (confectioners') sugar.

If you do want to ice them you can make chocolate icing by melting 200 g (6½ oz) of chopped dark chocolate in a bowl set over a saucepan of barely simmering water, stirring occasionally, until smooth. Stir in ½ cup of sour cream and ¼ cup of icing (confectioners') sugar and mix until smooth. Remove from the heat and spread over the muffins.

Makes 12

chocolate peanut butter cake.

Chocolate and peanut butter is the perfect combination for me – and this is a cake for the child in all of us. This recipe gives good results and is an adaptation of a cake I found in *The Chocolate Book*, written by Christine France.

75 g (2½ oz) dark chocolate, chopped

1 cup plain (all-purpose) flour

1 teaspoon baking powder

salt

110 g (3½ oz) unsalted butter, softened

110 g (3½ oz) crunchy peanut butter

1 cup brown sugar

2 large eggs, beaten

¼ cup milk

Preheat the oven to 180°C (350°F, Gas Mark 4). Grease a 19 × 9 × 6.5 cm (7½ × 3½ × 2½ in) loaf tin and line the base with baking paper.

Melt the chocolate in a heatproof bowl set over a saucepan of barely simmering water, stirring occasionally, until smooth. Allow to cool.

Sift together the flour, baking powder and a pinch of salt.

In an electric mixer, beat the butter, peanut butter and sugar for 3–4 minutes, or until pale and creamy. Gradually add the beaten eggs, alternating with spoonfuls of the flour, mixing well after each addition. Lightly fold in the remaining flour, alternating with the milk until just blended.

Pour half the mixture into a second bowl, add the chocolate and stir.

Using a large spoon, drop alternate spoonfuls of each mixture into the prepared tin. When all the mixture is in the tin, pull a large, flat knife through the batters to create a marbled effect. Bake for 45–55 minutes, or until golden and firm to the touch. A skewer inserted into the centre should come out clean. Turn out onto a wire rack to cool. Serve dusted with a little icing (confectioners') sugar.

chocolate puddings.

This is a simple, quick and easy dessert. As the puddings cook,
the batter turns magically into a rich chocolate sauce, topped with
a soft chocolate sponge.

1 cup self-raising (self-rising) flour

⅓ cup cocoa

salt

½ cup caster (superfine) sugar

½ cup milk

1 egg, lightly beaten

60 g (2 oz) unsalted butter, melted

½ teaspoon vanilla essence

½ cup lightly packed brown sugar

Preheat the oven to 180°C (350°F, Gas Mark 4). Grease 4 × 1-cup-capacity ramekins or small pudding bowls.

In a mixing bowl, sift together the flour, half the cocoa and a pinch of salt. Stir in the caster sugar and make a well in the centre.

In a separate bowl, combine the milk, egg, melted butter and vanilla. Pour into the well in the dry mixture and mix until smooth.

Spoon the mixture into the prepared ramekins and place on an oven tray. Combine the brown sugar and the remaining cocoa and sprinkle evenly over the top of each pudding. Bring 1 cup of water to the boil and carefully pour enough of the boiling water over the back of a spoon to fill each pudding to three-quarters. Bake for 20–25 minutes, or until the puddings have risen and are firm to the touch. Serve immediately, lightly dusted with icing (confectioners') sugar.

These puddings are delicious served with thick cream or good-quality vanilla ice-cream.

One large pudding can be made in a 4-cup-capacity soufflé dish. In this case, bake for 40–50 minutes.

Serves 4

chocolate sauce.

This easy-to-make, all-time favourite sauce is fantastic served warm
over ice-cream, pancakes, waffles, poached fruit or puddings.

250 g (8 oz) dark chocolate,
   roughly chopped
½ cup cream

40 g (1¼ oz) unsalted butter
1 tablespoon golden syrup

Place all the ingredients in a small saucepan over low heat. Stir until the chocolate has melted and the sauce is smooth.

Chocolate sauce is delicious flavoured with a little alcohol. Add 1 tablespoon of brandy or liqueur at the end of the cooking time and remove from the heat.

Any excess sauce may be stored in the fridge for up to 1 week. Gently reheat before serving.

Makes 2 cups

chocolate truffles.

Chocolate truffles are the ultimate in chocolate treats, and this rich, elegant and highly treasured confectionery is easy to make.

½ cup cream
250 g (8 oz) dark chocolate,
    roughly chopped

40 g (1¼ oz) unsalted butter, cubed
1 tablespoon cognac or brandy
cocoa, to coat

Heat the cream in a small saucepan and gently bring to the boil. Remove from the heat and add the chocolate and butter. Mix with a spoon or whisk until smooth. Add the cognac or brandy and stir well until combined. Cover and refrigerate until firm.

Using a melon-baller or two teaspoons, shape the mixture into balls 2 cm (¾ in) in diameter. Roll each ball between the palms of your hands to smooth them out. If the weather is humid and this is difficult to do, roll them into rough shapes, freeze for 10 minutes and re-roll.

Coat the truffles by tossing in cocoa. The truffles are best eaten fresh, but will keep in an airtight container in the refrigerator for up to 2 weeks.

Be sure to use the best-quality chocolate you can find. It really makes a difference.

Try rolling the truffles in finely chopped hazelnuts, macadamia nuts or almonds instead of cocoa.

Vary the flavour by replacing the cognac with Cointreau, Grand Marnier or cherry-flavoured brandy.

Makes 20

christmas pudding.

My favourite Christmas pudding recipe comes from British food writer Katie Stewart.

110 g (3½ oz) self-raising (self-rising) flour

1 teaspoon mixed spice

salt

75 g (2½ oz) fresh white breadcrumbs

30 g (1 oz) flaked almonds

350 g (11 oz) mixed dried fruits

1 tart dessert apple, peeled, coarsely grated

2 large eggs

juice and grated zest of 1 lemon

1 tablespoon black treacle

175 g (6 oz) light muscovado sugar

110 g (3½ oz) butter

2 tablespoons brandy or rum, plus extra, to serve

Sift the flour, mixed spice and a pinch of salt into a large mixing bowl. Add the breadcrumbs, flaked almonds, dried fruit and apple.

In a jug, combine the eggs, lemon juice, zest and the treacle. Melt the muscovado sugar and butter in a saucepan over low heat. Pour the butter mixture and the egg mixture into the dry ingredients and mix. Cover with a cloth and allow to stand for 1 hour.

Mix again. Butter a 1.2-litre pudding basin. Spoon in the mixture, ensuring the top is level. Cover with buttered baking paper containing a few small pleats, then cover the top of the basin with pleated foil or baking paper and secure with string.

To steam the pudding, preheat the oven to 150°C (300°F, Gas Mark 2). Place the pudding in a deep baking tin and pour boiling water into the baking tin to a depth of 2.5 cm (1 in). Cover the tin with a tent of foil and cook for 4–5 hours.

Let the pudding cool completely. Discard the coverings. Spoon over the brandy and re-cover. Store somewhere cool for up to 4 months – the refrigerator is a good place.

To serve the pudding, let it come to room temperature, re-cover with buttered baking paper and secure with foil, and steam for 2 hours. Invert the pudding onto a warm serving plate and remove the bowl. Flame the pudding with brandy, if desired.

Serves 8–10

cinnamon toast.

½ cup caster (superfine) sugar

2 teaspoons ground cinnamon

6 slices white bread

50 g (1¾ oz) unsalted butter, softened

In a small bowl, combine the sugar and cinnamon.

Preheat the griller (broiler).

Toast the bread lightly on both sides, then butter each slice, spreading the butter right to the edges. Using a shaker or spoon, sprinkle each slice of toast evenly with plenty of the cinnamon–sugar mixture.

Return the slices to the griller and toast until the sugar starts to melt. Remove, trim away the crusts and cut into quarters. Serve hot.

Any unused cinnamon and sugar mixture can be stored in a screw-top jar.

Serves 3–4

cocoa.

½ cup Dutch cocoa
⅓ cup caster (superfine) sugar
3 cups milk

1 teaspoon vanilla essence
whipped cream and marshmallows
(optional), to serve

Sift the cocoa and sugar into a medium-sized saucepan. Add 1 cup of water and whisk over low heat for 2–3 minutes, or until the sugar has dissolved and the mixture is smooth. Add the milk, increase the heat to medium and cook for 10–12 minutes, whisking regularly, or until steam rises from the surface and tiny bubbles form around the edge. Do not let the mixture boil – taste it occasionally with a spoon to check the temperature. The regular whisking helps make the cocoa nice and frothy.

Stir in the vanilla. Pour the cocoa into four cups or mugs, top with whipped cream and marshmallows, if desired, and serve immediately.

The secret to cocoa with a deep chocolate flavour is to use both water and milk.

If you want to increase or decrease the quantity of the recipe above, the key ratio to remember is 1½ tablespoons of cocoa to 1 heaped tablespoon of sugar per cup of liquid.

Serves 4

coconut fish curry.

This is a simple variation of a Thai green curry. The coconut milk adds smoothness and balances the spices and the heat.

1 tablespoon vegetable oil

1 shallot or small onion, thinly sliced

1 teaspoon grated fresh ginger

3–4 tablespoons homemade Thai green curry paste (see page 331), or good-quality bought Thai green curry paste

2 cups coconut milk

1 teaspoon palm or brown sugar

1 kg (2 lb) blue-eye cod fillets or other large white fish fillets, cut into 5 cm (2 in) pieces

1 tablespoon Thai fish sauce

juice of 1 lime

1 cup lightly packed coriander (cilantro) or basil leaves, to serve

salt

1 lime, to serve

Heat the oil in a large saucepan and add the shallot and ginger. Cook over medium heat, stirring occasionally, for 3 minutes. Add the curry paste and cook, stirring, for a further minute.

Add the coconut milk and sugar and bring to the boil. Reduce the heat and simmer gently, stirring occasionally, for 15 minutes – this allows the flavours to develop.

Add the fish pieces, stir well and cook for 5 minutes, or until tender. Use a spoon to remove any oil that rises to the top. Stir in the fish sauce, lime juice and half the coriander. Season to taste with salt. Serve with steamed rice and a lime quarter, and garnish with the remaining coriander.

Vary the amount of curry paste to suit your taste.

Serves 4

coleslaw.

½ Savoy cabbage or red cabbage,
   finely shredded

2 carrots, coarsely grated

1 red (Spanish) onion, finely sliced

1 clove garlic, finely chopped

3 spring onions (scallions), finely sliced

1 tablespoon olive oil

1 tablespoon lemon juice

salt and freshly ground black pepper

½ cup mayonnaise (see page 192)

Mix together the cabbage, carrot, red onion, garlic, spring onions, oil and lemon juice. Season to taste with salt and freshly ground black pepper. Stir through the mayonnaise. Add a little extra mayonnaise if necessary to coat the cabbage evenly.

Coleslaw can be made 2–3 hours ahead of time. Simply cover and chill until needed.

One to two tablespoons of plain yoghurt or sour cream is delicious stirred into the mayonnaise before mixing into the coleslaw.

To make an Asian-style coleslaw, add 1 seeded and chopped large red chilli, 2 tablespoons of finely chopped mint and 100 g (3½ oz) of bean sprouts to the salad. Omit the mayonnaise and make a dressing by thoroughly combining 1 tablespoon of Thai fish sauce, 2 tablespoons of lime juice, 2 teaspoons of soy sauce, 1 teaspoon of brown sugar and 1 tablespoon of olive oil. Pour the dressing over the salad and set aside for 10 minutes to allow the flavours to develop before serving.

Serves 4–6

corn on the cob.

This is the true taste of summer. Whether you boil or barbecue your corn on the cob, make sure you eat it with lots of butter, sea salt and freshly ground black pepper. You are definitely supposed to get messy when eating corn on the cob!

To boil corn on the cob, discard the husk and silk from the cob and place the cob in a large saucepan of unsalted boiling water. Add 1 tablespoon of olive oil and boil for 8–10 minutes, or until a kernel can be pried easily from a cob with the point of a knife. The kernels should be tender but slightly chewy, with a juicy, sweet flavour.

To grill or roast corn on the cob, strip back the husk, remove the silk, brush the corn with melted butter or oil and rewrap the corn in the husk. Tie the husk back into position with string, or tightly twist the husk ends together to secure. Soak in a bowl of water for 10 minutes. Grill for 15 minutes on a hot barbecue or preheated grill plate, or roast in a preheated 220°C (425°F, Gas Mark 7) oven for 15–20 minutes, turning every 5 minutes.

Corn on the cob is delicious served with herb butter (see page 310) or garlic butter (see page 135).

corned beef (silverside).

1 × 1.5–2 kg (3–4 lb) piece corned beef
    (silverside)
4 onions, peeled and quartered
6 carrots, cut into 5 cm (2 in) pieces
2 bay leaves
handful of parsley stems
6–8 whole black peppercorns
½ star anise (optional, but good)

6 carrots, extra, sliced into 1 cm (½ in)
    pieces
12 small potatoes, scrubbed
1 small cabbage, halved, cored and cut into
    4 cm (1½ in) wedges
350 g (11 oz) fresh or frozen shelled peas
2 tablespoons chopped parsley
mustard-flavoured mayonnaise (see below)

Soak the corned beef in a very large saucepan of cold water for 3–4 hours (or over-night). Drain off the liquid and cover the meat with plenty of fresh cold water. Add the onion, carrot, bay leaves, parsley stems, peppercorns and star anise. Bring to the boil and simmer gently for 2½ hours.

Skim off the fat with a large spoon. Remove and discard the vegetables and ladle off half of the cooking liquid. Add the extra carrots and the potatoes and cabbage, and bring back to the boil. Cook for 20 minutes. Add the peas and cook for a further 5 minutes, or until the vegetables are tender.

Remove the beef and carve it into 1 cm (½ in) thick slices. Serve in large pasta bowls, surrounded by the vegetables. Ladle over a little cooking liquid and sprinkle with the parsley. Serve with a dollop of mustard-flavoured mayonnaise.

Make mustard mayonnaise by stirring 1 teaspoon of hot, ready-made mustard and 1 teaspoon of lemon juice into ½ cup of good-quality bought or homemade mayonnaise (see page 192).

Serves 6

couscous.

Couscous is the perfect healthy convenience food and is used in salads,
as well as to accompany tagines or braised dishes. Most varieties available are
precooked and only need moistening and steaming,
so preparation time is minimal.

1 cup couscous

1¼ cups chicken stock (see page 68)
   or water

2 tablespoons butter or vegetable oil

salt

Place the couscous in a medium-sized heatproof bowl and pour over the stock or boiling water. Add the butter or oil and a pinch of salt. Cover with plastic wrap and stand for 5 minutes, or until the liquid has been absorbed.

If using in a salad or serving at room temperature, simply fluff the grains with a fork. If serving hot as an accompaniment to a braised dish or tagine, place the bowl containing the couscous over a saucepan of simmering water for 5–10 minutes, or until warmed through. Fluff with a fork to help separate the grains.

Traditionally, couscous is placed in a steamer lined with muslin or cheesecloth and heated over simmering water for 5–10 minutes to warm through.

Chopped mint, coriander (cilantro) or flat-leaf parsley may be folded through couscous before serving.

Make a delicious couscous salad by folding through roasted pumpkin, shredded rocket (arugula) or basil, finely grated lemon zest, chopped red (Spanish) onion, crushed garlic, chopped fresh chilli, salt and pepper and a drizzle of olive oil.

Serves 4

cranberry sauce.

Cranberry sauce is wonderful with turkey or ham, in sandwiches,
or served simply with cheese.

500 g (1 lb) fresh or frozen and thawed
    cranberries
½ cup orange juice
2 teaspoons finely grated orange zest

⅓ cup port
1 cinnamon stick
1–1½ cups caster (superfine) sugar

Place the cranberries, orange juice and zest, port and cinnamon stick in a medium-sized stainless-steel saucepan and slowly bring to the boil over low heat. Simmer gently, stirring occasionally, for 10–15 minutes, or until the cranberries have burst and the sauce has reduced slightly.

Add the sugar and stir until dissolved. Cranberries can be quite tart; taste and add a little extra sugar if needed. Discard the cinnamon stick. Transfer the mixture to a bowl and allow to cool. The sauce will thicken slightly. Serve cold.

The port may be replaced with water or extra orange juice, if you prefer.

Other spices work well with cranberry sauce. One whole star anise used in place of the cinnamon stick makes an interesting variation.

Makes 2 cups

creamed corn.

Proper homemade creamed corn makes a great side dish to grilled steak or barbecued sausages, and a delicious companion to roast chicken.
Corn is in season from summer to early autumn, so take advantage of this sweet-tasting vegetable while it's available.

4 fresh cobs of corn
30 g (1 oz) butter
1 small onion, chopped

¾ cup cream
salt and freshly ground black pepper

To prepare the corn, discard the husks and silk from the cobs. Rinse quickly and pat dry. Stand a cob upright on a chopping board and, using a sharp knife, slice downwards, cutting the kernels from the cob. Repeat with the remaining cobs.

Melt the butter in a medium-sized saucepan over gentle heat and add the onion. Sauté for 4–5 minutes, or until tender. Add the corn kernels and cook over medium heat, stirring occasionally, for 8 minutes. Stir in the cream, cover the pan, reduce the heat a little and cook, stirring occasionally, for 10 minutes, or until the corn is tender and the mixture is slightly thickened. Season well with salt and pepper.

The kernels should be nicely coated with cream – add a little extra if needed, or reduce the sauce over high heat if there is too much liquid. Be careful not to let the cream catch. Serve hot.

Buy corn as fresh as possible and eat it soon after purchasing. When selecting corn to buy, look for firm green cobs with clean white silks.

Creamed corn is also good with the addition of a little chopped red chilli and some freshly snipped chives.

Serves 4–6

crème anglaise.

2¹⁄₂ cups milk

1 vanilla bean

6 egg yolks

¹⁄₂ cup caster (superfine) sugar

Pour the milk into a small saucepan. Using a sharp knife, split the vanilla bean in half lengthways. Scrape out the seeds and add the pod and the seeds to the saucepan of milk. Bring the mixture to simmering point over low heat.

In a large mixing bowl, whisk together the egg yolks and sugar for 4–5 minutes, or until the sugar has dissolved and the mixture is thick and pale. Gently whisk the hot milk mixture, including the vanilla bean pod, into the yolk mixture. Return this mixture to the saucepan and cook over low heat, stirring constantly with a wooden spoon, until the mixture thickens slightly to form a custard which coats the back of the spoon. Do not allow the mixture to boil or it will curdle. Remove from the heat and strain into a bowl, discarding the vanilla bean pod.

Serve warm or at room temperature with puddings, fruit pies or poached or fresh fruit. Crème anglaise can be stored in an airtight container in the fridge for up to 5 days. Simply bring to room temperature before use.

A richer version can be made by replacing the milk with half milk and half cream.

Brandy crème anglaise can be made by adding 2 tablespoons of brandy to the mixture after removing from the heat.

Makes 3 cups

crème brûlée.

2½ cups cream

1 vanilla bean or 1 teaspoon vanilla essence

8 egg yolks

¼ cup caster (superfine) sugar

caster (superfine) sugar, extra, to serve

Preheat the oven to 180°C (350°F, Gas Mark 4).

Pour the cream into a medium-sized saucepan. Using a sharp knife, split the vanilla bean in half lengthways. Scrape out the seeds and add the pod and the seeds to the saucepan of cream. Bring the mixture to simmering point over low heat.

In a large mixing bowl, whisk together the egg yolks and sugar for 2 minutes. Gently whisk the hot milk mixture, including the vanilla bean, into the yolk mixture. Return this mixture to the saucepan and cook over low heat, stirring constantly with a wooden spoon, until the mixture thickens slightly to form a custard that coats the back of the spoon. Do not allow the mixture to boil or it will curdle. Remove from the heat and strain into a jug, discarding the vanilla pod. Divide the mixture between 6 × 7.5 cm (3 in) diameter ramekins, filling each almost to the top.

Transfer the ramekins to a large baking tin and fill the tin with enough boiling water to come halfway up the sides of the ramekins. Carefully transfer to the oven and bake for 20–25 minutes, or until the custard has just set.

Remove ramekins from the water bath, allow to cool and chill overnight.

To finish the crème brûlées, cover the top of the custards with a thin, even layer of caster sugar. Place the ramekins on an oven tray and set them under a very hot grill, until the sugar has melted and coloured, adding a little more sugar if needed.

If using a grill to finish the brûlée, a good tip is to place the ramekins in a shallow dish and surround them with ice — this helps to stop the custard becoming soft under the heat.

Makes 6–8

crêpes with lemon and sugar.

125 g (4 oz) plain (all-purpose) flour

salt

1 large egg

1 large egg yolk

1 cup milk

30 g (1 oz) butter, melted

20 g (¾ oz) butter, extra, for cooking

caster (superfine) sugar, to serve

lemon juice, to serve

Sift the flour and a pinch of salt into a mixing bowl. Add the egg, egg yolk and half of the milk. Using a wooden spoon, stir from the centre, gradually drawing in the flour from around the sides of the bowl. Gradually add the remaining milk and stir in ¼ cup of water and the melted butter. Beat well with the spoon until smooth.

Transfer the mixture to a jug and allow to stand for 30 minutes in a cool place. The batter will thicken on standing, so add a little more milk if needed before cooking – the batter should be the thickness of cream.

Heat an 18–20 cm (7–8 in) frying or crêpe pan over medium heat and, when hot, add a little butter. Pour approximately ¼ cup of batter into the pan and tilt the pan in a circular motion so that the batter evenly coats the surface. Cook for 2 minutes, or until the underside is light brown. Use a spatula to flip it and cook the other side. Remove to a warm plate.

Wipe the pan with a little extra butter and repeat the cooking process with the remaining batter. Layer the crêpes between slices of greaseproof paper to keep warm.

To serve, fold each crêpe in half, sprinkle with sugar and lemon juice and fold in half again. Serve extra sugar and wedges of lemon at the table.

Makes 8

cupcakes.

1½ cups self-raising (self-rising) flour

125 g (4 oz) unsalted butter, softened

¾ cup caster (superfine) sugar

1 teaspoon vanilla essence

2 eggs, beaten

½ cup milk

Preheat the oven to 180°C (350°F, Gas Mark 4). Line a 12-hole cupcake tin with paper patty cases.

Sift the flour into a large mixing bowl. Add the remaining ingredients and beat with a wooden spoon or an electric mixer on low speed until the mixture is just combined. Don't over-beat the mixture. Increase the speed to medium and beat for 3 minutes, or until pale and smooth.

Spoon the mixture evenly into the patty cases. Bake for 15–20 minutes, or until golden and firm to the touch. A skewer inserted into the centre of a cupcake should come out clean. Cool on a wire rack. Ice and decorate as desired.

For orange cupcakes, substitute ½ cup of freshly squeezed orange juice for the milk and add 1 tablespoon of finely grated orange zest to the cake batter. Bake as above.

To make lemon icing (frosting), combine 1 cup of sifted icing (confectioners') sugar, 20 g (¾ oz) of softened unsalted butter and 1–2 tablespoons of lemon juice. Beat until smooth and spread over the cupcakes.

To make strawberry icing (frosting), mash 6 large ripe strawberries with a fork. Combine the strawberries, 1 cup of sifted icing (confectioners') sugar, 1–2 drops of pink food colouring and 1–2 tablespoons of lemon juice. Beat until smooth and spread over the cupcakes.

Makes 12

curry powder.

Making your own freshly ground and blended curry powder will fill your kitchen with exotic scents and your cupboard with a useful and delicious preparation. There are many variations of this popular Indian curry mix; the following blend is spicy, but not too hot. Homemade blends allow you to vary and adjust the flavour and spice to your individual taste.

¼ cup coriander seeds

1 tablespoon cumin seeds

1 tablespoon mustard seeds

1 teaspoon cardamom seeds, pods removed

8 whole cloves

1 × 5 cm (2 in) cinnamon stick, broken up

½ teaspoon freshly grated nutmeg

1–2 dried red chillies

2 tablespoons ground turmeric

Place the coriander, cumin, mustard and cardamom seeds, and the cloves and cinnamon, in a small frying pan. Place the pan over medium heat and toast the spices, stirring frequently, for 1–2 minutes. The spices will colour slightly and give off a wonderfully aromatic scent.

Allow to cool in the pan, then combine with the remaining ingredients. Grind to a fine powder in a mortar and pestle, spice mill or electric coffee grinder. Store in an airtight container in a cool, dark place for up to 6 months.

Increase the heat, if that's what you like, by adding more dried or powdered chillies.

An electric coffee grinder makes a great tool for grinding spices, but remember to use it just for spices.

custard.

75 ml (2½ fl oz) milk

2½ cups cream

1 vanilla bean

6 egg yolks

100 g (3½ oz) caster (superfine) sugar

1 heaped tablespoon cornflour (cornstarch)

Pour the milk and cream into a small saucepan. Using a sharp knife, split the vanilla bean in half lengthways. Scrape out the seeds and add the pod and the seeds to the saucepan. Bring the mixture to simmering point over low heat.

In a large mixing bowl, whisk together the egg yolks, sugar and cornflour for 2–3 minutes. Gently whisk the hot milk mixture, including the vanilla bean pod, into the yolk mixture. Return this mixture to the saucepan and cook over low heat, stirring constantly with a wooden spoon, until the mixture comes just below simmering point and is thick and smooth. Remove from the heat and strain through a coarse sieve into a bowl, discarding the vanilla bean pod.

Serve warm or at room temperature. If not using immediately, cover the surface with plastic wrap to prevent a skin forming.

Nothing beats the flavour of a fresh vanilla bean, but if you don't have one to hand use 1 teaspoon of pure vanilla essence.

Makes 3 cups

damper.

Damper is true Australian bush food – traditionally made by the campfire in the outback and cooked in the coals of a fire. It's a quick and easy bread risen with the use of baking powder rather than yeast.

3 cups self-raising (self-rising) flour

1 teaspoon baking powder

2 teaspoons caster (superfine) sugar

1 teaspoon salt

30 g (1 oz) butter, chilled and chopped

300 ml (9½ fl oz) milk, soured with

1 teaspoon lemon juice

Preheat the oven to 200°C (400°F, Gas Mark 6). Lightly grease an oven tray.

Sift the flour, baking powder, sugar and salt into a large mixing bowl. Rub the butter into the flour mixture with your fingertips until it resembles breadcrumbs. Make a well in the centre.

Mix together the milk and lemon juice – the mixture will curdle slightly – and pour into the flour mixture. Mix gently, just until a soft dough forms. If the dough is too dry, add milk, a tablespoon at a time, and mix.

Gather into a rough ball shape, turn out onto a lightly floured surface and knead gently. The dough should feel slightly damp. With floured hands, pat the dough into a round loaf shape and place it on the prepared oven tray. Sprinkle the loaf with a little flour and slash a cross in the top with a sharp knife, if desired.

Bake for 25–30 minutes, or until risen and golden and the loaf sounds hollow when tapped on the base. Remove from the tray and wrap in a clean cloth. Serve warm or cold.

Makes 1 loaf

dumplings.

Dumplings are a great addition to a soup or a casserole. Prepare them about 30 minutes before you are ready to serve the dish, then, approximately 20 minutes before the end of cooking time, arrange the dumplings on top of the soup or casserole, cover and continue cooking.

125 g (4 oz) self-raising (self-rising) flour
50 g (1½ oz) shredded suet

2 tablespoons chopped parsley
salt and freshly ground black pepper

Sift the flour into a bowl and stir in the suet and parsley. Season with a little salt and freshly ground black pepper. Add enough cold water (approximately 3–4 tablespoons) to form a soft dough. Using lightly floured hands, pinch off walnut-sized pieces of dough and roll them into small dumplings.

Arrange the dumplings on top of the soup or casserole, cover and cook for a further 20 minutes.

Cheese and chive dumplings can be made by adding 30 g (1 oz) of grated cheddar or parmesan to the basic recipe and replacing the parsley with 1 tablespoon of snipped fresh chives.

Makes about 12

eggplant dip.

2 large eggplants (aubergines)

3–4 cloves garlic, chopped

2 tablespoons lemon juice

1 tablespoon olive oil

salt and freshly ground black pepper

paprika, to serve

Preheat the oven to 180°C (350°F, Gas Mark 4).

Pierce the eggplants a few times with a skewer. Place in a baking tin and bake for 40 minutes, or until tender. Allow to cool.

Cut the eggplants in half lengthways and scoop out the flesh. Place the flesh in a fine sieve and allow to drain for 20 minutes.

Transfer the eggplant flesh to a food processor or blender. Add the garlic, lemon juice and oil and purée until smooth. Season to taste with salt and freshly ground black pepper. Add a little extra lemon juice or oil if the mixture is very thick.

Serve in a bowl sprinkled with paprika. This dip can be stored in an airtight container in the refrigerator for 2–3 days.

Makes 2 cups

eggplant parmigiana.

4 medium-sized eggplants (aubergines)

salt

2 × 400 g (13 oz) cans chopped tomatoes

1 clove garlic, chopped

¼ cup torn basil

salt, extra, and freshly ground black pepper

vegetable oil, for frying

2 × 200 g (6½ oz) mozzarella balls

100 g (3½ oz) parmesan, freshly grated

Cut the eggplants lengthways into slices about 1 cm (½ in) thick. Place in a large colander, sprinkle generously with salt and leave for at least 1 hour.

Rinse eggplant and dry well with kitchen paper.

Meanwhile, place the tomato, garlic and 1 tablespoon of the basil in a small saucepan and cook, stirring occasionally, over medium heat for about 15 minutes, or until thickened a little. Season well with salt and freshly ground black pepper.

Preheat the oven to 180°C (350°F, Gas Mark 4).

Cover the base of a large frying pan with vegetable oil. Place over medium–high heat and fry the eggplant slices in batches, until golden on both sides. Drain well on kitchen paper.

Cut the mozzarella balls into thin slices. Place a layer of eggplant in a 25 cm (10 in) square ovenproof dish and cover with a thin layer of the tomato sauce. Top with slices of mozzarella, a sprinkling of the parmesan and a little of the chopped basil. Lightly season with salt and pepper. Repeat these layers until the dish is full, finishing with tomato sauce and a sprinkling of parmesan.

Bake for 50–60 minutes, or until golden and bubbling. Leave to rest for 20 minutes before serving.

Salting eggplant helps to remove any bitter juices. It also retards oil absorption during cooking.

Serves 4

feta, cheddar and chive muffins.

2¹/₂ cups self-raising (self-rising) flour

¹/₂ teaspoon bicarbonate of soda
  (sodium bicarbonate)

salt

2 teaspoons snipped chives

75 g (2¹/₂ oz) feta, cut into ¹/₂ cm (¹/₄ in)
  cubes

50 g (1³/₄ oz) parmesan, grated

freshly ground black pepper

150 g (5 oz) cheddar, grated

300 ml (9¹/₂ fl oz) buttermilk

2 eggs, lightly beaten

100 g (3¹/₂ oz) butter, melted

Preheat the oven to 190°C (375°F, Gas Mark 5). Grease a 12-cup muffin tin or line with paper patty cases.

Sift the flour, bicarbonate of soda and a pinch of salt into a mixing bowl. Stir in the chives, feta, parmesan, a couple of grindings of black pepper and most of the cheddar – reserve a little to sprinkle on the top of the muffins. Make a well in the centre.

Whisk together the buttermilk, eggs and melted butter. Pour the egg mixture into the well in the flour mixture and stir until the ingredients are just combined. Do not over-mix – the batter should not be smooth.

Divide the mixture evenly between the muffin cups. Sprinkle with the remaining cheddar and bake for 25–30 minutes, or until the tops are firm to the touch and golden. Allow to cool in the tin for 5 minutes before turning out onto a wire rack.

If you don't have any buttermilk, use 1 teaspoon of lemon juice mixed with 300 ml (9¹/₂ fl oz) low-fat milk.

These muffins are best eaten on the day they are made and are delicious with a little butter.

Makes 12

fish cakes.

450 g (14 oz) potatoes, peeled and cut into
    chunks
650 g (1 lb 5 oz) cooked fish fillets, flaked
6 spring onions (scallions), finely chopped
2 tablespoons chopped flat-leaf parsley
    or basil
finely grated zest of 1 lemon
1 tablespoon lemon juice

½ teaspoon English mustard
1 egg yolk
salt and freshly ground black pepper
1 cup plain (all-purpose) flour
1 egg, beaten
½ cup milk
1 cup dry breadcrumbs
¼ cup olive oil

Place the potato pieces in a large saucepan of salted water. Bring to the boil and cook for 20–25 minutes, or until tender. Drain and return the potatoes to the saucepan. Cook over low heat for 1–2 minutes to remove any remaining moisture. Mash well.

In a mixing bowl, combine the mashed potato, fish, spring onions, parsley, lemon zest and juice, mustard and egg yolk. Season well with salt and freshly ground black pepper.

Press the mixture firmly into eight patties. Lightly coat each patty in the flour and shake off any excess.

Whisk together the beaten egg and milk in a shallow bowl. Place the breadcrumbs in a second shallow bowl.

Dip each fishcake into the egg mixture and then into the breadcrumbs, making sure each is well coated. Refrigerate for 20 minutes, or until ready to cook.

Heat the oil in a frying pan over medium heat. Cook the fish cakes, in batches if necessary, for 3–4 minutes on each side, or until golden. Serve with lemon wedges, a little homemade mayonnaise (see page 192) and a green salad.

Fish cakes are also delicious made with either tinned or freshly cooked salmon.

Serves 4

fish lasagne.

750 g (1½ lb) smoked haddock or
    cod fillets

3 cups milk

3 eggs, at room temperature

4 rashers bacon

250 g (8 oz) uncooked tiger prawns
    (shrimp), shelled

75 g (2½ oz) butter

50 g (1¾ oz) plain (all-purpose) flour

150 ml (4½ fl oz) cream

175 g (6 oz) cheddar, roughly grated

salt and freshly ground black pepper

250 g (8 oz) fresh lasagne sheets

2 heaped tablespoons freshly grated
    parmesan

Preheat the oven to 190°C (375°F, Gas Mark 5). Place the fish in a baking tin, pour over the milk, cover with foil and bake for 25–30 minutes, or until just cooked.

Meanwhile, hardboil the eggs, peel, and roughly chop. Set aside in a large bowl.

Grill the bacon until cooked, then chop and add to the eggs, along with the prawns.

Remove the fish, reserving the milk. Flake the fish into bite-sized pieces, discarding the skin, and add it to the bacon and eggs.

Melt the butter in a medium-sized saucepan over low heat. Mix in the flour, cook for 1 minute, then slowly pour in the reserved milk, stirring constantly, then the cream. Stir until thickened. Add the cheddar, let it melt, then season lightly with salt and freshly ground black pepper. Remove from the heat and set aside.

Lightly grease a 20 × 20 × 6 cm (8 × 8 × 2½ in) ovenproof dish.

Layer the lasagne, starting with a third of the fish mixture. Cover with a thin layer of sauce and top with a layer of lasagne sheets. Repeat this process twice more, finishing with a final layer of sauce. Scatter with the parmesan.

Bake for 35 minutes, or until the lasagne is cooked. Cover with foil if the top becomes too brown during cooking.

Serves 6

fish pie.

1 quantity mashed potato (see page 190)

500 g (1 lb) firm white fish fillets

250 g (8 oz) smoked fish
   (haddock or cod) fillets

2 cups milk

1 bay leaf

4 black peppercorns

50 g (1¾ oz) butter

1 small brown onion, chopped

¼ cup plain (all-purpose) flour

250 g (8 oz) small cooked prawns
   (shrimp), shelled

pinch of cayenne pepper

2 tablespoons chopped flat-leaf parsley

salt and freshly ground black pepper

3 hard-boiled eggs, peeled and quartered

20 g (¾ oz) butter, extra

First, make the mashed potato according to the instructions on page 190.

Preheat the oven to 180°C (350°F, Gas Mark 4).

Place the white fish, smoked fish, milk, bay leaf and peppercorns in a saucepan over medium heat. Bring to the boil then reduce the heat and simmer for 5 minutes. Strain the mixture, reserving the fish and the strained milk.

Skin the fish, remove any bones, flake into bite-sized pieces and place in a bowl.

Melt the butter in a clean saucepan over low–medium heat. Add the onion and cook for 7 minutes, stirring frequently, until soft and translucent. Add the flour, stir well and cook for 1 minute. Slowly whisk in the reserved milk. Bring the mixture to the boil, whisking frequently, until smooth and thick. Allow to cool.

Add the prawns, cayenne pepper and parsley to the bowl containing the fish, and pour over the white sauce. Season well with salt and freshly ground black pepper.

Spoon the mixture into a large soufflé dish or other ovenproof dish. Top mixture with the boiled egg pieces. Spread with the mashed potato and fluff up with a fork. Dot with the extra butter. Bake for 30–35 minutes, or until golden and bubbling.

Serves 4–6

fish roasted in paper.

4 snapper, blue-eye cod, jewfish or other
    firm white fish fillets
sea salt and freshly ground black pepper
8 thin slices of lemon

1 tablespoon chopped chives
8 mint leaves, roughly chopped
30 g (1 oz) butter
1 lemon, quartered, to serve

Preheat the oven to 200°C (400°F, Gas Mark 6).

Cut four sheets of baking paper 35 cm (14 in) square. Place one sheet on your work surface and place a fish fillet to the right of centre of the paper, narrow end towards you. Season the fillet well with salt and freshly ground black pepper and top with two slices of lemon. Sprinkle with some of the herbs and add a small knob of the butter.

Fold over the left half of the paper to enclose the fish and then fold the remaining two edges over twice to seal well, making a tight parcel. My mum used wooden pegs or sometimes paper clips to seal the parcel (remove before serving). Lift the parcel onto an oven tray. Repeat with the remaining fillets, leaving space on the oven tray between each parcel.

Bake for 12–15 minutes – the paper parcel should puff up a little. Transfer the parcels to serving plates so they can be opened at the table. Serve with lemon quarters and a crisp, green salad.

Serves 4

flaky pastry.

This pastry is useful for covering a meat or other savoury pie.

300 g (9½ oz) plain (all-purpose) flour
salt

175 g (6 oz) butter, frozen for 30 minutes
before use
80–100 ml (2¾–3½ fl oz) chilled water

Sift the flour and a pinch of salt into a large bowl. Using the largest holes of a grater, grate the frozen butter into the flour. Gently mix with a knife or flat spatula, making sure that all the pieces of butter are coated in flour – the butter should be left in chunky grated pieces, not worked into the dough.

Add about 80 ml (2¾ fl oz) of the chilled water to the flour and butter mixture and mix in with the spatula. The pastry should come together in clumps – add a little extra water if necessary. When the dough holds together, roll it into a ball and flatten slightly to form a disc. Cover with plastic wrap and refrigerate for at least 30 minutes before using.

It is important to use frozen butter and to handle the dough as little as possible.

Any leftover pastry can be placed in a freezer bag and frozen for up to 2 months.

Makes enough to cover a 28 cm (11 in) pie dish

focaccia.

1 × 7 g (¼ oz) sachet (2 teaspoons) dry
    yeast
1 teaspoon sugar
2½ cups bread flour
½ teaspoon salt

⅓ cup olive oil
2–3 tablespoons extra-virgin olive oil,
    plus extra to serve
sea salt, to sprinkle

Dissolve the yeast and sugar in a small bowl with 200 ml (6½ oz) of tepid water. Stir well and set aside for 10 minutes, or until the mixture froths.

Place the flour and salt in a large mixing bowl. Make a well in the centre and add the yeast mixture and olive oil. Mix until a firm dough forms.

Knead on a lightly floured surface for 5–7 minutes, or until smooth and elastic. Place in a clean, lightly oiled bowl, cover with a cloth or plastic wrap and stand in a warm place for 1–1½ hours, or until the dough has doubled in size.

Punch down the dough with your fist to expel the air. Gently knead for 2 minutes and place on an oven tray. Using your fingertips, press the dough into a 30 × 18 cm (12 × 7 in) rectangle. Cover and leave in a warm spot to rise for 45 minutes.

Preheat the oven to 220°C (425°F, Gas Mark 7).

Press dimples into the surface of the dough. Brush well with the extra-virgin olive oil and sprinkle with sea salt. Bake for 20 minutes, spraying the oven with water from an atomiser at least three times during the first 10 minutes. Then slide the loaf off the tray onto the oven shelf and cook for a further 5 minutes, or until golden brown. Remove and serve drizzled with a little extra-virgin olive oil.

Make rosemary focaccia by brushing the dough with a combination of 2 tablespoons of roughly chopped rosemary and the extra-virgin olive oil before baking.

free-form blueberry pie.

1 quantity homemade regular shortcrust
    pastry (see page 290), or 1 × 380 g
    (12 oz) packet bought frozen
    shortcrust pastry, thawed
100 g (3½ oz) crushed amaretti biscuits or
    cake crumbs

500 g (1 lb) fresh blueberries
⅓ cup caster (superfine) sugar
1 egg, beaten
sugar, to sprinkle

Prepare the pastry according to the instructions on page 290 and refrigerate for at least 30 minutes.

Preheat the oven to 200°C (400°F, Gas Mark 6).

On a lightly floured surface, roll out the pastry to make a 35 cm (14 in) circle. Sprinkle the pastry with the biscuit crumbs, leaving a 5 cm (2 in) border. Pile on the blueberries, keeping them within the border, and sprinkle with the caster sugar. Fold up the edges of the pastry to form a freeform-shaped pie (see picture). Brush the pastry with the beaten egg and sprinkle the pastry with sugar, to decorate.

Bake for 25–30 minutes, or until the pastry is golden and the berries have softened. Serve warm or cold.

This pie is good with vanilla ice-cream.

If making your own pastry, add 1 tablespoon of caster (superfine) sugar to the flour mixture as a variation.

Serves 6–8

french toast.

These slices of thick bread, dipped in a rich mix of egg, milk, sugar and vanilla, make a delicious, indulgent start to the day – especially when delivered to your bed on a tray.

4 eggs

2 tablespoons caster (superfine) sugar

½ cup milk or cream

½ teaspoon vanilla essence

salt

1 white cob or cottage loaf

unsalted butter, for frying

maple syrup, to serve

In a shallow bowl, mix together the eggs, sugar, milk, vanilla and a pinch of salt.

Cut four slices of bread, about 2 cm (¾ in) thick, from the loaf of bread.

Heat a little butter in a frying pan over medium heat. Dip two slices of bread in the egg mixture for 30–60 seconds, or until the mixture is well absorbed by the bread. Fry the soaked bread for 1 minute on each side, or until crisp and golden. Repeat with the remaining slices of bread.

Serve warm, drizzled with maple syrup.

French toast is delicious served with a little crispy bacon or fresh berries on the side.

Slices of brioche or split croissants instead of the bread make a good variation.

Serves 2

fresh vietnamese spring rolls.

30 g (1 oz) rice vermicelli (cellophane)
    noodles
24 medium-sized cooked prawns (shrimp),
    shelled and roughly chopped
juice of 1 lime
1/2 teaspoon Thai fish sauce
1/2 Lebanese cucumber, peeled and
    thinly sliced

1 carrot, peeled and very thinly sliced
1 cup pea shoots
1/2 cup mint leaves
1/2 cup coriander (cilantro) leaves
salt and freshly ground black pepper
12 × 15 cm (6 in) square Asian rice paper
    wrappers
dipping sauce (see below)

Place the noodles in a heatproof bowl and cover with boiling water. Leave to soak for 5 minutes, or until tender. Drain well, blot with kitchen paper and cut into 5 cm (2 in) strips with scissors.

Combine the noodles, prawns, lime juice, fish sauce, cucumber, carrot, pea shoots, mint and coriander in a bowl. Season with salt and pepper.

Fill a shallow bowl with hot water. Dip six rice paper wrappers in the water for a minute to soften. Remove and place in a single layer on a clean tea towel.

Divide half the noodle mixture between the wrappers, spreading the mixture down the centre of each wrapper in a log shape. Fold up the base of each wrapper and then tightly roll sideways. Transfer to a serving plate and cover with a damp cloth. Repeat with the remaining rice paper wrappers and mixture. Serve with the dipping sauce.

To make the dipping sauce, stir together 2 teaspoons of brown sugar, 2 tablespoons of fresh lime juice, 2 teaspoons of Thai fish sauce and 1 chopped small red chilli. Serve in a small bowl.

Makes 12

friands.

These delicious, moist almond cakes are easy to make at home.

180 g (6 oz) unsalted butter

⅓ cup plain (all-purpose) flour

180 g (6 oz) icing (confectioners') sugar

100 g (3½ oz) ground almonds

2 teaspoons finely grated lemon zest

5 egg whites

icing (confectioners') sugar, extra,
   to serve

Preheat the oven to 200°C (400°F, Gas Mark 6). Lightly grease eight friand tins.

Melt the butter in a small saucepan over low heat, then cook for a further 1 minute, or until golden. Be careful not to burn the butter.

Sift the flour and icing sugar into a mixing bowl. Stir in the ground almonds and lemon zest.

Lightly beat the egg whites with a fork and pour into the bowl containing the dry ingredients. Add the warm butter and mix with a wooden spoon until smooth.

Spoon the mixture into the prepared friand tins, filling each to three-quarters full. Bake for 5 minutes, then reduce the heat to 180°C (350°F, Gas Mark 4) and cook for a further 10–15 minutes, or until golden and risen.

Allow to cool in the tins for 5 minutes before turning out onto a wire rack to cool completely. Dust with icing sugar to serve.

If you don't have friand tins, bake these little cakes in muffin tins or deep patty pan tins.

In place of the lemon zest, try orange zest.

To make berry friands, top each with a few fresh or frozen raspberries, blackberries or blueberries before baking.

Makes 8

fried rice.

The recipe for this favourite Cantonese dish can be readily varied, depending on what ingredients are at hand.

1 tablespoon vegetable oil

2 eggs, lightly beaten

2 tablespoons peanut oil

5 spring onions (scallions), chopped

1 clove garlic, crushed

½ cup frozen peas, thawed

1 tablespoon grated fresh ginger

1 cup shredded Chinese barbecue pork

4 cups cooked rice, chilled

1 tablespoon soy sauce or XO sauce

salt and ground white pepper

Heat the vegetable oil in a moderately hot wok and add the beaten egg, swirling it around to coat the wok. When set, turn out onto a board and allow to cool. Cut into strips.

Heat the peanut oil in the wok. Add the spring onions, garlic, peas and ginger. Stir-fry for 2–3 minutes. Add the pork and allow to warm through. Add the rice and egg strips. Stir-fry vigorously, breaking up any lumps of rice, until heated through. Add the soy sauce and mix until well combined. Season with salt and ground white pepper and serve immediately.

Always begin with cold rice cooked the day before. Boil 2 cups of long-grain rice in a large saucepan of boiling salted water for 10–15 minutes, or until tender. When cooked, drain and rinse. Store overnight in the refrigerator.

Chinese barbecue pork is available in Asian food stores and restaurants. If it is unavailable, substitute chopped ham, chopped cooked bacon or chopped cooked chicken.

Peeled, cooked prawns (shrimp) added towards the end of the cooking time are also delicious in this dish.

Serves 4

frittata.

Frittatas can vary from thin and pancake-like to thick with a golden crust and creamy centre. The following recipe for this popular Italian omelette is a classic flavour combination and is perfect picnic fare.

6 large eggs
100 g (3½ oz) baby spinach leaves,
    roughly chopped
1¼ cups freshly grated parmesan

pinch of freshly grated nutmeg
salt and freshly ground black pepper
1 tablespoon olive oil

In a mixing bowl, beat the eggs lightly with a fork. Stir through the spinach, 1 cup of the parmesan and the nutmeg. Season to taste with salt and freshly ground black pepper.

Heat the olive oil in a 23 cm (9 in) non-stick frying pan over medium heat. Swirl the pan to coat with oil. Pour in the egg mixture. Reduce the heat to low and cook, stirring once, for 12–15 minutes. The bottom should be firm and the top a little runny. Sprinkle with the remaining ¼ cup of parmesan.

Place the frying pan under a preheated griller (broiler) for just long enough to set the top. A good frittata should be firm but moist, never stiff and dry. Remove from the heat and allow to cool for 2 minutes. Serve straight from the pan, or place a large, flat plate over the top of the pan and invert the frittata onto it. Serve warm or at room temperature, sliced into wedges.

Variations on this recipe are only limited by what ingredients you have at hand. Try incorporating cooked zucchini (courgettes), sautéed mushrooms, cooked asparagus, prosciutto, marinated artichokes, goat's cheese or cooked potato slices.

Serves 4

fruit cake.

250 g (8 oz) unsalted butter, chopped

1 cup lightly packed brown sugar

½ cup brandy

1 kg (2 lb) mixed dried fruit

100 g (3½ oz) mixed peel

100 g (3½ oz) glacé cherries, halved

5 eggs, beaten

2 tablespoons treacle

2 teaspoons finely grated lemon zest

2 tablespoons finely grated orange zest

1¾ cups plain (all-purpose) flour

½ cup self-raising (self-rising) flour

1 teaspoon bicarbonate of soda
   (sodium bicarbonate)

1½ teaspoons mixed spice

150 g (5 oz) almonds

Place the butter, sugar, brandy, dried fruit, mixed peel, glacé cherries and ½ cup of water in a large saucepan. Bring to the boil and simmer gently, stirring frequently, for 10 minutes. Allow to cool.

Preheat the oven to 150°C (300°F, Gas Mark 2). Grease a 23 cm (9 in) round cake tin. Line the base and sides with a double layer of baking paper, extending the paper 5 cm (2 in) above the cake tin.

Transfer the cool fruit mixture to a large mixing bowl. Add the beaten eggs, treacle, lemon and orange zest, and mix well. Sift the flours, bicarbonate of soda and mixed spice into the bowl and mix until combined. Roughly chop half the almonds and stir these into the mixture. Spoon the mixture into the prepared cake tin. Decorate the top of the cake with the remaining whole almonds. Wrap the cake tin in a double layer of brown paper, extending the paper 5 cm (2 in) above the cake tin, to match the baking paper. Tie securely with string.

Bake for 2–2½ hours, or until firm and a skewer inserted into the centre comes out clean. Allow to cool in the tin. Wrap in foil and store for up to 3 months in a cool, dark place.

A good combination of mixed dried fruit is 375 g (12 oz) of chopped raisins, 250 g (8 oz) of sultanas, 250 g (8 oz) of currants, and 125 g (4 oz) of chopped dates, figs and prunes.

fruit tart.

2 tablespoons apricot jam

1 sheet frozen puff pastry, thawed

3 ripe nectarines or plums

2 tablespoons sugar

20 g (¾ oz) unsalted butter

Preheat the oven to 200°C (400°F, Gas Mark 6).

Place the jam and 2 tablespoons of water in a small saucepan and warm until the mixture forms a syrup. Brush half the syrup over the sheet of pastry, leaving a 2 cm (¾ in) border all around.

Halve the nectarines or plums, remove the seeds and thinly slice the fruit. Lay the slices, overlapping slightly, over the pastry, again leaving a 2 cm (¾ in) border all around. Sprinkle over the sugar and dot the fruit with the butter.

Bake the tart for 20–25 minutes, or until the pastry is golden and puffed up. Glaze the tart by brushing lightly with the remaining jam. Cut into slices and serve warm or at room temperature with cream or ice-cream.

Two peeled and thinly sliced pears or apples may be substituted for the stone fruit.

Serves 4

garlic bread.

1 baguette or bread stick
salt and freshly ground black pepper

GARLIC BUTTER
200 g (6½ oz) unsalted butter, softened
4 cloves garlic, chopped
2 tablespoons finely chopped
    flat-leaf parsley
1 teaspoon lemon juice

Preheat the oven to 180°C (350°F, Gas Mark 4).

To make the garlic butter, mix together the ingredients thoroughly in a small mixing bowl. Season with salt and freshly ground black pepper.

Cut slashes into the baguette at 2.5 cm (1 in) intervals, cutting almost to the bottom crust, and spread each side of the cut liberally with the garlic butter.

Wrap the bread in foil and bake for 10 minutes. Open the foil at the top and cook for another 5–7 minutes, or until crisp. Serve immediately.

Any leftover garlic butter can be rolled in foil and kept in the fridge for up to 2 weeks.

Add a little finely chopped chilli or a dash of Tabasco sauce to the garlic butter for a hotter version.

Serves 4

garlic prawns.

The combination of butter, garlic and parsley is a true classic.

24 large uncooked prawns (shrimp)

80 g (2¾ oz) unsalted butter

2 tablespoons olive oil

3 cloves garlic, finely chopped

½ large red chilli, seeded and
    finely chopped

2 tablespoons chopped flat-leaf parsley

juice of 1 lemon

sea salt and freshly ground black pepper

1 tablespoon chopped flat-leaf
    parsley, extra

2 teaspoons finely grated lemon zest

Peel and devein the prawns, leaving the tails intact. Set aside.

Melt the butter and olive oil in a large frying pan or wok over medium heat. Add the garlic and chilli and cook, stirring, for 3 minutes. Add the prawns and cook, untouched, for 2 minutes. Turn the prawns, add the parsley and squeeze over the lemon juice. Cook for a further 2–3 minutes, or until the prawns are pink. Season with sea salt and freshly ground black pepper.

In a small bowl, combine the extra chopped parsley and the lemon zest, and sprinkle this mixture over the prawns. Serve at once with good crusty bread to mop up the juices.

As a variation, add ½ teaspoon of grated fresh ginger at the beginning with the garlic and chilli. Cook as above, but replace the lemon with lime, and the parsley with coriander (cilantro).

Fresh scallops are also delicious cooked this way.

Serves 4

gazpacho.

Few dishes taste as refreshing on a hot summer's day as this simple,
no-cook, chilled soup.

1 kg (2 lb) ripe tomatoes, peeled and
    chopped
1 small cucumber, roughly chopped
1 red capsicum (bell pepper), seeded
    and chopped
2 cloves garlic, chopped

½ red (Spanish) onion, chopped
2 thick slices good white bread
¼ cup sherry vinegar or red wine vinegar
salt and freshly ground black pepper
extra-virgin olive oil, to drizzle

Place the tomatoes, cucumber, capsicum, garlic and onion in a large mixing bowl. Remove the crusts from the bread. Chop the bread and add it to the bowl. Stir through 1½ cups of water.

Transfer the mixture to a food processor or blender and pulse until the mixture is roughly combined. (This may need to be done in batches.) The mixture should still be slightly chunky. Add a little extra water if the soup needs thinning.

Chill for at least 2 hours, or preferably overnight, to allow the flavours to develop.

Just before serving, stir through the vinegar. Season to taste with salt and freshly ground black pepper. Serve well chilled with a good drizzle of extra-virgin olive oil.

To peel tomatoes, use a sharp knife to cut a cross in the base of each tomato. Place in a heatproof bowl and cover with boiling water. Leave for 45 seconds, then transfer to cold water and peel the skin away, beginning at the cross.

Decent tomatoes are essential for a good gazpacho. If possible, use home-grown ones.

Crabmeat or cooked prawns are delicious additions to this soup.

Serves 4

ginger cake.

This cake is a great addition to your recipe collection. It's delicious and easy to make – it falls into that stress-free 'melt and mix' category of baking.

60 g (2 oz) unsalted butter, cubed

½ cup golden syrup

¾ cup plain (all-purpose) flour

¼ cup self-raising (self-rising) flour

1 teaspoon bicarbonate of soda
   (sodium bicarbonate)

1 heaped teaspoon ground ginger

½ teaspoon mixed spice

½ cup caster (superfine) sugar

salt

½ cup milk

1 egg, beaten

Preheat the oven to 170°C (325°F, Gas Mark 3). Thoroughly grease a 23 × 12 cm (9 × 5 in) loaf tin and line the base with baking paper.

Place the butter and golden syrup in a small saucepan. Melt, stirring occasionally, over low heat. Remove from the heat.

Sift both flours, the bicarbonate of soda and the spices into a mixing bowl. Stir in the sugar and a pinch of salt, then add the milk and egg and mix until smooth. Gradually add the melted butter mixture, stirring until well incorporated.

Pour the batter into the prepared loaf tin and bake for 50–55 minutes, or until risen and firm to the touch. A skewer inserted into the middle of the cake should come out clean. Allow the cake to cool in the tin for 5 minutes before turning out onto a wire rack to cool. Serve dusted with icing (confectioners') sugar.

If you like, you can turn this into a simple syrup cake. Place ½ cup of sugar, ½ cup of water and 1 tablespoon of finely grated fresh ginger in a small saucepan. Bring the mixture to the boil and simmer for 5 minutes. Spoon a little syrup over the hot cake.

gingerbread biscuits.

125 g (4 oz) unsalted butter

¼ cup golden syrup

⅓ cup lightly packed brown sugar

2 cups plain (all-purpose) flour

¼ cup self-raising (self-rising) flour

1 teaspoon bicarbonate of soda
   (sodium bicarbonate)

1 tablespoon ground ginger

½ teaspoon mixed spice

salt

1 egg, lightly beaten

Place the butter, golden syrup and sugar in a small saucepan over low heat. Cook, stirring, until the butter has melted and the mixture is smooth. Remove from the heat and allow to cool.

Sift both flours, the bicarbonate of soda, the spices and a pinch of salt into a large mixing bowl and make a well in the centre. Pour in the melted butter mixture and the beaten egg and mix well.

Turn out onto a lightly floured surface and knead until smooth. Wrap in plastic wrap and refrigerate for 30 minutes.

Preheat the oven to 170°C (325°F, Gas Mark 3). Line two oven trays with baking paper.

Roll out the dough between two sheets of baking paper to a thickness of 5 mm (¼ in). Cut out shapes with cookie cutters and bake for 8–10 minutes, or until firm and golden brown. Allow to cool on a wire rack.

To decorate your biscuits, beat 1 egg white with an electric mixer until foamy. Gradually add 1 teaspoon of lemon juice and 1½ cups of sifted icing (confectioners') sugar, beating all the while until the mixture is thick and smooth. Tint the mixture with a couple of drops of food colouring. Attach a fine nozzle to a piping bag and pipe decorative shapes onto the biscuits.

Makes 24–30

granola.

The perfect granola should be chewy, crisp and crumbly, with a combination of sweet and tart flavours. The trick is selecting the right ingredients and combining them in the proper proportions. Try this basic recipe, substituting different nuts, seeds or fruit as desired.

3 cups rolled oats	¼ cup wheatgerm
1 cup almonds	1 teaspoon finely grated lemon zest
½ cup roughly chopped pecans	⅓ cup vegetable oil
½ cup shredded coconut	½ cup honey
2 tablespoons sesame seeds	1 cup chopped dried apricots
2 tablespoons pepitas (pumpkin seeds)	1 cup sultanas

Preheat the oven to 170°C (325°F, Gas Mark 3).

Place the oats, almonds, pecans, coconut, sesame seeds, pepitas, wheatgerm and lemon zest in a large mixing bowl.

In a small saucepan over low heat, warm the vegetable oil and honey.

Pour the honey mixture over the oat mixture and mix thoroughly.

Tip the mixture into a baking tin and bake, stirring every 5 minutes, for 20 minutes, or until golden. Allow the mixture to cool completely.

Stir through the apricots and sultanas.

Granola can be stored in an airtight container for up to 3 months.

When experimenting with different combinations of ingredients, keep in mind that the total volume of nuts and fruit should be equal to or slightly greater than the volume of oats.

Vary the dried fruit component by using dried apples, pears or peaches.

Makes 8 cups

gravlax.

This Swedish dish preserves fresh salmon by marinating it in a mixture of salt and sugar. The preparation time is minimal and the curing process occurs in the refrigerator.

2 tablespoons roughly chopped fresh dill

150 g (5 oz) sea salt

100 g (3½ oz) sugar

2 tablespoons freshly ground black pepper

1 tablespoon vodka or vermouth

2 large salmon fillets – total weight about 1.25 kg (2 lb 7 oz)

In a bowl, combine the dill, salt, sugar, pepper and vodka. Spread a quarter of the mixture on the base of a ceramic dish that is big enough to hold the salmon fillets.

Place one fillet, skin-side down, on top of the mixture. Cover with slightly more than half of the remaining salt mixture. Place the second fillet on top, skin-side up, and scatter the remaining salt mixture over the skin. Seal the dish with plastic wrap, then weigh down the salmon with tins or a heavy breadboard. Refrigerate for at least 24 hours (maximum 48 hours), turning the fish every 12 hours.

When ready to serve, drain off any liquid, brush off the marinade and wipe dry with kitchen paper. Slice the salmon thinly – it will look slightly translucent. Serve as you would smoked salmon.

Gravlax is traditionally served with rye bread and a mustard dressing. Make the dressing by combining 1 tablespoon of Dijon mustard, 1 teaspoon of caster (superfine) sugar and 2 tablespoons of wine vinegar. Gradually whisk in ½ cup of vegetable oil until amalgamated. Stir in 1 tablespoon of chopped dill and season to taste with salt and freshly ground black pepper.

Once cured, the salmon will keep in the refrigerator for up to 5 days.

gravy.

pan juices from roast meat
2–3 tablespoons plain (all-purpose) flour
½ cup wine

2 cups stock or water
salt and freshly ground black pepper

After removing the roast meat from the baking tin, pour off all but about ½ cup of the fat. Place the baking tin over medium heat on the stove top and sprinkle over the flour. Stir constantly with a wooden spoon for 1–2 minutes, or until the flour has browned slightly.

Gradually add the wine and stock, stirring constantly to loosen any browned bits stuck to the bottom of the tin, until the gravy has thickened and is smooth. Simmer gently for 5–10 minutes, adding a little extra stock or water if necessary to reach the desired consistency. Season to taste with salt and freshly ground black pepper.

As a rule, use white wine to make gravy for poultry dishes and red wine for red meat dishes.

Serves 4–6

greek salad.

As per the authentic Athenian way, this version of a Greek salad serves everything nice and chunky, without any lettuce. This delicious recipe is from Terry Durack.

3 ripe tomatoes

1 crisp cucumber, unpeeled

2 tablespoons Greek olive oil

1 tablespoon lemon juice or red-wine
    vinegar

sea salt and freshly ground black pepper

200 g (6½ oz) Greek feta, in one piece

20 Kalamata olives

½ red (Spanish) onion, sliced into
    thin rings

1 teaspoon chopped fresh oregano or dill

½ teaspoon dried oregano

Cut the tomatoes into quarters or eighths. Cut the cucumber in half lengthwise, and roughly chop. Toss the tomato and cucumber with the olive oil and lemon juice, and season to taste with salt and freshly ground black pepper. Top with the feta in one piece and scatter with the olives, onion rings and herbs. Break up the feta with a fork as you serve.

This recipe serves two people as a light lunch. The quantities can easily be doubled if needed.

Serves 2

grilled peaches.

A sweet, sun-ripened peach is a real summer treat. Take advantage of this delicious fruit by creating this simple and tasty dessert. Grilling peaches seems to bring out their natural flavour. Serving them with fresh raspberries is a perfect match.

4 ripe slipstone peaches
⅓ cup sugar

cream or ice-cream, to serve
raspberries, to serve

Preheat the grill to hot.

Peel the peaches, if desired, then cut in half and remove the stones.

Place the peach halves cut-side up in a baking tin. Sprinkle with the sugar and grill for 5–8 minutes, or until the sugar has caramelised and the fruit has begun to brown. Transfer to four serving plates and serve immediately with dollops of thick cream or with scoops of good-quality vanilla ice-cream and fresh raspberries.

Choose large, ripe peaches that smell fragrant and are slightly soft when pressed.

Grilled peaches are also delicious sprinkled with a little Cointreau or amaretto before cooking.

Dollops of mascarpone or vanilla yoghurt also go particularly well with this dessert.

Nectarines make a good substitute for peaches.

Serves 4

hamburgers.

250 g (8 oz) minced (ground) beef

2 tablespoons tomato sauce (ketchup)

dash of Worcestershire sauce

salt and freshly ground black pepper

1 tablespoon vegetable oil

butter

2 good-quality bread rolls, split in half

50 g (2 oz) rocket (arugula) leaves

1 ripe tomato, sliced

1 cooked beetroot, sliced

Combine the meat, tomato sauce and Worcestershire sauce. Season with plenty of salt and freshly ground black pepper. Divide the mixture in two and shape each portion into a 10 cm (4 in) diameter patty. Do not over-handle the meat – it will toughen the hamburgers.

Heat the oil in a heavy frying pan over medium–high heat. When the oil is hot, add the burgers and cook for 1–2 minutes, or until browned. Turn and cook for a further minute, or until well browned.

Meanwhile, lightly butter the rolls and cover the bottom half of each with a layer of rocket leaves. Top each with a burger and then a layer of tomato and beetroot. Season lightly and top with the other half of the roll.

Don't use low-fat minced meat for burgers, as a little bit of fat will make the burgers juicier. I often add 2 finely chopped rashers of bacon to the burger mixture.

Don't forget to offer tomato sauce, barbecue sauce or mayonnaise with the burgers.

Makes 2

hazelnut slice.

120 g (4 oz) skinned hazelnuts

50 g (1¾ oz) dark chocolate, chopped

60 g (2 oz) butter, chopped

1 teaspoon instant coffee powder

1 cup caster (superfine) sugar

½ cup plain (all-purpose) flour

½ teaspoon baking powder

2 eggs, lightly beaten

1 teaspoon vanilla essence

icing (confectioners') sugar, to serve

Preheat the oven to 180°C (350°F, Gas Mark 4). Lightly grease a shallow 20 cm (8 in) square cake tin and line the base and sides with baking paper, leaving the paper over-hanging on two opposite sides.

Place the hazelnuts in a baking tin and roast in the oven for 5 minutes, tossing occasionally, or until lightly toasted. Cool and roughly chop.

Melt the chocolate and butter with the coffee powder in a heatproof bowl set over a saucepan of barely simmering water, stirring occasionally, until melted and smooth. Remove from the heat.

Sift the sugar, flour and baking powder into the chocolate and butter mixture. Add the eggs, vanilla and half of the hazelnuts. Mix with a wooden spoon until combined.

Spoon the mixture into the prepared cake tin and bake for 15 minutes. Remove, top with the remaining hazelnuts and return to the oven for a further 20 minutes, or until firm and nicely coloured. Leave to cool in the tin for 10 minutes before removing the slice using the overhanging baking paper. Allow to cool on a wire rack. To serve, dust with icing (confectioners') sugar and cut into squares.

Makes 16

herb omelette.

3 large organic eggs
salt and freshly ground black pepper

1 tablespoon chopped chives, parsley,
chervil or basil
15 g (½ oz) butter

Lightly beat the eggs in a bowl. Season well with salt and freshly ground black pepper and stir through the chopped herbs.

Heat the butter in a small non-stick frying pan over medium heat until it is foaming, then immediately add the eggs to the pan. Using a fork or spatula, move the eggs around the pan until they begin to set – this will take less than a minute. Quickly tip the pan a little and lift the edges of the omelette, so that any runny egg flows underneath and starts to set. If you are adding a filling (see suggestions below), place this over one half of the omelette now. Ease the fork or spatula under the edge of the omelette and, tilting the pan slightly, fold it in half. Leave to cook for a further 30 seconds, then slide the omelette onto a plate. The eggs should be completely cooked on the outside, but still creamy and soft in the centre.

If making omelettes for a few people, I tend to undercook the first few and keep them warm in a preheated 160°C (315°F) oven – they have usually firmed up and are perfect by the time I'm ready to serve.

Good fillings for omelettes include cheese, crumbled crisp bacon, grilled mushrooms, steamed asparagus and smoked salmon.

Makes 1

hollandaise sauce.

Hollandaise sauce is wonderful served with fish, steamed asparagus
or with poached eggs, as in eggs Benedict.

125 g (4 oz) unsalted butter

1 tablespoon lemon juice

3 egg yolks

salt and freshly ground black pepper

Melt the butter in a small saucepan over low heat. Pour the melted butter into a small jug, leaving behind any white sediment in the bottom of the pan. Allow to cool slightly.

Place the lemon juice, egg yolks and 1 tablespoon of water in a heatproof bowl over a saucepan of simmering water. Whisk the yolk mixture until combined. Gradually add the melted butter, whisking until the sauce is smooth and thick. If the sauce thickens too much, whisk in a spoonful of hot water. Do not allow the mixture to boil or the sauce will separate. Season to taste with salt and freshly ground black pepper, and keep warm until ready to serve.

You can make hollandaise sauce in a food processor or blender by processing the lemon juice, egg yolks and 1 tablespoon of water in the machine. While the machine is running, gradually add the warm melted butter until the sauce is smooth and thick. Season to taste with salt and freshly ground black pepper.

To make orange hollandaise, replace the lemon juice with 2 tablespoons of strained freshly squeezed orange juice and proceed as above.

Makes 1 cup

honeycomb.

A candy thermometer is a useful piece of kitchen equipment and a good investment.
Using a candy thermometer enables you to know when the correct temperature
is reached – very important when making candies, fudge or jam.

2 cups sugar

¼ cup golden syrup

1 teaspoon bicarbonate of soda
(sodium bicarbonate)

Lightly grease a 20 × 30 cm (8 × 12 in) shallow cake tin.

Combine the sugar, golden syrup and 1 cup of water in a medium-sized saucepan. Place over medium heat and bring to the boil, stirring to dissolve the sugar. Gently boil the mixture, without stirring, for 5–10 minutes, or until it reaches 154°C (310°F) or hard-crack stage on the thermometer. Remove the pan from the heat and sprinkle the bicarbonate of soda over the mixture. It will immediately froth and foam up. Beat quickly with a balloon whisk for about 5 seconds, then pour the mixture into the prepared tin.

Allow to cool for a few minutes before scoring into bars or squares. When completely cool, turn out of the tin onto a breadboard and cut into pieces.

Honeycomb is delicious broken into bite-sized pieces and dipped in melted chocolate.

Make hokey-pokey ice-cream by stirring crushed pieces of honeycomb into softened vanilla ice-cream. Refreeze before serving.

hot chocolate.

The perfect hot chocolate isn't made from powder spooned from a tin, it's made using real chocolate. Hot chocolate should be very rich – wonderful for a cold, wintry night.

2 cups milk
100 g (3½ oz) dark chocolate, chopped

sugar, to taste

Gently heat the milk in a saucepan over low heat for 2 minutes. Add the chocolate and stir occasionally, until melted and smooth. Bring the mixture to just under boiling point and whisk briskly for a couple of minutes to make it frothy.

Taste for sweetness and stir in a little sugar if needed. Pour the hot chocolate into cups and serve immediately.

For an extra treat, add marshmallows to the cup before pouring over the hot chocolate. Or try topping with a dollop of lightly whipped cream and sprinkling with a little coarsely grated chocolate.

For extra richness, use couverture chocolate, which has a high cocoa butter content and melts beautifully.

Serves 2

hummus.

1 × 425 g (14 oz) can chickpeas (garbanzo
    beans), drained and rinsed
3 cloves garlic, crushed
¼ cup lemon juice
¼ cup tahini (sesame paste)

1 teaspoon ground cumin
pinch cayenne pepper
¼ cup olive oil
salt and freshly ground black pepper

Place the chickpeas, garlic, lemon juice, tahini, cumin and cayenne pepper in the bowl of a food processor. With the motor running, slowly add the olive oil and process until smooth. Add a little extra oil or lemon juice if the mixture is too thick. Season to taste with salt and freshly ground black pepper.

Serve with pita bread. Leftover hummus can be stored in an airtight container in the refrigerator for 2–3 days.

Makes 1 cup

indian-style lamb curry.

1 cup plain natural yoghurt

juice of 1 lemon

2 teaspoons cornflour (cornstarch)

2 cloves garlic, crushed

1 teaspoon grated fresh ginger

1 kg (2 lb) shoulder or leg of lamb, trimmed
and cubed

2 tablespoons vegetable oil

1 onion, finely chopped

1 tablespoon curry powder (see page 106)

1 × 400 g (13 oz) can chopped tomatoes

2 tablespoons tomato paste

1 long red chilli, seeded and finely chopped

½ cup beef stock or water

½ teaspoon salt

1 bay leaf

salt, extra, and freshly ground black pepper

½ cup coarsely chopped coriander
(cilantro) leaves

In a large bowl, combine the yoghurt, lemon juice, cornflour, garlic and ginger. Add the lamb pieces and toss to coat thoroughly. Cover and allow to marinate in the refrigerator overnight.

Heat the oil in a large saucepan over medium heat and sauté the onion for 4–5 minutes, or until golden. Add the curry powder and cook, stirring, for 2 minutes. Add the lamb and its marinade to the saucepan and cook, stirring, for 10 minutes. Stir in the tomatoes, tomato paste, chilli, stock, salt and bay leaf. Cover and simmer over gentle heat for 1½–2 hours, or until the meat is tender. Taste and add extra curry powder, if desired. Add extra water or stock if the sauce becomes too thick during cooking.

Season to taste with salt and freshly ground black pepper and stir in the coriander. Serve with steamed rice.

Serves 4–6

jelly.

This recipe is a grown-up version of that favourite wobbly, nostalgic treat.
Fresh fruit jelly is delicious served with good-quality ice-cream.

1 litre (32 fl oz) freshly squeezed orange
   juice, strained
2 × 10 g (¼ oz) sachets (1½ tablespoons)
   powdered gelatine

2–3 tablespoons sugar
¼ cup Grand Marnier

Place 1 cup of the orange juice in a small bowl, sprinkle over the gelatine and leave to soften for 5 minutes.

Bring the remaining juice to the boil in a medium-sized saucepan. Taste and add sugar until the jelly is sweet enough for you. Stir until the sugar has dissolved. Remove from the heat and stir through the softened gelatine mixture until it has completely dissolved. Add the Grand Marnier and mix well.

Pour the mixture into small individual decorative moulds, or simply into a bowl or shallow dish. Allow to cool to room temperature. Refrigerate for 3–4 hours until set, and turn out. Serve with ice-cream.

Any fresh fruit juice or juice combination can be used in this recipe – all except pineapple juice, which inhibits the gelatine setting.

Delicious jellies can be made using store-bought cranberry or berry juices and substituting schnapps or vodka for the Grand Marnier.

Fresh raspberries or strawberries can be set in the jelly.

Use powdered or leaf gelatine, depending on what is available. Six leaves will set 1 litre (32 fl oz) of liquid.

Serves 6

kedgeree.

Kedgeree is a dish the British brought home from their days in India – the rice and spices are typically Indian, and the smoked fish and eggs are the result of Anglo adaptation. The recipe I always use is by Katie Stewart.

900 g (1 lb 13 oz) smoked fish (haddock or cod) fillets
1 bay leaf
a few parsley stalks
1 tablespoon vegetable oil
100 g (3½ oz) butter
1 onion

½ teaspoon curry powder (see page 106)
450 g (14 oz) basmati or long-grain rice
3 large hard-boiled eggs
125 g (4 oz) unsalted cashews
⅓ cup chopped parsley
juice of ½ lemon
lemon or lime wedges, to serve

Cut the fish fillets into pieces about 5 cm (2 in) square, discarding any skin or bones. Place in a large saucepan with the bay leaf and parsley stalks, and cover with 1 litre (32 fl oz) of water. Bring to a simmer and poach the fish for 6 minutes, or until tender. Remove the fish pieces with a slotted spoon. Strain the cooking liquid and reserve. When the fish is cool, break the flesh into loose flakes.

Heat the oil and half of the butter in a saucepan over low heat. Add the onion and cook gently for 5 minutes, or until softened. Add the curry powder and rice and stir into the butter and onion for a moment. Add the reserved poaching liquid. Bring to a simmer, stirring occasionally, then cover and cook over gentle heat for 20–25 minutes, or until the rice is tender and all the liquid has been absorbed.

Shell and chop the hard-boiled eggs. Using a fork, fold the eggs, fish, cashews, parsley, lemon juice and remaining butter into the cooked rice. Heat gently until hot, then serve at once with lemon wedges.

Serves 6–8

laksa.

I usually cheat a little and use a ready-made laksa paste to make this dish.

1 tablespoon vegetable oil

3–4 tablespoons laksa paste

600 ml (19 fl oz) coconut milk

600 ml (19 fl oz) chicken stock
(see page 68) or fish stock

4 fresh kaffir lime leaves, thinly sliced
(optional)

200 g (6½ oz) rice vermicelli (cellophane)
noodles

24 medium-sized uncooked prawns
(shrimp), shelled and deveined, or
2–3 cooked skinned chicken breasts,
chopped

100 g (3½ oz) bean sprouts

1 cup coriander (cilantro) leaves

8 bean curd puffs, each cut into 3 pieces

Thai fish sauce, to serve

2–3 teaspoons sambal oelek

1 lime, quartered

Heat the oil in a large frying pan over medium heat. Add the laksa paste and cook, stirring, for 2–3 minutes, or until fragrant. Add the coconut milk and stock and bring to the boil. Stir in the lime leaves. Reduce the heat and simmer for 10 minutes.

Meanwhile, place the noodles in a heatproof bowl and cover with boiling water. Leave to soak for 5 minutes, or until tender. Drain.

Add the prawns to the simmering broth and cook for 2 minutes, or until pink.

Divide the noodles between four deep bowls. Add the prawns or chicken to the bowls and ladle the broth over the noodles. Garnish with the bean sprouts, coriander leaves and bean curd puffs. Drizzle each bowl with a little fish sauce and top with sambal oelek. Serve with lime quarters.

Serves 4

lamb shanks.

8 lamb shanks

⅓ cup plain (all-purpose) flour

¼ cup vegetable oil

4 cloves garlic, crushed

2 onions, sliced

3 sticks celery, sliced

2 × 400 g (13 oz) cans chopped tomatoes

2 cups white wine

2 cups chicken stock (see page 68)
   or beef stock

2 large red chillies

2 sprigs rosemary

salt and freshly ground black pepper

GREMOLATA

1 clove garlic, finely chopped

¼ cup finely chopped flat-leaf parsley

grated zest of 1 lemon

Preheat the oven to 160°C (315°F, Gas Mark 2–3). Coat the shanks with the flour.

Heat half the oil in a large frying pan over medium heat. Cook the shanks two or three at a time, adding a little extra oil if needed, until browned. Do not overcrowd the pan – the meat will start to stew. Transfer to a large casserole dish.

Heat the remaining oil in the frying pan over medium heat. Add the garlic, onion and celery and cook, stirring occasionally, for 6–7 minutes, or until the vegetables are tender but not coloured. Transfer to the casserole dish.

Stir the tomato, wine and stock into the casserole and bring to the boil over medium heat. Tuck the whole chillies and rosemary into the pot. Cover, transfer to the oven and cook for 2 hours. Turn the shanks occasionally as they cook.

Remove from the oven and check the sauce for seasoning.

To make the gremolata, combine the garlic, parsley and lemon zest. Serve up the shanks in their sauce, sprinkled with the gremolata.

Serves 4

lamingtons.

CAKE

150 g (5 oz) unsalted butter, softened

1¾ cups self-raising (self-rising) flour

1 teaspoon baking powder

1 cup caster (superfine) sugar

3 eggs, lightly beaten

1 teaspoon vanilla essence

½ cup milk

COATING

3 cups icing (confectioners') sugar

⅓ cup cocoa

30 g (1 oz) unsalted butter, melted

¾ cup milk

3 cups desiccated (shredded) coconut

Preheat the oven to 180°C (350°F, Gas Mark 4). Grease a 20 × 30 cm (8 × 12 in) shallow cake tin and line the base with baking paper.

Place all the cake ingredients in a large mixing bowl and beat with an electric mixer on medium speed for 3 minutes, or until the mixture is smooth. Spoon into the prepared tin and smooth the surface.

Bake for 45–50 minutes, or until golden and firm to the touch. Allow to cool in the tin for 5 minutes before turning out onto a wire rack to cool completely.

Make the coating by sifting the icing sugar and cocoa into a heatproof bowl. Stir in the melted butter and milk. Place the bowl over a saucepan of simmering water and stir until smooth and shiny. Remove from the heat. The mixture should be thin – add a little boiling water if necessary.

Place the coconut in a shallow bowl.

Trim away the edges of the cool cake and cut the cake lengthways into three even strips. Cut each strip into eight even pieces. Using two forks, dip each piece of cake into the chocolate mixture then roll in the coconut. Transfer to a wire rack to dry. Repeat with the remaining pieces of cake.

Makes 24

lemon curd.

Lemon curd makes a great filling for cakes or small tarts or a topping for ice-cream or pavlova. Alternatively, simply spread onto buttered bread, hot toast, scones or English muffins.

3 lemons
220 g (7 oz) caster (superfine) sugar

110 g (3½ oz) unsalted butter
3 eggs, lightly beaten

Wash and dry the lemons. Finely grate the zest of one of the lemons. Place the zest, along with the sugar and butter, in a small, heavy-based saucepan over very low heat. Stir with a wooden spoon until the butter has melted and the sugar has dissolved.

Squeeze the three lemons and strain the juice. Add the juice and beaten eggs to the saucepan. Continue to cook over low heat, stirring constantly, until the mixture is thick enough to coat the back of the spoon. Do not allow the mixture to boil.

Stir the mixture well, pour into clean screw-top jars and seal. Allow to cool to room temperature before storing in the refrigerator for up to 1 month.

Lemon curd requires slow cooking and constant stirring, so don't rush the process by increasing the heat.

To make lime curd, substitute the lemon zest with the zest of 2 limes, and the lemon juice with the juice of 5 medium-sized limes.

To make orange curd, substitute the lemon zest with 1 tablespoon of finely grated orange zest, and the lemon juice with the juice of 2 medium-sized oranges.

To make passionfruit curd, substitute the lemon juice with the strained pulp of 8 passionfruit and the unstrained pulp of 2 passionfruit.

Makes 1½ cups

lemon c

2 chicken breasts
2 chicken thighs with drumsticks attached
salt and freshly ground black pepper
2 lemons
2 cloves garlic, unpeeled

Preheat the oven to 200°C (400°F, Gas

Place the chicken pieces in a bakin

black pepper. Quarter one of the lemo

ters over the chicken pieces. Add the

ones) to the tin. Add the garlic cloves

30–35 minutes, or until tender and go

Remove the chicken and keep w

tin, and discard the lemon quarters. A

along with enough chicken stock to

heat on the stove top, bring to the b

any bits stuck to the bottom of the ti

release any juices. Simmer gently for

to taste with salt and freshly ground

Pour the sauce over the chicker

with a salad or steamed vegetables.

lem

This is the perfect cake to add to y
sugary topping. (And yes, b

185 g (6 oz) unsalted butter, softened
¾ cup caster (superfine) sugar
1 tablespoon finely grated lemon zes
3 eggs, lightly beaten

Preheat the oven to 160°C (315°
tin and line the base with baking
Place the butter, caster sugar
the flour into the mixture. Use
beat until just smooth. (It is imp
Spoon the batter into the
50–60 minutes, or until golden
should come out clean. Turn o
Mix together the sugar an
sugar dissolve. Quickly spoon
juice will sink into the cake a

lemon curd.

Lemon curd makes a great filling for cakes or small tarts or a topping for ice-cream or pavlova. Alternatively, simply spread onto buttered bread, hot toast, scones or English muffins.

3 lemons

220 g (7 oz) caster (superfine) sugar

110 g (3½ oz) unsalted butter

3 eggs, lightly beaten

Wash and dry the lemons. Finely grate the zest of one of the lemons. Place the zest, along with the sugar and butter, in a small, heavy-based saucepan over very low heat. Stir with a wooden spoon until the butter has melted and the sugar has dissolved.

Squeeze the three lemons and strain the juice. Add the juice and beaten eggs to the saucepan. Continue to cook over low heat, stirring constantly, until the mixture is thick enough to coat the back of the spoon. Do not allow the mixture to boil.

Stir the mixture well, pour into clean screw-top jars and seal. Allow to cool to room temperature before storing in the refrigerator for up to 1 month.

Lemon curd requires slow cooking and constant stirring, so don't rush the process by increasing the heat.

To make lime curd, substitute the lemon zest with the zest of 2 limes, and the lemon juice with the juice of 5 medium-sized limes.

To make orange curd, substitute the lemon zest with 1 tablespoon of finely grated orange zest, and the lemon juice with the juice of 2 medium-sized oranges.

To make passionfruit curd, substitute the lemon juice with the strained pulp of 8 passionfruit and the unstrained pulp of 2 passionfruit.

Makes 1½ cups

lemon bars.

BASE

125 g (4 oz) unsalted butter, softened

1 cup caster (superfine) sugar

1⅓ cups plain (all-purpose) flour

LEMON TOPPING

1 cup caster (superfine) sugar

4 eggs

1 teaspoon grated lemon zest

½ cup freshly squeezed lemon juice

⅓ cup plain (all-purpose) flour

½ teaspoon baking powder

icing (confectioners') sugar, to serve

Lightly grease a 20 × 30 cm (8 × 12 in) shallow cake tin and line the base and sides with baking paper, leaving the paper overhanging along the two long sides.

Make the base by beating the butter and sugar together in a bowl for 3–4 minutes, or until pale and fluffy. Sift in the flour and fold through with a large metal spoon until combined and the mixture forms a firm dough. Press the mixture into the prepared tin, making sure there are no holes, and chill for 15 minutes.

Preheat the oven to 180°C (350°F, Gas Mark 4).

Bake the base for 20 minutes, or until firm and golden. Allow to cool in the tin.

Make the lemon topping by placing the sugar, eggs and lemon zest in a mixing bowl and beating with a hand-held electric mixer for 2–3 minutes, or until thickened and increased in volume. Stir in the lemon juice. Sift over the flour and baking powder and use the mixer on low speed to gradually whisk in.

Spoon the mixture onto the cool base, return to the oven and bake for 25–30 minutes, or until the topping is just set. Remove and allow to cool in the tin. Lift out using the baking paper and cut into 5 cm (2 in) squares. Serve dusted with icing (confectioners') sugar.

Makes 24

lemon cake.

This is the perfect cake to add to your repertoire – big lemon flavour and a crunchy sugary topping. (And yes, baking a great cake really can be this easy.)

185 g (6 oz) unsalted butter, softened

¾ cup caster (superfine) sugar

1 tablespoon finely grated lemon zest

3 eggs, lightly beaten

1½ cups self-raising (self-rising) flour, sifted

½ cup sugar

¼ cup lemon juice

Preheat the oven to 160°C (315°F, Gas Mark 2–3). Grease a 23 × 12 cm (9 × 5 in) loaf tin and line the base with baking paper.

Place the butter, caster sugar and lemon zest in a mixing bowl. Add the eggs and sift the flour into the mixture. Use a large wooden spoon to combine the ingredients and beat until just smooth. (It is important not to over-beat the batter.)

Spoon the batter into the prepared loaf tin and smooth the surface. Bake for 50–60 minutes, or until golden and firm to the touch. A skewer inserted in the centre should come out clean. Turn out onto a wire rack.

Mix together the sugar and lemon juice until just combined, without letting the sugar dissolve. Quickly spoon the sugar mixture over the top of the warm cake. The juice will sink into the cake and the sugar will form a crunchy topping.

Serves 8

lemon chicken.

2 chicken breasts

2 chicken thighs with drumsticks attached

salt and freshly ground black pepper

2 lemons

2 cloves garlic, unpeeled

2 tablespoons olive oil

about 2 cups chicken stock (see page 68)
   or water

2 tablespoons roughly chopped
   flat-leaf parsley

Preheat the oven to 200°C (400°F, Gas Mark 6).

Place the chicken pieces in a baking tin. Season well with salt and freshly ground black pepper. Quarter one of the lemons and squeeze the juice from two of the quarters over the chicken pieces. Add the four lemon quarters (including the squeezed ones) to the tin. Add the garlic cloves and drizzle the chicken with the oil. Roast for 30–35 minutes, or until tender and golden.

Remove the chicken and keep warm. Pour or spoon off any fat from the baking tin, and discard the lemon quarters. Add the juice from the remaining lemon to the tin, along with enough chicken stock to cover the bottom of the tin. Place over medium heat on the stove top, bring to the boil and stir well with a wooden spoon to loosen any bits stuck to the bottom of the tin. Squash the garlic with the back of the spoon to release any juices. Simmer gently for 5–7 minutes or until reduced by half, and season to taste with salt and freshly ground black pepper.

Pour the sauce over the chicken and sprinkle with the parsley. Serve immediately with a salad or steamed vegetables.

Serves 4

lemon curd.

Lemon curd makes a great filling for cakes or small tarts or a topping for ice-cream or pavlova. Alternatively, simply spread onto buttered bread, hot toast, scones or English muffins.

3 lemons	**110 g (3½ oz) unsalted butter**
220 g (7 oz) caster (superfine) sugar	**3 eggs, lightly beaten**

Wash and dry the lemons. Finely grate the zest of one of the lemons. Place the zest, along with the sugar and butter, in a small, heavy-based saucepan over very low heat. Stir with a wooden spoon until the butter has melted and the sugar has dissolved.

Squeeze the three lemons and strain the juice. Add the juice and beaten eggs to the saucepan. Continue to cook over low heat, stirring constantly, until the mixture is thick enough to coat the back of the spoon. Do not allow the mixture to boil.

Stir the mixture well, pour into clean screw-top jars and seal. Allow to cool to room temperature before storing in the refrigerator for up to 1 month.

Lemon curd requires slow cooking and constant stirring, so don't rush the process by increasing the heat.

To make lime curd, substitute the lemon zest with the zest of 2 limes, and the lemon juice with the juice of 5 medium-sized limes.

To make orange curd, substitute the lemon zest with 1 tablespoon of finely grated orange zest, and the lemon juice with the juice of 2 medium-sized oranges.

To make passionfruit curd, substitute the lemon juice with the strained pulp of 8 passionfruit and the unstrained pulp of 2 passionfruit.

Makes 1½ cups

lemon delicious pudding.

This simple dessert consists of a rich, creamy lemon base topped with a light golden sponge.

60 g (2 oz) unsalted butter, softened

¾ cup sugar

3 eggs, separated

2 teaspoons finely grated lemon zest

¼ cup self-raising (self-rising) flour

¾ cup milk

⅓ cup lemon juice

Preheat the oven to 180°C (350°F, Gas Mark 4). Grease a deep 5-cup-capacity soufflé dish.

In an electric mixer, beat the butter, sugar, egg yolks and lemon zest until light and fluffy. Alternately fold in the flour and mix through the milk to make a smooth batter. Stir in the lemon juice. The batter may look like it has separated at this stage, but this is fine.

In a separate clean bowl, whisk the egg whites until firm. Gently fold the whites into the batter.

Pour the batter into the prepared dish. Place the dish in a large baking tin and fill the tin with enough boiling water to come a third of the way up the sides of the dish. Carefully transfer to the oven and bake for 50–55 minutes, or until the top is golden and risen. Dust with icing (confectioners') sugar and serve with cream.

This pudding may also be cooked in six individual dishes, which take about 30 minutes to cook.

Lime zest and juice can be substituted for the lemon, if you prefer.

Serves 6

lemon ice-cream.

This rich ice-cream can be easily made without an ice-cream churn.

grated zest of 2 lemons
juice of 3 lemons
¾ cup icing (confectioners') sugar

1½ cups cream
½ cup plain natural yoghurt

Mix the lemon zest, juice and icing sugar in a small bowl until combined.

In a separate, clean bowl, whip the cream until it holds soft peaks, then stir through the yoghurt.

Gently whisk the lemon juice mixture into the cream mixture, until smooth and combined. Pour into a shallow, lidded container, cover with a layer of baking paper and the lid, then place in the freezer for 4 hours, or until firm and frozen. Freeze, covered, for up to 2 weeks.

Prior to serving, soften the ice-cream by transferring it to the refrigerator for about 15 minutes.

The yoghurt gives this ice-cream a nice depth of flavour. Alternatively, you can make it with more cream instead of the yoghurt, if desired.

Serves 6

lemon posset.

This simple pudding is well pedigreed and was very popular in the 19th century, when sweet creams and syllabubs were much favoured. This dish is definitely worth reviving, as it magically sets to form a sweet lemon custard using only cream, sugar and lemon juice. It is particularly delicious served with ripe berries.

600 ml (19 fl oz) double or thick cream
¾ cup caster (superfine) sugar

juice of 2 lemons

Place the cream and sugar in a saucepan and slowly bring to the boil over low heat, stirring to dissolve the sugar. Boil gently for 3 minutes.

Remove from the heat and whisk in the lemon juice. Allow to cool slightly and pour into 4 × 200 ml (6½ fl oz) ramekins, small tea cups or glasses. Chill for 12 hours or until set.

Serves 4

lemon tart.

1 quantity sweet shortcrust pastry
(see page 290)

4 eggs

2 egg yolks

1 cup caster (superfine) sugar

2 tablespoons finely grated lemon zest

1 cup lemon juice

¾ cup cream

Prepare the pastry according to the instructions on page 290. Chill the pastry for at least 30 minutes before using.

Lightly grease a 25 cm (10 in) loose-based tart tin. Roll out the pastry between two sheets of baking paper so that it is large enough to fit the tart tin. Line the tin with the pastry, leaving a little pastry overhanging the tin. Refrigerate for 15 minutes.

Preheat the oven to 200°C (400°F, Gas Mark 6).

Line the pastry case with baking paper. Half-fill the pastry case with pie weights, uncooked dried beans or rice, and bake for 12 minutes. Remove the weights and baking paper, return the tin to the oven and cook for a further 10–15 minutes, or until the pastry is dry and lightly coloured. Set aside to cool. If the pastry case has any holes, plug them with a little uncooked pastry. With a sharp knife, cut off the overhanging pastry.

Reduce the oven temperature to 150°C (300°F, Gas Mark 2).

Whisk together the whole eggs, egg yolks and sugar until well combined. Whisk in the lemon zest and juice. Stir through the cream. Place the tart tin on a flat oven tray. Pour the egg and lemon mixture into the pastry case, filling almost to the top of the tart shell. Bake for 35–40 minutes, or until it is just set – the centre should wobble a little. The tart will firm up as it cools. Allow to cool for at least 1 hour before serving. Serve dusted with icing (confectioners') sugar.

Serves 8

lemonade.

Pop six extra lemons into your basket next time you go shopping. Homemade lemonade is worth making, not only for its simplicity but because of its ability to refresh and revive. The following recipe gives you a concentrated base. Pour a little into a glass or jug, add ice and top up with still or sparkling water to taste.

1¹/₂ cups sugar | **6 lemons**

Place the sugar and 1¹/₂ cups of water in a small saucepan. Finely grate the zest of two of the lemons and add this to the saucepan. Bring the mixture to the boil, stirring constantly. Simmer for 5 minutes, or until the sugar has dissolved.

Squeeze the juice of all six lemons and add to the saucepan. Allow to cool.

Strain the mixture into a bottle, seal and store in the refrigerator for up to 5 days. Dilute as required.

Choose ripe, bright yellow lemons that feel heavy for their size.

Add some freshly chopped mint leaves as a tasty variation.

Try this syrup with a dash of gin or vodka and diluted with soda or tonic water.

Makes 3 cups concentrated syrup

macaroni cheese.

A big thanks to Nigel Slater for letting me include his 'really good macaroni cheese' recipe – a jolly nice supper dish.

350 g (11 oz) small macaroni, penne or
   other short, hollow dried pasta
1 litre (32 fl oz) milk
1 bay leaf
60 g (2 oz) butter
3 tablespoons plain (all-purpose) flour

6 rashers smoked streaky bacon
¾ cup grated mature farmhouse cheddar
2 teaspoons Dijon mustard
salt and freshly ground black pepper
2 handfuls fresh breadcrumbs
⅓ cup freshly grated parmesan

Preheat the oven to 200°C (400°F, Gas Mark 6).

Cook the pasta in plenty of boiling salted water until it is al dente.

Meanwhile, warm the milk in a saucepan over medium heat and add the bay leaf. When the milk comes to the boil, remove it from the heat.

In another saucepan, melt the butter. Add the flour and stir over moderate heat until you have a pale, biscuit-coloured paste. Pour in the hot milk, discarding the bay leaf, and whisk until there are no lumps. Simmer until the sauce is the consistency of double cream, stirring regularly so it does not catch.

Grill the bacon until lightly crisp, then break it into small pieces. Drain the pasta and fold it into the sauce, along with the bacon, cheddar cheese and mustard, and season to taste with salt and freshly ground black pepper.

Tip the mixture into a 2 litre (64 fl oz) gratin dish, avoiding the temptation to smooth the top. Toss the breadcrumbs with the parmesan and scatter over the top. Bake for 35–40 minutes or until topping is golden.

Serves 4

madeleines.

2 eggs

60 g (2 oz) caster (superfine) sugar

1 teaspoon vanilla essence

⅓ cup plain (all-purpose) flour

50 g (1¾ oz) butter, melted

icing (confectioners') sugar, to sprinkle

Preheat the oven to 180°C (350°F, Gas Mark 4). Generously grease and flour a 12-hole madeleine tin.

Whisk together the eggs, sugar and vanilla essence for 2–3 minutes, or until the sugar has dissolved and the mixture is thick and pale and has increased in volume. Sift the flour on top and fold in gently with a large metal spoon. Gently stir in the melted butter until combined.

Fill each hole in the prepared tin to three-quarters full. Bake for 7–10 minutes, or until risen, golden and firm to the touch. Cool on a wire rack. Sprinkle lightly with icing sugar while still warm. Eat within a couple of hours of baking.

Madeleines are traditionally made in a tin with shallow, shell-shaped holes. Alternatively, you can use a shallow 12-cup muffin tin.

Madeleines are even more delicious with 1 teaspoon of grated orange or lemon zest added to the mixture.

Makes 12

maître d'hôtel butter.

Maître d'hôtel butter is traditionally served with steak, but it is also good with grilled fish. Top a grilled steak or fish fillet with a slice of butter.

100 g (3½ oz) unsalted butter, diced and
   softened
2 tablespoons finely chopped parsley
1 teaspoon chopped chervil (optional)

½ teaspoon salt
freshly ground black pepper
1 tablespoon lemon juice

Place the butter, parsley, chervil and salt and a good grinding of freshly ground black pepper into a small bowl. Using a fork or wooden spoon, beat the mixture until the ingredients are combined. Slowly add the lemon juice, beating as you go, until combined.

Roll the butter into a small log. Wrap in baking paper and chill until firm. Store, wrapped in baking paper, in the refrigerator for up to 2 weeks. To serve, cut the butter into 1 cm (½ in) slices.

mango chutney.

My favourite mango chutney is based on a recipe from the remarkable
Joan Campbell, which appeared in her book *From Market to Table*.

3 large unripe mangoes, peeled and diced

¾ cup sugar

1 cup apple cider vinegar

juice and grated zest of 1 lemon

4 long red chillies, chopped

1 tablespoon grated fresh ginger

1 cloves garlic, crushed

½ cup sultanas

½ teaspoon ground cumin

½ teaspoon ground cinnamon

1 teaspoon salt

Place all the ingredients in a large stainless-steel saucepan – the pan should be no more than half full, to allow space for the mixture to simmer safely. Cook over medium heat, stirring to dissolve the sugar, until the mixture comes to the boil.

Reduce heat and simmer, stirring occasionally, for 35–45 minutes, or until the mixture thickens. Spoon into sterilised jars, seal and label.

To sterilise jars, you can either put them through the dishwasher or wash them by hand in hot soapy water; if hand washing, rinse the jars with boiling water and drain on a clean tea towel before use.

This chutney will keep for 6 months in a cool, dark place. After opening, refrigerate and use within 3 weeks.

Makes about 2½ cups

mango sorbet.

Easy to make, ultra refreshing and full of flavour, this sorbet is virtually fat free. It can easily be made without an ice-cream churn. Mango sorbet is perfect served simply in a cone or bowl.

170 g (5½ oz) caster (superfine) sugar
juice of 1 lime

2 large ripe mangoes, flesh removed and chopped

Place the sugar in a heatproof bowl and pour over 1 cup of boiling water. Stir well until dissolved, then set aside to cool.

Purée the lime juice, mango and sugar syrup in a blender until smooth. Taste and add extra lime juice or sugar if desired. Churn in an ice-cream machine until firm. If you don't have a machine, pour the mixture into a shallow, lidded container and place, covered, in the freezer for about 2 hours, or until firm on top and frozen around the edges. Transfer to an electric mixer or food processor and beat or whiz until smooth. Return to the freezer until firm, then beat and freeze once more.

Freeze, covered, for up to 2 weeks. Prior to serving, soften the sorbet by transferring it to the refrigerator for about 15 minutes.

Variations to this recipe are numerous. Try one or all of the following: raspberry sorbet – replace the mango flesh with 500 g (1 lb) of raspberries (frozen raspberries are fine); strawberry sorbet – replace the mango flesh with 400 g (13 oz) of hulled strawberries; peach or nectarine sorbet – replace the mango flesh with 5 large ripe peaches or nectarines, peeled and roughly chopped.

Serves 4

marinated olives.

500 g (1 lb) black or green olives

3 cloves garlic, finely sliced

1 large red chilli, seeded
   and finely chopped

2 teaspoons finely grated lemon zest

2 teaspoons chopped rosemary

3 sprigs thyme

2 bay leaves

olive oil, to cover

In a mixing bowl, combine the olives, garlic, chilli, lemon zest, rosemary, thyme and bay leaves, then spoon into a large glass jar. Add enough olive oil to cover the olives. Seal the jar and tap gently to dislodge any air bubbles.

Marinate in the refrigerator for 1–2 weeks before eating.

You can use many other flavour combinations for this versatile dish. Grated orange zest, basil leaves or anchovies are just a few other ingredients that work well. Vary the recipe above with one or more of these ingredients.

mashed potato.

1 kg (2 lb) floury potatoes, peeled and cut
 into chunks
1 cup milk

100 g (3½ oz) butter, cubed
salt and freshly ground black pepper

Place the potato pieces in a large saucepan of salted water. Bring to the boil and cook for 20–25 minutes, or until tender. Drain and return the potatoes to the saucepan. Cook over low heat for 1–2 minutes to remove any remaining moisture.

Meanwhile, heat the milk in a small saucepan over medium heat.

Mash the potatoes with the butter and ¾ cup of the hot milk until smooth. Beat well with a wooden spoon to fluff up the potato, adding a little more milk if needed. The mash should be soft and fluffy. Season to taste with salt and freshly ground black pepper.

The best mashed potato is made from varieties that are high in starch. Choose varieties such as bison, coliban, kennebec, sebago or spunta.

If you like a coarse texture to your mash, use a potato masher. Or for a really light, fluffy mash, push the potatoes through a mouli or potato ricer.

Try adding other vegetables, such as parsnip, celeriac or sweet potato (garnet yam) to the mash.

Add some gruyère cheese or pesto for a variation on standard mashed potato.

Serves 4–6

marinated pork fillets.

2 large pork fillets, each about 500 g (1 lb)

4 teaspoons fennel seeds

1 teaspoon sea salt flakes

2 teaspoons freshly ground black pepper

2 cloves garlic, finely chopped

1 teaspoon dried chilli flakes

1 teaspoon brown sugar

1/2 teaspoon dried sage

2–3 tablespoons olive oil

Pat the pork fillets dry with kitchen paper. With a sharp knife, make a few slashes across each piece of pork to allow the marinade to penetrate the meat, but take care not to cut right through. Transfer the fillets to a glass or ceramic dish.

Grind the fennel seeds with a pestle and mortar, then mix in the salt, pepper, garlic, chilli, sugar and sage. Add enough olive oil to make a thick but spreadable paste. Alternatively, blend the spices in a small food processor, adding a little olive oil while the motor is running to make a paste. Spread the paste over the pork fillets then drizzle with a little more olive oil. Leave in the fridge to marinate for 1–2 hours.

Preheat oven to 220°C (425°F, Gas Mark 7). Transfer the marinated fillets to a roasting tray and cook on the top shelf of the oven for 25–30 minutes, or until cooked through and lightly browned. To test, insert a skewer into the thickest part of the meat; the juices should run clear. Remove the pork fillets from the oven, cover loosely with foil and set aside to rest in a warm place for 10 minutes.

Slice and serve with a salad or steamed green vegetables.

You need a hot oven for this, so make sure it is fully preheated to the correct temperature.

This spice paste is also delicious rubbed into pork chops or a roasting joint of pork before cooking.

Serves 4

marmalade.

1 kg (2 lb) Seville oranges
juice of 1 large lemon

2 kg (4 lb) sugar

Scrub the oranges to remove any wax on the peel. Place the whole oranges in a large saucepan with 2 litres of water. Bring to the boil, then simmer gently for 2 hours, or until the skin of the oranges is very soft and can be easily pierced with a fork.

Remove the fruit from the saucepan, reserving the cooking liquid. When cool enough to handle, quarter each orange and cut each segment into thin shreds, saving the juice. Remove any pips and place them on a 20 cm (8 in) square of muslin or cheese cloth. Tie the bag tightly with a piece of string – the string should be long enough to secure the bag and to allow it to be tied to the handle of the saucepan but reach the bottom of the pan.

Place a saucer in the freezer.

Return the cooking liquid to medium heat, add the pips and lemon juice and boil for 10 minutes. Remove the pips, then add the chopped fruit and reserved juice and boil until reduced by one third.

Add the sugar, stirring well to dissolve. Increase the heat and boil rapidly for about 20 minutes, or until setting point is reached. To test for setting point, drop a spoonful of marmalade onto the chilled saucer and allow to cool. If the jam forms a skin and wrinkles when pushed with a fingertip, it has reached setting point. Remove marmalade from heat when testing.

Allow the jam to cool, stir well, then spoon into sterilised jars, seal and label.

Makes 2½ litres

mashed potato.

1 kg (2 lb) floury potatoes, peeled and cut
    into chunks
1 cup milk

100 g (3½ oz) butter, cubed
salt and freshly ground black pepper

Place the potato pieces in a large saucepan of salted water. Bring to the boil and cook for 20–25 minutes, or until tender. Drain and return the potatoes to the saucepan. Cook over low heat for 1–2 minutes to remove any remaining moisture.

Meanwhile, heat the milk in a small saucepan over medium heat.

Mash the potatoes with the butter and ¾ cup of the hot milk until smooth. Beat well with a wooden spoon to fluff up the potato, adding a little more milk if needed. The mash should be soft and fluffy. Season to taste with salt and freshly ground black pepper.

The best mashed potato is made from varieties that are high in starch. Choose varieties such as bison, coliban, kennebec, sebago or spunta.

If you like a coarse texture to your mash, use a potato masher. Or for a really light, fluffy mash, push the potatoes through a mouli or potato ricer.

Try adding other vegetables, such as parsnip, celeriac or sweet potato (garnet yam) to the mash.

Add some gruyère cheese or pesto for a variation on standard mashed potato.

Serves 4–6

minestrone.

2 tablespoons olive oil

3 rashers bacon or pancetta, chopped

2 brown onions, chopped

1 leek, sliced

1 carrot, chopped

2 sticks celery, chopped

1 clove garlic, crushed

2 zucchini (courgettes), diced

400 g (13 oz) can crushed tomatoes

1.5 litres (48 fl oz) chicken stock
    (see page 68)

2 cups shredded spinach leaves

120 g (4 oz) small pasta shapes,
    such as orzo

400 g (13 oz) can cannellini beans, rinsed
    and drained

2 tablespoons chopped flat-leaf parsley
    or basil

salt and freshly ground black pepper

extra-virgin olive oil, to serve

freshly grated parmesan, to serve

Heat the oil in a large saucepan over low heat. Add the bacon or pancetta and cook, stirring, for 2 minutes. Add the onion, leek, carrot, celery and garlic. Cook, stirring, for 7–8 minutes, or until softened. This mixture gives the soup its flavour base.

Add the zucchini and crushed tomatoes to the saucepan. Cook, stirring, for 2 minutes. Add the chicken stock and 2 cups of water. Bring to the boil. Skim off any scum, reduce the heat and simmer gently for 30 minutes.

Add the spinach and pasta. Simmer for 20 minutes, stirring occasionally.

Add the cannellini beans and parsley. Add extra water or stock if there is not enough liquid, but remember, this is a thick soup. Season to taste with salt and freshly ground black pepper. Continue to cook for a further 10 minutes.

Ladle the soup into bowls, drizzle with extra-virgin olive oil and sprinkle with freshly grated parmesan.

Serves 4–6

mayonnaise.

Mayonnaise is simple to make at home. I mix it by hand with a wire whisk, rather than whizzing it in the food processor, because I prefer the silky texture of a handmade mayonnaise.

2 egg yolks
1 teaspoon Dijon mustard
1 tablespoon lemon juice
salt

¼ cup olive oil
¾ cup vegetable oil
freshly ground black pepper

Place the egg yolks, mustard, lemon juice and a pinch of salt into a small bowl and whisk until smooth.

Combine the olive oil and vegetable oil in a jug. Pour it very slowly, drop by drop, into the egg mixture, whisking constantly. As the mixture thickens, start adding the oil in a steady stream. Continue until all the oil has been incorporated and the mixture is thick. Season to taste with salt and freshly ground black pepper. Taste and add a little more lemon juice if desired. The mixture can be thinned with boiling water, if necessary.

It's a good idea to stand the mixing bowl on a damp cloth while you're making mayonnaise. This prevents it from moving as you whisk.

The mixture may separate if the oil has been added too quickly. To remedy this, simply whisk up another egg yolk and gradually whisk this through the separated mixture in small amounts.

Mayonnaise can easily be flavoured. Chopped fresh herbs, garlic, anchovies, lemon zest, capers or chilli are just a few suggestions.

Makes 1½ cups

meatballs.

1 thick slice Italian-style bread

milk, to soak

650 g (1 lb 5 oz) minced (ground) veal

2 cloves garlic, finely chopped

⅓ cup freshly grated parmesan

2 tablespoons chopped flat-leaf parsley

1 tablespoon chopped oregano

1 teaspoon finely grated lemon zest

1 large egg, lightly beaten

salt and freshly ground black pepper

plain (all-purpose) flour, to coat

2–3 tablespoons olive oil

1 × 400 g (13 oz) can crushed tomatoes

2 cloves garlic, peeled, extra

200 g (6½ oz) mozzarella, sliced or grated

chopped flat-leaf parsley, extra, to garnish

Remove the crust from the bread, break the bread into pieces and soak in a little milk. Squeeze dry, crumble and place in a large bowl. Add the minced veal, garlic, parmesan, parsley, oregano, lemon zest and beaten egg, and mix well. Season with plenty of salt and freshly ground black pepper. To check the seasoning, fry a small amount of the mixture until cooked through, and taste it. Adjust the seasoning to taste.

Shape the mixture into balls 5 cm (2 in) in diameter. Roll them in flour and shake off any excess.

Heat the oil in a large frying pan over medium heat. Add the meatballs and cook, turning, until brown all over. Remove and drain on kitchen paper.

Add the crushed tomatoes and whole garlic cloves to the frying pan. Bring to the boil, reduce the heat and simmer gently for 5 minutes. Return the meatballs to the pan and cook, turning them occasionally, for 5 minutes.

Preheat the oven to 180°C (350°F, Gas Mark 4).

Transfer the meatballs and sauce to an ovenproof dish. Top with the mozzarella and bake for 20 minutes. Sprinkle with the extra chopped parsley and serve with crusty bread to mop up the juices.

Serves 4–6

meatloaf.

This dish is inspired by a recipe that originally came from Delia Smith.

500 g (1 lb) minced (ground) veal

500 g (1 lb) minced (ground) pork

4 rashers streaky bacon, chopped

2 onions, finely chopped

2 cloves garlic, chopped

2 tablespoons chopped parsley

2 teaspoons chopped thyme

1 egg, lightly beaten

1 cup fresh white breadcrumbs

¼ cup milk

2 teaspoons Dijon mustard

2 teaspoons Worcestershire sauce

¼ cup beef stock or vegetable stock

salt and freshly ground black pepper

3 hard-boiled eggs, shells removed

Preheat the oven to 160°C (315°F, Gas Mark 2–3). Grease a 20 × 12 × 9 cm (9 × 5 × 3½ in) loaf tin.

In a large bowl, combine the veal, pork, bacon, onion, garlic, herbs and egg. Mix well with your hands or with a large wooden spoon.

In a separate bowl, lightly mash together the breadcrumbs and the milk, then add to the meat mixture. Stir in the mustard, Worcestershire sauce and stock. Season well.

Half fill the prepared tin with the mixture. Place the hard-boiled eggs end to end down the centre of the tin, then cover with the remaining mixture. Level the top and cover the tin with foil. Place in a large baking tin and fill the baking tin with enough boiling water to come one-third of the way up the sides of the loaf tin. Carefully transfer to the oven and bake for 2 hours, or until cooked. A skewer inserted into the centre and pressed should produce clear liquid, not pink liquid. Allow to cool in the tin for 15 minutes before serving. Serve hot or cold.

Meatloaf is delicious served hot with a spicy fresh tomato sauce or cold with pickles or chutney.

Serves 8

meringues.

3 large egg whites
salt

175 g (6 oz) caster (superfine) sugar

Preheat the oven to 140°C (275°F, Gas Mark 1). Line two oven trays with baking paper.

Place the egg whites and a pinch of salt in a large, clean, dry bowl. Whisk with an electric mixer or hand-held electric beater on low speed for a couple of minutes. Increase the speed to medium and whisk for a further 2 minutes, or until stiff peaks form – if you lift the beater out of the bowl, the mixture should cling to the beaters, keeping stiff and moist-looking peaks. Continue to whisk the mixture, gradually adding the sugar 1 tablespoon at a time and beating well after each addition. Continue beating until the mixture is stiff and glossy – this may take 5–10 minutes.

Using a large metal spoon, spoon free-form shapes (2 rounded tablespoons in size) onto the prepared trays.

Bake the meringues for 15–20 minutes, or until pale and dry. Turn off the oven and allow to cool in the oven with the door ajar. Store in an airtight container for up to 2 weeks.

Instead of spooning the mixture onto the oven trays, alternatively you can use a piping bag. The easiest way to do this is to sit the bag in a large, tall glass or container and fold the top of the bag over the edge of the glass. Spoon in the mixture and secure the top of the bag with a few twists. Keeping the bag upright, pipe small shapes onto the tray.

Makes 40

minestrone.

2 tablespoons olive oil

3 rashers bacon or pancetta, chopped

2 brown onions, chopped

1 leek, sliced

1 carrot, chopped

2 sticks celery, chopped

1 clove garlic, crushed

2 zucchini (courgettes), diced

400 g (13 oz) can crushed tomatoes

1.5 litres (48 fl oz) chicken stock
    (see page 68)

2 cups shredded spinach leaves

120 g (4 oz) small pasta shapes,
    such as orzo

400 g (13 oz) can cannellini beans, rinsed
    and drained

2 tablespoons chopped flat-leaf parsley
    or basil

salt and freshly ground black pepper

extra-virgin olive oil, to serve

freshly grated parmesan, to serve

Heat the oil in a large saucepan over low heat. Add the bacon or pancetta and cook, stirring, for 2 minutes. Add the onion, leek, carrot, celery and garlic. Cook, stirring, for 7–8 minutes, or until softened. This mixture gives the soup its flavour base.

Add the zucchini and crushed tomatoes to the saucepan. Cook, stirring, for 2 minutes. Add the chicken stock and 2 cups of water. Bring to the boil. Skim off any scum, reduce the heat and simmer gently for 30 minutes.

Add the spinach and pasta. Simmer for 20 minutes, stirring occasionally.

Add the cannellini beans and parsley. Add extra water or stock if there is not enough liquid, but remember, this is a thick soup. Season to taste with salt and freshly ground black pepper. Continue to cook for a further 10 minutes.

Ladle the soup into bowls, drizzle with extra-virgin olive oil and sprinkle with freshly grated parmesan.

Serves 4–6

mocha.

Chocolate and coffee are flavours made for each other. Just as the depth and flavour of a chocolate cake is improved with the addition of a little coffee, this hot chocolate drink is delicious when combined with coffee. This is a perfect lazy Sunday afternoon treat.

100 g (3½ oz) dark chocolate, chopped

2 teaspoons sugar

1 cup milk

a plunger or pot of freshly brewed coffee

whipped cream, to serve

cocoa, drinking chocolate or grated chocolate, to serve

Combine the chocolate, sugar and milk in a small saucepan. Place over low heat and stir until the sugar and chocolate have melted and the mixture is smooth. As it comes to the boil, whisk hard to create a bit of froth, then remove from the heat.

Divide the mixture between two large mugs and add enough freshly brewed coffee to almost fill the mugs. Top with a dollop of whipped cream and sprinkle with a little cocoa or grated chocolate. Taste and add extra sugar if desired.

Use good-quality couverture chocolate or dark chocolate with a high cocoa butter content, if available.

Mocha is also good with a dash of brandy, whisky or a flavoured liqueur, such as Frangelico or Grand Marnier.

Serves 2

muffins.

Muffins are fast, easy and infinitely variable.

2¼ cups plain (all-purpose) flour

2 teaspoons baking powder

½ teaspoon bicarbonate of soda
    (sodium bicarbonate)

salt

300 ml (9½ fl oz) buttermilk

2 eggs

1 teaspoon vanilla essence

¾ cup lightly packed brown sugar

125 g (4 oz) unsalted butter, melted

Preheat the oven to 190°C (375°F, Gas Mark 5). Grease a 12-cup muffin tin or line with paper patty cases.

Sift the flour, baking powder, bicarbonate of soda and a pinch of salt into a mixing bowl and make a well in the centre.

Whisk together the buttermilk, eggs, vanilla, sugar and melted butter. Pour the egg mixture into the well in the flour mixture and stir until the ingredients are just combined. Do not over-mix – the batter should not be smooth.

Divide the mixture evenly between the muffin cups. Bake for 20–25 minutes, or until the tops are golden and a skewer inserted into the centre of a muffin comes out clean. Allow to cool in the tin for 5 minutes before turning out onto a wire rack. Muffins are delicious served warm.

If you can't find buttermilk, use 150 ml (4½ fl oz) of natural yoghurt mixed with 150 ml (4½ fl oz) of milk.

To make blueberry muffins, fold 200 g (6½ oz) of fresh or frozen blueberries into the batter.

To make pecan muffins, fold in ¾ cup of chopped pecans. Sprinkle the top of each muffin with a little ground cinnamon and extra chopped nuts before baking.

Makes 12

mussel broth.

6 large ripe Roma (egg) tomatoes

2 tablespoons olive oil

2 leeks, thinly sliced

1 clove garlic, crushed

2 sticks celery, thinly sliced

1 large red chilli, seeded and sliced

1 cup white wine

1 cup vegetable stock or fish stock

2 kg (4 lb) fresh mussels, cleaned and
debearded

1/4 cup roughly chopped flat-leaf parsley

salt and freshly ground black pepper

Cut a cross in the base of each tomato, then place tomatoes in a large heatproof bowl and pour over enough hot water to cover. Let them sit for 1 minute, then drain off the water. Peel the tomatoes by pulling the skin away from the end with the cross. Chop the peeled tomatoes and place them and any juice in a bowl.

Heat the oil in a large saucepan and add the leek, garlic, celery and chilli. Cook over medium heat, stirring occasionally, for 5 minutes, or until the vegetables have softened. Add the wine, stock and tomato (with the juice) and simmer over gentle heat for 5 minutes.

Add the mussels and increase the heat to high. Cover with a tight-fitting lid and cook for 3–4 minutes, giving the saucepan an occasional shake to help the mussels release their juices. Uncover, add the parsley and stir well. Season to taste with salt and freshly ground black pepper. Serve the mussels and broth in large, wide bowls with plenty of crusty bread.

When buying mussels, choose only those that have perfect shells. Prior to cooking, use only those that close firmly after giving them a good tap. If they haven't already been cleaned, soak mussels in fresh water for 15 minutes, then scrub them and pull off their beards with a sharp tug. Discard any mussels that don't open after cooking.

Serves 4

mussels.

Mussels are perfect for a simple, fast and easy supper. For two people you will need 1–1.25 kg (2–2½ lb) of fresh mussels. Choose mussels that have perfect shells and that close firmly after they've been given a good tap. Soak the mussels in fresh water for 15 minutes, and then pull off their beards with a sharp tug.

2 tablespoons olive oil

1 onion, chopped

2 cloves garlic, crushed

1 tablespoon chopped flat-leaf parsley

1 cup white wine

¼ cup cream

1.25 kg (2½ lb) fresh mussels, cleaned and debearded

salt and freshly ground black pepper

chopped flat-leaf parsley, extra, to serve

Place a large saucepan or wok over medium heat. Add the oil, onion, garlic, parsley, wine and cream. Bring to the boil and simmer for 5 minutes. Add the mussels and increase the heat to high. Cover with a tight-fitting lid and cook for 3 minutes, giving the pan an occasional shake to help the mussels release their flavour.

Uncover and stir well. As the mussels open, transfer them to two deep serving bowls. Discard any that haven't opened after 5 minutes. Boil the broth for 2 minutes, season to taste with salt and freshly ground black pepper, and then strain over the mussels. Discard the solids. Sprinkle the mussels with the extra chopped parsley and serve immediately. Serve with crusty bread to mop up the delicious creamy broth.

Mussels are at their best from midwinter to the end of summer.

Serves 2

onion marmalade.

This is great served alongside cold meats or cheese, or as part of a ploughman's lunch.

2 tablespoons olive oil

1.5 kg (3 lb) red (Spanish) onions, thinly sliced

2 cloves garlic, finely chopped

1 tablespoon mustard seeds

2 bay leaves

½ cup lightly packed brown sugar

1 cup white wine

1 cup white-wine vinegar

finely grated zest of 1 orange

juice of 2 oranges

Heat the oil in a large saucepan over low heat. Add the onion and garlic and cook, stirring occasionally, for 15 minutes, or until soft and lightly coloured. Add all the remaining ingredients, increase the heat and bring to the boil, stirring to dissolve the sugar. Reduce the heat and simmer, stirring frequently, until the mixture has reduced to a jam consistency – this will take 35–50 minutes.

Allow to cool, then spoon into sterilised screw-top jars and store in the refrigerator for up to 2 weeks.

Makes 3 cups

orange biscuits.

These biscuits are adapted from a recipe I found in a delightful old book titled
Kitchen Essays, written by Agnes Jekyll (sister of the famed Victorian
garden designer Gertrude Jekyll) in 1922.

125 g (4 oz) ground almonds (almond meal)

½ cup sugar

90 g (3 oz) butter

60 g (2 oz) plain (all-purpose) flour

grated zest and juice of 2 oranges

Preheat the oven to 180°C (350°F, Gas Mark 4). Line two oven trays with baking paper.

Place all the ingredients into a mixing bowl and beat with a wooden spoon until smooth and combined.

Using a tablespoon, scoop up small walnut-sized pieces of dough and place them on the prepared trays, leaving room for each to spread a little.

Bake for 8–10 minutes, or until firm and coloured. You may need to bake a third tray if any mixture remains. Cool on a wire rack.

Agnes's biscuits are delicious served with afternoon tea, or for dessert with ice-cream or to accompany a creamy dish.

Makes about 24

orange cordial.

Wonderfully refreshing on a hot summer's day, make this cordial in advance and have it chilled ready for use. The following gives you a concentrated syrup.

1½ cups caster (superfine) sugar | juice of 6 oranges
zest of ½ orange | juice of 2 lemons

Place the sugar and zest in a large heatproof bowl. Pour over 1½ cups of boiling water and stir until the sugar dissolves. Set aside to cool for 5 minutes.

Stir in the orange and lemon juice. Allow to cool to room temperature.

Strain the cordial into a jug or bottle, seal and store in the refrigerator for up to 7 days.

To serve, dilute 1 part syrup to 5 parts water, or to taste, and serve in tall glasses with plenty of ice. Garnish with fresh mint leaves and slices of lemon or orange.

Dilute the syrup with still or sparkling water.

Makes 3 cups concentrated syrup

orange poppy seed cake.

½ cup poppy seeds

¾ cup milk

juice of ½ lemon

250 g (8 oz) unsalted butter, softened

1 cup caster (superfine) sugar

grated zest of 1 orange

4 eggs

2 cups plain (all-purpose) flour

2 teaspoons baking powder

½ teaspoon bicarbonate of soda
      (sodium bicarbonate)

orange syrup (see below)

Soak the poppy seeds in the milk and lemon juice for 1–2 hours.

Preheat the oven to 180°C (350°F, Gas Mark 4). Lightly grease a 25 cm (10 in) kugelhopf or bundt cake tin.

Beat the butter, sugar and orange zest in an electric mixer until fluffy and pale. Beat in the eggs one at a time, alternating with a little flour, until combined. Sift together the remaining flour and the baking powder and bicarbonate of soda, then fold into the mixture. Gently stir in the milk mixture until smooth and combined.

Spoon the batter into the prepared tin. Bake for 55–60 minutes, or until the cake feels firm to the touch and a skewer inserted into the centre comes out clean. Allow to cool in the tin for 5 minutes, then turn out onto a large plate and brush hot orange syrup over the top and sides of the cake. Leave to cool.

To make the orange syrup, combine the juice from 2 oranges and ½ cup caster (superfine) sugar in a small saucepan. Bring to the boil over medium heat, stirring to dissolve the sugar, then simmer gently for 5 minutes.

orange semolina cake.

Semolina adds an interesting texture to cakes. This delicious version of orange cake keeps well and is good as a dessert or with a cup of tea.

125 g (4 oz) self-raising (self-rising) flour

1 teaspoon baking powder

1½ cups semolina

1 cup caster (superfine) sugar

3 eggs, lightly beaten

200 ml (6½ fl oz) plain natural yoghurt

½ cup milk

grated zest and juice of 1 orange

juice of ½ lemon

½ cup vegetable oil

orange syrup (see opposite)

Preheat the oven to 180°C (350°F, Gas Mark 4). Lightly grease a 23 cm (9 in) round cake tin and line the base with baking paper.

Sift the flour, baking powder, semolina and sugar into a large bowl and make a well in the centre.

In a separate bowl, combine the eggs, yoghurt, milk, orange zest and juice, lemon juice and oil. Pour the egg mixture into the flour mixture, stirring until just combined.

Pour the batter into the prepared tin. Bake for 40–45 minutes, or until firm to the touch and golden. A skewer inserted into the centre should come out clean. Allow to cool in the tin for 5 minutes, then turn out onto a large plate and brush the hot syrup over the top and sides of the cake. Leave to cool.

pancakes.

1 cup plain (all-purpose) flour

1 teaspoon baking powder

salt

2 tablespoons caster (superfine) sugar
(optional)

2 eggs, lightly beaten

1 cup milk

30 g (1 oz) butter, melted

Sift the flour, baking powder and a pinch of salt into a bowl, and make a well in the centre. If you want to make sweet pancakes, stir in the caster sugar now. In a separate bowl, combine the beaten eggs, milk and melted butter. Pour the wet ingredients into the centre of the dry ingredients and mix until combined – don't worry about a few lumps. The batter should be the consistency of thick or double cream.

Grease a small non-stick frying pan and place over medium heat for 1 minute. Pour a ladleful of batter into the hot pan and cook for about 1 minute, or until bubbles appear on the surface of the pancake and the underside is golden. Using a spatula or fish slice, flip the pancake over and cook for a further 45–60 seconds before turning out.

The pancake mixture can be made ahead of time and left to rest for up to 2 hours.

Serve sweet pancakes with maple syrup or a squeeze of lemon juice and a sprinkling of sugar.

For savoury pancakes, fill with ratatouille, or mushrooms cooked in a little cream.

A little grated zucchini (courgette), chopped fresh herbs or spring onions (scallions) added to the batter also make delicious variations.

Makes 6–8

pannacotta.

Pannacotta is a traditional creamy pudding from Piedmont in northern Italy.
This rich and delicious version is flavoured with orange and vanilla.

½ cup milk

1 × 10 g sachet (3 teaspoons)
    powdered gelatine

600 ml (20 fl oz) cream

¾ cup caster (superfine) sugar

1 teaspoon finely grated orange zest

1 teaspoon vanilla essence

Lightly grease 6 × ½-cup-capacity pudding moulds.

Pour the milk into a small bowl. Stir in the gelatine and set aside.

Place the cream, sugar, orange zest and vanilla in a saucepan. Slowly bring to the boil, stirring until the sugar dissolves. Remove from the heat, add the gelatine mixture and stir until the gelatine dissolves. Set aside to cool for 15 minutes.

Strain the mixture and pour into the prepared moulds. Refrigerate for at least 4 hours, or until set.

To serve, dip the outside of each mould in hot water for 10 seconds, run a sharp knife around the inside of each mould and invert onto a serving plate. Serve as is or with fresh seasonal fruit.

Pannacotta can be made ahead of time and stored, covered, in the fridge for up to 3 days.

Serves 6

passionfruit ice-cream.

I love to see how a recipe changes as it travels from one person to the next. Many
years ago I ate a delicious orange and cardamom ice-cream at Stephanie Alexander's
restaurant in Melbourne. Gently flavoured and subtly spiced, the ice-cream was
a revelation. Stephanie credited Jane Grigson (the great English food writer)
with the recipe, who in turn had credited Jocelyn Dimbleby with the original.
I have made it many times and in the process adapted the method
to suit one of my favourite flavours – passionfruit.

8 passionfruit	salt
175 g (6 oz) caster (superfine) sugar	300 ml (9½ fl oz) cream
3 large eggs	

Push the pulp from the passionfruit through a small sieve to remove the seeds,
reserving 1 teaspoon of the seeds.

Place the sugar and 100 ml (3½ fl oz) of water in a small saucepan and bring to the
boil, stirring to dissolve the sugar. Boil steadily for 3 minutes.

Meanwhile, beat the eggs and a pinch of salt with an electric mixer until frothy.

Pour the sugar syrup into the egg mixture and continue to beat for 2–3 minutes,
or until the mixture has thickened. Stir the sieved passionfruit and the reserved seeds
into the mixture.

Lightly whip the cream and fold into the mixture. Churn in an ice-cream machine
until frozen.

*To make the original orange and cardamom version, follow the above but replace the passionfruit
with ½ cup of concentrated orange juice and the crushed seeds from 5 cardamom pods.*

Serves 6

passionfruit syllabub.

8 passionfruit

⅓ cup dessert wine

juice of ¼ lemon

50 g (1¾ oz) caster (superfine) sugar

1 cup cream

Halve the passionfruit and scoop the pulp into a sieve set over a small bowl. Press on the pulp with the back of a spoon to extract all the juices. Reserve the juice and discard all but 1 teaspoon of the seeds.

Mix together the wine, lemon juice and sugar. Add the cream and whip the mixture slowly using a balloon whisk until soft peaks form. Fold in the passionfruit juice and the reserved seeds.

Spoon into four wine glasses and chill for 1 hour before serving.

Serves 4

pasta.

Fresh pasta is not difficult to make and is preferable to dried pasta when making lasagne and stuffed or filled pasta dishes. This version of pasta dough is adapted from Anna del Conte's recipe. A hand-cranked pasta machine will help enormously with the rolling and cutting.

220 g (7 oz) unbleached strong or plain (all-purpose) flour
1 teaspoon salt

2 large free-range or organic eggs, lightly beaten

Place the flour and salt in a food processor. With the processor running, add the eggs and process until the dough clumps together – it should be elastic but not moist. If necessary, add more flour.

Knead on a lightly floured surface for 5 minutes, or until smooth. Wrap in plastic wrap and leave at room temperature for 30 minutes.

Knead for a further 2 minutes, then divide the dough into four roughly equal pieces. Flatten each piece with your hand.

Set the pasta machine rollers to the thickest setting and run a piece of dough through the machine. Fold it in half, turn it 180 degrees and run it through again. Do this about 6 times. Change to the next-thickest setting and run the sheet of pasta through, then continue through every setting until the pasta is the desired thickness. You may have to dust the dough with flour occasionally, to stop it sticking. Repeat with the remaining pieces of dough.

For lasagne, ravioli or cannelloni, roll pasta through the thinnest setting and use immediately.

For spaghetti or tagliatelle, stop rolling at the second-last setting. Leave sheets to dry a little before cutting them.

Makes about 250 g

pasta with zucchini.

Simple pasta dishes are my staple fare. This one is especially easy, as the grated zucchini cooks quickly and can be prepared while the pasta cooks.

200 g (6½ oz) dried pasta

3 medium-sized zucchini (courgettes)

2 tablespoons olive oil

1 clove garlic, crushed

salt and freshly ground black pepper

2 tablespoons chopped flat-leaf parsley

½ cup freshly grated parmesan, plus extra
 to serve

extra-virgin olive oil, to serve

Bring a large saucepan of salted water to the boil and add the pasta. Stir well and boil rapidly until the pasta is al dente.

Meanwhile, grate the zucchini using the coarsest side of the grater, or cut the zucchini into thin strips.

Heat the olive oil in a frying pan over medium heat. Add the garlic and zucchini and cook, stirring, for about 5 minutes, or until the zucchini has released its juice and started to colour. Season well with salt and freshly ground black pepper.

Drain the cooked pasta and return it to the saucepan. Add the cooked zucchini and garlic, and the parsley and parmesan. Taste and adjust the seasoning. Serve drizzled with a little extra-virgin olive oil and extra grated parmesan.

I prefer thick spaghetti for this dish, and dried rather than fresh pasta.

As a variation you can replace some of the parsley with chopped rocket (arugula). You can also add some chopped prosciutto and a little chopped fresh chilli.

Serves 2

peach pie.

1 quantity homemade shortcrust pastry
   (see page 290)
6 peaches
2 tablespoons demerara sugar or raw sugar

⅓ cup caster (superfine) sugar
2 egg yolks, lightly beaten
1 cup cream

Grease a 25 cm (10 in) loose-based tart tin.

Roll out the pastry between two sheets of baking paper, until large enough to line the base and sides of the tin. Line the tin with pastry, allowing any excess to hang over the sides. Chill for 15 minutes.

Preheat the oven to 200°C (400°F, Gas Mark 5).

Halve, stone and peel the peaches. Slice each half into four and line the pastry case with peaches. Sprinkle with the demerara sugar. Bake for 15 minutes. Remove from the heat and reduce the oven to 150°C (300°F, Gas Mark 2).

Lightly beat the caster sugar, egg yolks and cream together and pour over the peaches. Return the pie to the oven for 25–30 minutes, or until the custard is set. Trim the edges and serve warm.

Nectarines work well in this pie in place of the peaches.

Serves 8

pavlova.

Pavlova is often referred to as Australia's national dessert,
but nothing this good remains a secret for long.

4 egg whites

salt

1 cup caster (superfine) sugar

1 teaspoon white vinegar

$^{1}/_{2}$ teaspoon vanilla essence

2 teaspoons cornflour (cornstarch)

whipped cream, to serve

ripe seasonal fruit, to serve

Preheat the oven to 120°C (250°F, Gas Mark 1–2). Line a baking tray with baking paper. Draw a circle 20 cm (8 in) in diameter in the middle of the piece of baking paper.

Place the egg whites and a pinch of salt in a clean, dry bowl. Beat with an electric mixer until soft peaks form. Gradually add the sugar, beating well after each addition. Beat until the mixture is stiff and glossy. Fold in the vinegar, vanilla and cornflour.

Heap the mixture within the circle on the baking paper. Shape into a circle with a spatula, leaving the centre slightly hollowed. Cook for 1–1$^{1}/_{2}$ hours, or until crisp on the outside. Turn off the oven and allow to cool in the oven with the door ajar.

To serve, top with whipped cream and sliced seasonal fruit.

Traditionally, pavlova is served with strawberries and passionfruit, but any fruit will do.

The base of the pavlova may be made a few days ahead and stored in an airtight container until ready to use.

As a variation, make individual pavlovas and top with berries and a fruit purée or coulis (see raspberry coulis, page 254).

Serves 8

pea soup.

This is a simple and modern version of an old favourite – pea and ham soup. The ham bone is replaced with bacon and I use fresh or frozen peas instead of the traditional dried variety. This soup is delicious served hot or cold.

1 tablespoon olive oil

2 rashers bacon, roughly chopped

1 onion, roughly chopped

1 stick celery, roughly chopped

1 leek, sliced

1 litre (32 fl oz) chicken stock
(see page 68) or vegetable stock

500 g (1 lb) fresh or frozen peas

1 tablespoon roughly chopped mint

salt and freshly ground black pepper

Heat the oil in a large saucepan over medium heat. Add the bacon and cook, stirring occasionally, for 2 minutes. Add the onion, celery and leek, and cook, stirring constantly, for 4–5 minutes, or until the vegetables are tender but have not browned. Add the stock and bring to the boil. Reduce the heat and simmer for 15 minutes. Add the peas, return to the boil and simmer for 10 minutes.

Remove from the heat and allow to cool a little. Purée the soup in batches in a blender or with a hand-held blender until smooth. Season to taste with salt and freshly ground black pepper. Serve garnished with mint.

For a vegetarian version of this soup, omit the bacon and use vegetable stock.

Serves 4

peach pie.

1 quantity homemade shortcrust pastry
    (see page 290)
6 peaches
2 tablespoons demerara sugar or raw sugar

$\frac{1}{3}$ cup caster (superfine) sugar
2 egg yolks, lightly beaten
1 cup cream

Grease a 25 cm (10 in) loose-based tart tin.

Roll out the pastry between two sheets of baking paper, until large enough to line the base and sides of the tin. Line the tin with pastry, allowing any excess to hang over the sides. Chill for 15 minutes.

Preheat the oven to 200°C (400°F, Gas Mark 5).

Halve, stone and peel the peaches. Slice each half into four and line the pastry case with peaches. Sprinkle with the demerara sugar. Bake for 15 minutes. Remove from the heat and reduce the oven to 150°C (300°F, Gas Mark 2).

Lightly beat the caster sugar, egg yolks and cream together and pour over the peaches. Return the pie to the oven for 25–30 minutes, or until the custard is set. Trim the edges and serve warm.

Nectarines work well in this pie in place of the peaches.

Serves 8

peanut biscuits.

125 g (4 oz) unsalted butter, chopped and
softened
½ cup lightly packed brown sugar

1 cup self-raising (self-rising) flour
1 cup roasted salted peanuts
2 tablespoons strong coffee, freshly made

Preheat the oven to 180°C (350°F, Gas Mark 4). Grease two oven trays and line with baking paper.

Place the butter in a medium-sized mixing bowl and add the sugar. Beat with an electric mixer for 2–3 minutes, or until smooth and fluffy. Sift in the flour and add the peanuts and coffee. Mix with a wooden spoon until combined.

Roll tablespoons of the mixture into balls and place on the prepared trays, leaving 5 cm (2 in) between each to allow for spreading. Flatten each ball with your thumb or the back of a fork.

Bake for 10–12 minutes, or until golden. Remove from the oven and allow to cool on the trays for 5 minutes, then transfer to wire racks to cool completely. Store in an airtight container for up to 1 week.

Use salted or unsalted peanuts depending on your preference. If using unsalted peanuts, add a pinch of salt to the mixture with the flour.

Makes about 24

pecan pie.

1 quantity sweet shortcrust pastry
   (see page 290)
1¹⁄₂ cups pecans
100 g (3¹⁄₂ oz) unsalted butter, melted
¹⁄₂ cup golden syrup

¹⁄₂ cup lightly packed brown sugar
3 eggs
¹⁄₂ teaspoon mixed spice
finely grated zest and juice of 1 lemon

Prepare the pastry according to the instructions on page 290. Chill the pastry for at least 30 minutes before using.

Lightly grease a 25 cm (10 in) loose-based tart tin. Roll out the pastry between two sheets of baking paper so that it is large enough to fit the tart tin. Line the tin with the pastry, leaving a little pastry overhanging the tin. Refrigerate for 15 minutes.

Preheat the oven to 200°C (400°F, Gas Mark 6).

Line the pastry case with baking paper. Half-fill the pastry case with pie weights, uncooked dried beans or rice, and bake for 12 minutes. Remove the weights and baking paper, return the tin to the oven and cook for a further 10–15 minutes, or until the pastry is dry and lightly coloured. Set aside to cool. If the pastry case has any holes, plug them with a little uncooked pastry. With a sharp knife, cut off the overhanging pastry.

Reduce the oven temperature to 180°C (350°F, Gas Mark 4).

Roughly chop half the pecans and place them in a large mixing bowl. Add the melted butter, golden syrup, sugar, eggs, spice, lemon zest and juice and mix well. Pour the mixture into the pastry case and top with the remaining whole pecans.

Bake for 25–30 minutes, or until firm. Remove from the oven and allow to cool for at least 20 minutes before removing from the tin. Serve warm or cold with thick cream or ice-cream.

Serves 8–10

pesto.

Purists make pesto by hand in a mortar and pestle, but use a blender
or food processor for a simple and fast result.

⅓ cup pine nuts

2 cups basil leaves

⅓ cup freshly grated parmesan

3 cloves garlic, roughly chopped

1 cup extra-virgin olive oil

salt and freshly ground black pepper

Place the pine nuts, basil, parmesan and garlic in a food processor or blender and process until the mixture is roughly chopped.

With the motor running, slowly add the olive oil in a thin stream, and process until the mixture is smooth but retains some texture. It will remain a good green colour so long as it is not over-processed. Season to taste with salt and freshly ground black pepper. Store in a screw-top jar, cover with a thin film of oil, and keep in the fridge for up to 2 weeks.

Pesto is delicious stirred though a bowl of pasta or gnocchi. A teaspoon added to a bowl of vegetable soup is the perfect finishing touch.

Always use a good-quality extra-virgin olive oil and freshly purchased pine nuts for pesto.

Makes 2 cups

piri piri sauce.

Piri Piri is the variety of chilli used to create this hot and spicy sauce. Piri Piri sauce is the key ingredient in the well-loved dish Portuguese chicken.

6 long red chillies, seeded
3 cloves garlic, crushed

juice of 1 lemon
½ cup olive oil

Place all the ingredients in a food processor and process until smooth. Store the sauce in an airtight container in the refrigerator for up to 5 days.

To make Portuguese chicken, cut a small chicken down the backbone with a sharp knife or scissors and press down on the breastbone to flatten it. Season lightly with salt and freshly ground black pepper. Brush the chicken well with Piri Piri sauce. Cover and refrigerate for at least 3 hours (or overnight). Cook the chicken skin-side down on a hot, ribbed grill pan, or a heavy frying pan, until golden, then transfer to a preheated 200°C (400°F, Gas Mark 6) oven and cook skin-side up for 35–40 minutes, or until nicely coloured and cooked. Serve accompanied with lemon wedges.

I use long red chillies for the sauce, but if you like your food really hot you can substitute a few short chillies for the longer, milder varieties.

Makes ¾ cup

pizza base.

Pizza dough is easy to make; it simply needs a little time to rise.

1 × 7 g (¹/₄ oz) sachet (2 teaspoons)
   dry yeast

1 teaspoon sugar

2¹/₂ cups bread flour

salt

2 tablespoons olive oil

Dissolve the yeast and sugar in a small bowl with 200 ml (6½ fl oz) of tepid water. Stir well and set aside for 10 minutes, or until the mixture froths.

Place the flour and a pinch of salt in a large mixing bowl. Make a well in the centre and add the yeast mixture and olive oil. Mix until a firm dough forms.

Knead on a lightly floured surface for 5–7 minutes, or until smooth and elastic. Place in a clean, lightly oiled bowl, cover with a cloth or plastic wrap and leave in a warm place for 1–1½ hours, or until the dough has doubled in size.

Preheat the oven to 210°C (415°F, Gas Mark 6–7).

Punch down the dough with your fist to release the air. Divide into two or three equal portions and roll out or press to a thickness of 5 mm (¼ in). Transfer to lightly oiled pizza trays.

Top with your choice of toppings and cook for 15 minutes. Then slide the pizza off the tray onto the oven shelf and cook for a further 3–4 minutes, to crisp up the base.

A good pizza base should have a little bit of chew, so don't roll out the dough any thinner than 5 mm (¼ in).

Pizza bases can be made and frozen, uncooked, for 2–3 months.

Don't overload your pizzas with toppings – less is definitely more.

Makes three 23 cm (9 in) or two 30 cm (12 in) pizza bases

pizza bianca.

In this recipe my basic pizza dough is brushed with olive oil, sprinkled with garlic and rosemary, and topped with mozarella – the simplest of all pizza toppings.

1 quantity basic homemade pizza dough
    (see page 229)
3 cloves garlic, crushed

2 teaspoons roughly chopped rosemary
1 tablespoon sea salt
1 × 200 g (6½ oz) mozzarella ball, sliced

Lightly oil two 30 cm (12 in) pizza trays or oven trays and sprinkle with a little cornmeal.

Make the basic pizza dough as described on page 229. After the first rise, punch down the dough with your fist to expel the air and gently knead for 1 minute. Divide the dough into two portions. Roll each portion into a 30 cm (12 in) diameter circle.

Preheat the oven to 220°C (425°F, Gas Mark 7).

Place the garlic and rosemary in a small bowl with the remaining oil.

Punch down the dough with your fist to release the air. Divide into two equal portions and roll out or press to a thickness of 5 mm (¼ in). Transfer to lightly oiled pizza trays.

Brush with the rosemary mixture and sprinkle with sea salt. Top with sliced mozzarella. Cook for 20 minutes, or until crisp underneath and molten on top.

Makes 2 × 30 cm (12 in) pizza bases

pizza margherita.

cornmeal or polenta, to sprinkle

1 quantity homemade basic pizza dough
  (see page 229), or 2 bought pizza bases

1 cup tomato pizza sauce, homemade (see
  below) or bought

2 × 150 g (5 oz) mozzarella balls, cut into
  thin rounds

¼ cup extra-virgin olive oil, plus extra,
  to serve

salt and freshly ground black pepper

12 small basil leaves

Lightly oil two 30 cm (12 in) pizza trays or oven trays and sprinkle with a little cornmeal.

Make the basic pizza dough as described on page 229. After the first rise, punch down the dough with your fist to expel the air and gently knead for 1 minute. Divide the dough into two portions. Roll each portion into a 30 cm (12 in) diameter circle.

Preheat the oven to 240°C (465°F, Gas Mark 9).

Transfer the pizza bases to the prepared trays. Spread each base with an even layer of tomato sauce. Top with the mozzarella slices and drizzle with the extra-virgin olive oil. Season well with salt and freshly ground black pepper.

Bake for 12–15 minutes, or until the base is golden and the cheese has melted. Remove from the oven, drizzle with a little extra oil and scatter over the basil.

To make an easy tomato pizza sauce, strain 2 × 400 g (13 oz) cans of chopped or crushed tomatoes in a fine sieve for about 10 minutes, discarding the liquid. Place the tomato flesh, 2 cloves of crushed garlic, ¼ cup of olive oil and ½ teaspoon of dried oregano in a medium-sized saucepan and cook over low heat, stirring frequently, for 20–30 minutes, or until thick. Season to taste with salt and freshly ground black pepper. Store in a sealed container in the refrigerator for up to 5 days, or freeze for up to 2 months.

Makes 2 × 30 cm (12 in) pizzas

pork satays.

1 kg (2 lb) pork fillet

salt and freshly ground black pepper

¼ cup vegetable oil

1 teaspoon grated fresh ginger

1 long red chilli, finely chopped

1 clove garlic, chopped

2 tablespoons soy sauce

juice of 1 lime

satay sauce (see page 282)

3 small red onions, each cut into eighths

Cut the pork fillet into 2 cm (¾ in) cubes and season lightly with salt and freshly ground black pepper.

Combine the oil, ginger, chilli, garlic, soy sauce and lime juice in a bowl. Add the pork pieces and mix well. Cover and allow to marinate in the refrigerator for at least 2 hours (but no longer than 4 hours).

If using bamboo skewers, soak them in water for 30 minutes.

Thread the pork onto the skewers alternating with the onion pieces.

Preheat a ribbed grill pan or heavy frying pan over high heat. Add the skewers and cook for 10 minutes, turning once or twice.

Meanwhile, heat the satay sauce in a small saucepan. Serve two skewers per person accompanied with the warmed sauce.

Serves 4

poached cherries.

This is a delicious way to preserve the last of the summer cherries.

500 g (1 lb) cherries

3 cups red wine

1½ cups caster (superfine) sugar

1 cinnamon stick

2 tablespoons redcurrant jelly

2 tablespoons brandy (optional)

Remove the stems from the cherries and place the cherries in a medium-sized saucepan. Pour over the red wine, making sure there is enough wine to cover the fruit – add extra if needed. Add the sugar and cinnamon stick. Bring the mixture slowly to the boil, stirring frequently to dissolve the sugar. Cover and simmer gently over low heat for 10 minutes. Remove the saucepan from the heat and set aside to cool.

Drain the cherries, reserving the syrup. Discard the cinnamon.

Sterilise two medium-sized screw-top jars by filling them with boiling water. Drain them on a clean tea towel.

Divide the cherries between the jars.

Bring the syrup back to the boil and simmer until the liquid has reduced by one third. Remove from the heat. Stir in the redcurrant jelly and brandy and pour over the cherries. Seal the jars and set aside to cool.

Store in the refrigerator for up to 2 months. Once opened, use the cherries within 7 days. The cherries and syrup are delicious served with vanilla ice-cream.

For the wine, use a light, Italian-style red wine or a pinot noir.

Choose cherries that are plump and shiny and have green stalks.

I never bother stoning cherries, but cherry stoners are available in kitchenware shops if you prefer no pips.

Makes 1 litre

poached eggs.

salt

white wine vinegar

4 fresh eggs

Half-fill a deep frying pan or wide saucepan with water. Add a teaspoon of salt and a dash of white vinegar. Bring the water to a gentle boil.

Carefully break one egg into a small, shallow dish or saucer and gently slide the egg into the simmering water. Repeat with the remaining eggs.

Lower the heat until the water is barely moving, allowing the eggs to cook gently without breaking. Cook for 4–5 minutes, or until the whites are set. Remove the eggs with a slotted spoon and drain.

The most successful poached eggs are made from very fresh eggs.

If the white separates from the yolk, it means the egg was not fresh, or that the water was not simmering sufficiently when the egg was added.

Only cook four eggs at a time in one frying pan or saucepan.

Serves 4

poached pears.

6 firm, ripe pears

1 lemon, halved

½ cup sugar

1 cinnamon stick

Carefully peel the pears, leaving the stalks attached if possible. Squeeze the juice of half a lemon over the pears as you peel them to stop them browning.

Place the peeled pears in a large saucepan. Add enough water to just cover. Remove the pears and set aside.

Add the sugar and cinnamon stick to the saucepan. Peel the zest from the remaining lemon half and add the zest to the saucepan. Bring the mixture to the boil, stirring to dissolve the sugar. Return the pears to the saucepan. Bring to the boil again, then reduce the heat and simmer for 15–20 minutes, or until the pears are tender.

Transfer the pears to a large serving dish. Strain the syrup, discarding the cinnamon and lemon zest, and return to the boil over high heat. Simmer rapidly until it is reduced by half. Pour the syrup over the pears. Serve warm or cold with cream or yoghurt.

Poached pears and chocolate are a classic combination. Serve pears with the chocolate sauce given on page 85.

Replacing 1 cup of the poaching water with 1 cup of red wine makes a delicious variation.

Serves 6

poached salmon with salsa verde.

4 salmon fillets
salt and freshly ground black pepper

SALSA VERDE
1 thick slice Italian-style bread
milk, to soak

1 cup loosely packed flat-leaf parsley

15 basil leaves

1 tablespoon capers

2 anchovy fillets

1 clove garlic, chopped

¼ cup olive oil

To make the salsa verde, remove the crust from the bread, break the bread into pieces and soak it in a little milk. Squeeze dry and set aside.

In a food processor or blender, process the parsley, basil, capers, anchovies and garlic until roughly chopped. Add the milk-soaked bread. With the machine running, gradually add the olive oil in a thin stream, and process until the sauce is thick and smooth. Season to taste with salt and freshly ground black pepper.

Lay a salmon fillet, skin-side down, on a sheet of foil. Season well with salt and freshly ground black pepper. Wrap the fillet tightly in the foil, making an airtight seal. Repeat with the remaining fillets.

Place the wrapped fillets in a large saucepan and cover completely with cold water. Bring to the boil over medium heat. Reduce the heat and simmer gently for 2 minutes.

Remove the parcels from the saucepan. Open each one and remove the skin from the fish. Serve the salmon with the salsa verde, plus steamed potatoes and a mixed green salad.

Serves 4

polenta.

Polenta makes a delicious accompaniment to roast chicken or quail, roast veal, sausages or grilled liver. The whisking method comes from my friend, the Italian food writer Anna Del Conte, who says that whisking the polenta aerates it, making it much lighter in texture and more delicate in flavour then polenta stirred with a wooden spoon.

salt

300 g (9½ oz) polenta

20 g (¾ oz) butter

Bring 1.5 litres (48 fl oz) of water and 2 teaspoons of salt to the boil in a large saucepan. With one hand, slowly trickle the polenta into the boiling water, whisking (using a large metal balloon whisk) with the other hand. It is important to keep whisking to stop the grains from clumping together. Maintain at a fast simmer for about 30–40 minutes, whisking constantly at first and then at regular intervals. The polenta will become quite thick. It is ready when it comes away from the sides of the pan. Stir through the butter.

Polenta may be served while still hot and soft, or allowed to cool and set in a greased dish (about 20–30 cm square) before being cut into slices or squares, then either shallow-fried in a little olive oil or brushed with olive oil and grilled.

Serves 6

pommes anna.

This delicious, golden and crispy potato cake is perfect with just about anything (think roast chicken, lamb or beef, or steak).

1.35 kg (2 lb 11 oz) potatoes, peeled and thinly sliced

50 g (1¾ oz) butter
salt and freshly ground black pepper

Preheat the oven to 200°C (400°F, Gas Mark 6).

Melt the butter over medium heat in a 20 cm (8 in) heavy-based frying pan with an ovenproof handle. Remove from the heat and place the potato slices in a single overlapping layer on the bottom of the pan. Season with salt and freshly ground black pepper. Repeat the layering process with the rest of the potato, seasoning each layer as you go. You should end up with potato to a depth of 3 cm (1¼ in).

Return the frying pan to the heat and cook for 1–2 minutes, to colour the potatoes. Cover with foil, transfer to the oven and bake for 30 minutes. Remove foil and cook for a further 30 minutes, or until the potatoes are golden and a sharp knife is easily inserted into their centres. Remove from the oven and let sit for 5 minutes, then invert the potato cake onto a serving plate. Cut into wedges.

I use desiree potatoes for this dish.

Serves 6

pork satays.

1 kg (2 lb) pork fillet

salt and freshly ground black pepper

¼ cup vegetable oil

1 teaspoon grated fresh ginger

1 long red chilli, finely chopped

1 clove garlic, chopped

2 tablespoons soy sauce

juice of 1 lime

satay sauce (see page 282)

3 small red onions, each cut into eighths

Cut the pork fillet into 2 cm (¾ in) cubes and season lightly with salt and freshly ground black pepper.

Combine the oil, ginger, chilli, garlic, soy sauce and lime juice in a bowl. Add the pork pieces and mix well. Cover and allow to marinate in the refrigerator for at least 2 hours (but no longer than 4 hours).

If using bamboo skewers, soak them in water for 30 minutes.

Thread the pork onto the skewers alternating with the onion pieces.

Preheat a ribbed grill pan or heavy frying pan over high heat. Add the skewers and cook for 10 minutes, turning once or twice.

Meanwhile, heat the satay sauce in a small saucepan. Serve two skewers per person accompanied with the warmed sauce.

Serves 4

porridge.

2 cups rolled oats
salt

brown sugar, to serve
warm milk, to serve

Place the rolled oats and a pinch of salt in a medium-sized saucepan. Add 2 cups of water and set aside for 5–10 minutes. (This helps to soften the oats and makes the finished product smoother and creamier.)

Add an extra 2½ cups of water to the saucepan. Place over medium heat and bring to the boil, stirring frequently. Reduce the heat to low and simmer for 10–12 minutes, stirring frequently, until the mixture is soft and creamy.

Serve sprinkled with brown sugar and a jug of warm milk.

For a creamier version, replace 1 cup of water with 1 cup of milk and cook as above.

Add ½ cup of sultanas or a mixture of dried fruits to the dry oats before cooking.

A mashed ripe banana or a grated apple is delicious added to the porridge while cooking.

Serves 4

portuguese custard tarts.

4 egg yolks

½ cup caster (superfine) sugar

1 tablespoon plain (all-purpose) flour

finely grated zest of 1 orange

200 ml (6½ fl oz) milk

300 ml (10 fl oz) cream

1 x 500 g (1 lb) packet frozen puff pastry, thawed

½ teaspoon ground cinnamon

1 teaspoon caster (superfine) sugar

Place the yolks, sugar, flour and orange zest in a bowl and whisk with a hand-held beater for about 3 minutes, or until the mixture is pale and thick. Pour the milk and cream into a small saucepan and heat to boiling point. Stir into the egg-yolk mixture, then transfer to a saucepan and place over low heat, stirring constantly, until the custard has thickened – do not let it boil. Allow to cool.

Roll out the pastry to approximately 28 cm (11 in) square.

Combine the cinnamon and caster sugar and sprinkle over the pastry. Roll up tightly to form a log. Wrap in plastic wrap and chill for 30 minutes.

Lightly grease a 12-cup muffin tin.

Cut the pastry log into 2 cm (¾ in) discs. Roll each disc between two sheets of non-stick baking paper until it is about 13 cm (5 in) in diameter. Press into a cup of the muffin tin, then repeat with remaining pastry discs. Chill for 15 minutes.

Meanwhile, preheat the oven to 220°C (425°F, Gas Mark 7). Pour the custard into a jug and three-quarters-fill each pastry cup. Bake for 20–25 minutes, or until the custard is set and the pastry is golden. Eat warm or cold.

You can make the custard up to 24 hours beforehand, and keep it in the refrigerator.

To achieve the 'burnt top' look, lightly sprinkle each tart with a little icing sugar and pop under a hot grill for a minute or two.

Makes 12

pot of tea.

Throw out your teabags and return to the ritual of a *real* cuppa made from tea leaves! Personal taste, the strength of the brand of tea and the size of the pot will determine how much tea to use. As a guide, start by adding 2–3 teaspoons of tea leaves for an average-sized two-person pot.

Fill a kettle with fresh cold water and bring to the boil. When the water has almost reached the boil, pour a little into your teapot, swirl it around and pour it out. Add 2–3 teaspoons of tea leaves to the pot.

When the water is boiling, fill the teapot with boiling water. Put on the lid and leave to brew for 3–5 minutes.

The pot may be topped up later with more boiling water if needed.

Experiment by trying different types of tea. Look out for a specialist tea shop.

Black tea varieties include Orange Pekoe, Darjeeling, Assam, and blended varieties like English Breakfast and Earl Grey. These teas are dried and fermented to produce a dark-coloured leaf.

Green tea is made from the same plant as black tea but is not fermented. If making green tea, use water that has not quite come to the boil.

Serve full-flavoured teas such as Assam or English Breakfast in the morning. Orange Pekoe and Darjeeling are lighter, more aromatic teas and are perfect for an afternoon cuppa.

Serves 2

potato gratin.

600 ml (20 fl oz) cream

1 bay leaf

salt and freshly ground black pepper

1.5 kg (3 lb) desiree potatoes, peeled

2 cloves garlic, finely chopped

Preheat the oven to 170°C (325°F, Gas Mark 3). Grease a large, shallow ovenproof dish.

Place the cream and bay leaf in a large saucepan and season with freshly ground black pepper. Slowly bring to the boil, then simmer gently for 10 minutes. Remove the bay leaf.

Slice the potatoes very thinly. Add the slices to the saucepan, stir well and return the mixture to the boil. Simmer for 2–3 minutes, stirring gently.

Spoon a third of the potato mixture into the prepared dish, sprinkle with salt, pepper and a little chopped garlic. Repeat until the dish is full. Cover with foil and cook for 1 hour. Remove the foil and cook for a further 15–20 minutes, or until the top is golden and bubbling and the potato is tender.

Serves 6

potato salad.

1 kg (2 lb) waxy potatoes, scrubbed

2–3 tablespoons chopped flat-leaf parsley,
    chives or mint

4 finely sliced spring onions (scallions)

½ small red (Spanish) onion, finely sliced

salt and freshly ground black pepper

6 slices prosciutto or bacon

DRESSING

½ cup olive oil

1 tablespoon Dijon mustard

2 tablespoons white wine vinegar

Cook the potatoes in a large saucepan of gently boiling salted water for 12–15 minutes, or until just tender. Drain and allow to cool slightly.

While the potatoes are still warm, cut them into 2 cm (¾ in) pieces and place in a large bowl with the parsley, spring onions and red onion. Season well with salt and freshly ground black pepper.

Place the dressing ingredients in a screw-top jar and shake well to combine. Pour half the dressing over the warm potatoes and toss gently to coat the pieces, being careful not to break up the potato. Allow to stand until most of the dressing is absorbed.

Meanwhile, cook the prosciutto or bacon in a frying pan or under a hot griller (broiler) until crisp. Prosciutto should take 3–4 minutes, bacon 5–7 minutes. Allow to cool, then break into bite-sized pieces.

Gently stir half the prosciutto or bacon into the salad. Transfer to a serving dish, drizzle with the remaining dressing and sprinkle over the remaining prosciutto or bacon. Serve warm or at room temperature.

For best results, use waxy potatoes such as kipflers, desirees, pink eyes, bintje, chats or small new potatoes when available.

Serves 4–6

prawn cocktail.

24 medium-to-large cooked prawns
   (shrimp)
1 small iceberg lettuce
1 lemon, quartered, to serve

COCKTAIL SAUCE
1 cup mayonnaise (see page 192)
1/3 cup tomato sauce (ketchup)

1 tablespoon Worcestershire sauce
1 tablespoon brandy
1 tablespoon lemon juice
1/4 cup cream, whipped
salt and freshly ground black pepper

Peel and devein the prawns, leaving on the tails if desired.

Remove and discard any broken or limp outer leaves from the lettuce and cut it into four wedges with a sharp knife.

Make the cocktail sauce by combining the mayonnaise, tomato sauce, Worcestershire sauce, brandy and lemon juice. Stir in the whipped cream. Season with salt and freshly ground black pepper and adjust the quantities of the other ingredients to suit your taste.

To serve, place a wedge of lettuce on each plate, spoon over some sauce and surround with six prawns. Serve with a wedge of lemon.

I like to use fresh, ready-cooked prawns for this dish — they are usually cooked on the trawler in salt water, giving them a good flavour.

Add a drop or two of Tabasco sauce to the cocktail sauce if you like a little spice.

Serves 4

prawn toasts.

250 g (8 oz) uncooked prawns (shrimp), shelled and deveined
1 egg white
2 spring onions (scallions), chopped
1 teaspoon grated fresh ginger
1 tablespoon roughly chopped coriander (cilantro) leaves

1 tablespoon cornflour (cornstarch)
6 slices white bread
$\frac{1}{3}$ cup sesame seeds
vegetable oil, for frying

Roughly chop the prawns and place in a food processor with the egg white, spring onion, ginger, coriander and cornflour. Process using the pulse action until just combined but still a little chunky.

Spread each slice of bread evenly with the prawn mixture. Sprinkle generously with the sesame seeds. Trim the crusts off the bread and cut each slice into quarters.

Pour the oil into a large frying pan to a depth of 1 cm (½ in). Heat over medium heat to 180°C (350°F), or until a cube of bread dropped into the oil browns in about 20 seconds. Fry the toasts in batches, starting with the side spread with the prawn mixture face down and cooking for about 10 seconds. Turn the toasts and cook for a further 10 seconds, or until golden and crisp. Repeat with remaining toasts. Drain on kitchen paper and serve immediately.

Makes 24

pumpkin soup.

2 tablespoons vegetable oil

1 large onion, chopped

1 carrot, chopped

1 clove garlic, chopped

2 potatoes, peeled and chopped

500 g (1 lb) peeled and chopped pumpkin

1.25 litres (40 fl oz) chicken stock
   (see page 68)

salt and freshly ground black pepper

yoghurt or sour cream, to serve

Heat the oil in a large saucepan over medium heat. Add the onion, carrot, garlic, potato and pumpkin. Cook, stirring, for 5 minutes, or until the onion has softened.

Add the stock and bring to the boil. Cover and simmer for 25–30 minutes, or until the vegetables are tender.

Allow to cool a little, then purée the mixture in batches in a blender or with a hand-held blender.

Gently reheat the soup. Season to taste with salt and freshly ground black pepper. Serve garnished with a dollop of yoghurt.

For an Asian-inspired soup, cook the vegetables with 1 tablespoon of Thai red curry paste. Stir in ½ cup of coconut milk before serving.

Serves 4

quiche lorraine.

A homemade quiche, with its crisp pastry and slightly wobbly centre,
is a great dish – it wins hands down over any store-bought counterpart.

1 quantity homemade shortcrust pastry (see
    page 290), or 1 × 380 g (12 oz) packet
    bought frozen shortcrust pastry, thawed
5 rashers streaky bacon, diced
100 g (3½ oz) gruyere cheese, grated

¾ cup cream
½ cup milk
½ teaspoon Dijon mustard
3 eggs, lightly beaten
salt and freshly ground black pepper

Prepare the pastry according to the instructions on page 290 and refrigerate for at least 30 minutes before using.

Roll out the pastry between two sheets of baking paper to a size to fit a 23 cm (9 in) deep, fluted flan tin. Grease the tin. Line the tin with the pastry, pressing it into the edges. Trim any excess pastry. Chill for 30 minutes.

Preheat the oven to 190°C (375°F, Gas Mark 5).

Line the pastry case with foil or baking paper. Half-fill the pastry case with pie weights, uncooked dried beans or rice and bake for 15 minutes. Remove the weights and foil and bake the pastry case for a further 10 minutes, or until dry and lightly coloured.

Reduce the oven temperature to 170°C (325°F, Gas Mark 3).

Place the bacon in a small frying pan over medium heat and cook, stirring, until crisp. Sprinkle over the pastry case, along with the gruyere cheese.

Whisk the cream, milk, mustard and eggs in a bowl until smooth. Season well with salt and freshly ground black pepper. Pour into the pastry case and bake for 35–40 minutes, or until just set. Serve warm.

Serves 6

raspberry cordial.

Raspberries can make a delicious soft drink for the summer season.
The following recipe gives you a concentrated base.

300 g (9½ oz) raspberries, fresh, or frozen
and thawed
1¼ cups caster (superfine) sugar

juice of 5 lemons
lemon slices, to serve
sprigs of mint, to serve

Place the raspberries and sugar in a blender and pulse until smooth. Strain through a sieve into a large bowl. Add the lemon juice and stir until well mixed and the sugar has dissolved.

Transfer the mixture to a large bottle or storage container and refrigerate for up to 5 days. Dilute with still or sparkling water, as desired. Serve with ice, slices of lemon and a sprig of mint.

As a variation, replace the raspberries with an equal quantity of strawberries.

To give it a little kick, try this cordial with a dash of gin or vodka, and dilute it with soda or mineral water.

Makes 3 cups concentrated syrup

raspberry coulis.

250 g (8 oz) fresh raspberries
¼ cup icing (confectioners') sugar, sifted
1 tablespoon lemon juice

1–2 tablespoons raspberry-flavoured
brandy or raspberry-flavoured
liqueur (optional)

Purée the raspberries, icing sugar and lemon juice in a blender or food processor. Stir in the alcohol, if using. Pass the sauce through a strainer to remove any seeds.

Taste and add extra lemon juice or sugar if needed.

This coulis is good served with ice-cream, fresh or cooked fruit, chocolate cake, bavarois, pannacotta or tarts.

Thawed, frozen berries work equally well.

Replace the raspberries with an equal quantity of strawberries, blackberries or blueberries for a different berry coulis.

To make a mango coulis, use the flesh of two large ripe mangoes and follow the recipe above.

Makes 1½ cups

risotto with sausage and red wine.

1.35 litres (43 fl oz) chicken stock (see
  page 68), beef stock or veal stock
60 g (2 oz) butter
1 onion, chopped
400 g (13 oz) good-quality Italian-style
  sausages, skinned

1 cup arborio or Carnaroli rice
½ cup robust red wine
handful of flat-leaf parsley, chopped
¾ cup freshly grated parmesan, plus extra
  to serve
salt and freshly ground black pepper

Bring the stock to a gentle simmer in a large saucepan.

Meanwhile, melt 40 g (1½ oz) of the butter in a large, heavy-based saucepan over medium heat. Add the onion and cook, stirring, for 3 minutes, or until soft. Increase the heat a little and add the sausage meat. Cook, stirring, until the meat colours, breaking up any lumps with a fork. Add the rice and stir gently for 2 minutes. Add the wine. Stir and allow most of the liquid to evaporate.

Add enough of the simmering stock to just cover the rice. Stirring frequently, allow the rice to absorb most of the stock. Repeat the process, stirring well and adding stock as required. (If the stock runs out before the rice is cooked, continue with simmering water.) It will take 18–25 minutes to cook. Taste the rice for texture – it should be soft but still retain a little bite.

Remove from the heat and add the parsley, parmesan and the remaining butter. Season to taste with salt and freshly ground black pepper. Cover and allow to rest for 5 minutes before serving. Serve with extra grated parmesan, if desired.

Serves 4

ratatouille.

Although not traditional, this is my favourite way to make ratatouille.

2 tablespoons olive oil

1 onion, chopped

2 cloves garlic, chopped

2 zucchini (courgettes), sliced

1 eggplant (aubergine), diced

1 large red capsicum (bell pepper),
　seeded and chopped

1 × 400 g (13 oz) can chopped tomatoes

salt and freshly ground black pepper

2 tablespoons roughly chopped basil

1 tablespoon lemon juice

extra-virgin olive oil, to serve

Heat the olive oil in a large frying pan and fry the onion and garlic over medium heat for 10 minutes, or until soft. Add the zucchini, eggplant and capsicum and cook for a further 10 minutes, stirring occasionally. Stir in the tomatoes, cover and simmer, stirring occasionally, for 10 minutes.

Season with salt and freshly ground black pepper. Stir in the basil and lemon juice and remove from the heat.

Serve ratatouille hot or cold, drizzled with a little extra-virgin olive oil.

Ratatouille is delicious served with roast meat, or as a filling for vegetarian lasagne. It also makes a great pasta sauce.

Serves 4

rhubarb and apple crumble.

1 bunch rhubarb

4 apples, peeled, cored and chopped

¾ cup sugar

juice of 1 lemon

1 cup plain (all-purpose) flour

¾ cup lightly packed brown sugar

½ teaspoon ground ginger

125 g (4 oz) unsalted butter, chilled
   and diced

¼ cup flaked almonds

Grease a 4-cup-capacity ovenproof dish.

Trim the rhubarb and cut the stems into 2.5 cm (1 in) lengths. Set aside.

Heat a frying pan or large saucepan over medium heat and add the apples, sugar and lemon juice. Cook, stirring, for 3–4 minutes, or until tender.

Add the chopped rhubarb and cook for 4–5 minutes, or until the rhubarb is tender but still holds its shape. The rhubarb will give off a lot of liquid.

Use a slotted spoon to transfer the cooked fruit to the prepared dish. Leave behind any liquid remaining in the frying pan. Allow the fruit to cool a little. Taste and add extra sugar if needed.

Preheat the oven to 180°C (350°F, Gas Mark 4).

With your fingertips, rub together the flour, brown sugar, ginger and butter until the mixture resembles breadcrumbs and starts to clump together. Stir through the flaked almonds.

Sprinkle the crumble mixture evenly over the fruit. Bake for 30 minutes, or until golden and bubbling. Serve with cream or ice-cream.

Look for rhubarb with crisp red stalks. The deeper the colour, the sweeter the flavour.

Be careful to trim away any leaves from the rhubarb, as they are poisonous.

Granny Smith or any new-season apples make a good choice for this crumble.

Serves 4–6

rice.

To make the perfect fluffy rice, use the absorption method. Choose long-grain rice such as basmati that will separate into fluffy individual grains when cooked. This makes a delicious accompaniment to braised food, Indian dishes or roast meats.

1 cup long-grain rice | **salt**

Place 600 ml (19 fl oz) of water, the rice and ½ teaspoon of salt in a large saucepan and bring to the boil over high heat. Stir once, then reduce the heat to the lowest setting and cover with a tight-fitting lid. Cook for 15 minutes. Check that all the water has been absorbed. If not, cook for a further couple of minutes. Remove from the heat and allow to rest, covered, for 5–10 minutes. Fluff the rice with a fork before serving.

Use ¼ cup of rice and 150 ml (4½ fl oz) of water per person.

Don't be tempted to stir the rice while it cooks, as this releases the starch in the grain and makes it sticky.

Serve rice plain or tossed with herbs, spices or cooked vegetables.

Serves 4

rice pudding.

3 cups milk

1 cup cream

finely grated zest of 1 orange

3 cardamom pods

¹⁄₂ cup short-grain rice, pudding rice
or arborio rice

¹⁄₃ cup caster (superfine) sugar

Combine the milk, cream and orange zest in a medium-sized saucepan.

Remove the seeds from the cardamom pods and crush them with the back of a knife. Add the crushed seeds to the saucepan.

Bring the mixture to the boil over medium heat. Reduce the heat to low, add the rice and sugar, and stir well until the sugar has dissolved. Simmer, stirring frequently to prevent the rice from sticking, for 30–35 minutes, or until the rice is soft and creamy and the mixture has thickened. Remove from the heat, cover and set aside for 15 minutes. Spoon into a large serving dish or into individual decorative dishes. Serve warm or cold.

Short-grain or pudding rice is traditionally used for rice pudding because the starch breaks down easily as it is cooked, giving the pudding a delicious creamy texture.

It is important to stir the rice frequently as it cooks. This helps to release the starch in the grains as well as to prevent the rice sticking to the pan.

Rice pudding is delicious served as it is or accompanied with fresh berries, orange segments or poached stone fruit.

Serves 4–6

risotto.

1.25 litres (40 fl oz) chicken stock
  (see page 68) or vegetable stock
45 g (1½ oz) butter
1 onion, finely chopped

1½ cups arborio or Carnaroli rice
⅓ cup dry white wine
½ cup freshly grated parmesan

Bring the stock to a gentle simmer in a large saucepan.

Meanwhile, heat 30 g (1 oz) of the butter in a large, heavy-based saucepan. Add the onion and cook, stirring, over moderate heat for 5 minutes, or until soft. The onion should soften but not change colour. Add the rice to the onion and stir gently for 2 minutes to coat the grains with a little butter. Add the wine. Stir and allow most of the liquid to evaporate.

Add the simmering stock, a ladleful at a time, to the rice mixture. The first amount of stock added should just cover the rice. Allow the rice to absorb the liquid before more stock is added. Stir frequently, and add more stock as required. It will take 18–25 minutes to cook. Taste the rice for texture – it should be soft but still retain a little bite.

Remove from the heat and add the remaining 15 g (½ oz) of butter and the grated parmesan. Cover and allow to rest for 5 minutes before serving.

The grains should fall easily from a spoon, and the liquid thicken to a creamy consistency. If necessary, moisten the risotto with a little more stock just before serving.

You can add almost anything you like to risotto. Try different combinations of herbs, sautéed mushrooms, cooked vegetables, cooked meats and seafood. Add ingredients towards the end of cooking.

Don't be tempted to leave out the butter at the end. Called 'mantecare', this process of adding the butter softens and marries all the flavours.

The better the stock, the better the risotto. Try homemade stock, such as chicken stock (see page 68).

Serves 4

risotto with sausage and red wine.

1.35 litres (43 fl oz) chicken stock (see
    page 68), beef stock or veal stock
60 g (2 oz) butter
1 onion, chopped
400 g (13 oz) good-quality Italian-style
    sausages, skinned

1 cup arborio or Carnaroli rice
½ cup robust red wine
handful of flat-leaf parsley, chopped
¾ cup freshly grated parmesan, plus extra
    to serve
salt and freshly ground black pepper

Bring the stock to a gentle simmer in a large saucepan.

Meanwhile, melt 40 g (1½ oz) of the butter in a large, heavy-based saucepan over medium heat. Add the onion and cook, stirring, for 3 minutes, or until soft. Increase the heat a little and add the sausage meat. Cook, stirring, until the meat colours, breaking up any lumps with a fork. Add the rice and stir gently for 2 minutes. Add the wine. Stir and allow most of the liquid to evaporate.

Add enough of the simmering stock to just cover the rice. Stirring frequently, allow the rice to absorb most of the stock. Repeat the process, stirring well and adding stock as required. (If the stock runs out before the rice is cooked, continue with simmering water.) It will take 18–25 minutes to cook. Taste the rice for texture – it should be soft but still retain a little bite.

Remove from the heat and add the parsley, parmesan and the remaining butter. Season to taste with salt and freshly ground black pepper. Cover and allow to rest for 5 minutes before serving. Serve with extra grated parmesan, if desired.

Serves 4

roast beef fillet.

Fillet of beef is an expensive piece of meat but there is no waste, it requires little preparation and is easy to cook. Take care not to overcook the beef – because this cut is so lean, much of the meat's flavour and tenderness will be lost if you cook it beyond medium.

1.75–2 kg (3½–4 lb) fillet beef

2 tablespoons olive oil, plus extra for the
    roasting tray

salt and freshly ground black pepper

Remove the fillet from the fridge about 1 hour before cooking, to allow the meat to come to room temperature. Preheat oven to 220°C (425°F, Gas Mark 7).

If one end of the fillet is tapered or thin, fold it underneath and tie in place with a piece of string – this helps the meat to cook evenly. I also usually tie a few pieces of string around the fillet at regular 3–4 cm (1¼–1½ in) intervals so that it will keep its shape while cooking. Brush the fillet with the oil and season well with salt and freshly ground black pepper (as a variation, you can lightly spread with wholegrain mustard).

Lightly grease a roasting tray with a little extra oil then transfer the fillet to the tray. Roast in the preheated oven for about 25–30 minutes for rare, or about 35–40 minutes for medium. Remove from the oven, cover loosely with foil and set aside in a warm place to rest for 10 minutes. Serve the beef hot, warm or at room temperature with its juices.

This roast is delicious served with steamed new potatoes and lightly puréed fresh peas.

Serves 8

roast beetroot.

There is much more to beetroot than the vinegary purple slices you find in cans (where would an Aussie burger be without the stuff?). Give yourself a treat and try the delicious sweetness of roasted fresh beetroot.

6–8 small beetroots

2 tablespoons olive oil

salt and freshly ground black pepper

Preheated the oven to 180°C (350°F, Gas Mark 4).

Trim the tops of the beetroots, leaving a little of the stem attached, but don't peel them. Halve any large ones, and place them all in a baking tin. Drizzle with a little of the olive oil and cover with foil. Roast for 1½–2 hours, or until beetroot is tender when pierced with a skewer or sharp knife.

Allow to cool a little, then slip the skins off the beetroots and halve or quarter them. Drizzle with the remaining olive oil, or toss with butter or sour cream and herbs while hot. Season with salt and freshly ground black pepper.

Serve hot as a side dish or at room temperature as part of a salad.

Look for a bunch of small-to-medium-sized beetroots that has firm, nicely coloured flesh and fresh leaves.

If short of time, you can parboil the beetroots before roasting, then reduce the roasting time to 30 minutes.

Hot beetroots are also delicious dressed with balsamic vinegar and olive oil and sprinkled with fresh chives.

Serves 4–6

roast capsicum.

red capsicums (bell peppers) | **olive oil**

Preheat the oven to 190°C (375°F, Gas Mark 5).

Brush the capsicums with oil and place in a single layer in a baking tin. Place in the top half of the oven and roast, turning occasionally, for 25–30 minutes, or until the skin is blackened and bubbling. Remove and transfer to a large heatproof bowl. Cover with plastic wrap and set aside to cool.

When cool, quarter the capsicums, discard the seeds and juice, and peel off the skin.

Use within 2 days or store by placing the capsicum quarters in a screw-top jar and filling with enough olive oil to cover. Refrigerate for up to 2 weeks.

Roast capsicum makes a great addition to an antipasto platter. It is also delicious added to salads or a frittata or quiche.

Chopped fresh herbs or peeled garlic added to a jar of roast capsicum make delicious variations.

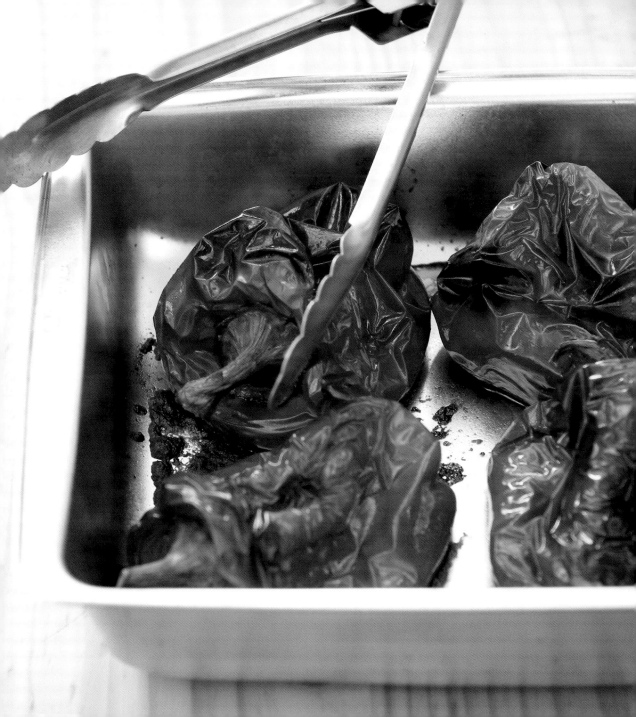

roast chicken.

1 medium-sized chicken

1 lemon, halved

5 cloves garlic, unpeeled

1 tablespoon olive oil

salt and freshly ground black pepper

½ cup white wine

1½ cups chicken stock (see page 68)
or water

Preheat the oven to 200°C (400°F, Gas Mark 6).

Rinse the chicken and pat dry with kitchen paper. Place in a baking tin, breast-side up, and squeeze the juice of half a lemon over the bird. Place the other lemon half inside the cavity, along with one of the garlic cloves. Tie the legs securely with string. Scatter the remaining garlic in the tin.

Drizzle the oil over the breast of the chicken. Sprinkle generously with salt and freshly ground black pepper.

Roast for 65–70 minutes, basting the bird with the pan juices every 20 minutes. To test if the chicken is cooked, insert a sharp knife or skewer into the thigh cavity – the juice should run clear.

Transfer the roasted chicken to a serving dish and allow to rest for 10 minutes. Warm the serving plates in the oven for 2–3 minutes.

To make a sauce, pour off the fat from the baking tin. Place the baking tin over medium heat on the stove top and add the wine and chicken stock. Stir well with a wooden spoon and scrape any bits stuck to the bottom of the tin, incorporating them into the sauce. Bring to the boil and simmer until the sauce is reduced and slightly thickened. Season to taste with salt and freshly ground black pepper. Alternatively, make a gravy by following the directions on page 144.

Use a free-range, chemical-free chicken if available.

A size 16 chicken (1.6 kg, 3¼ lb) will feed four people.

Serves 4

roast leg of lamb.

3 cloves garlic, peeled

1 medium-sized leg lamb

6–8 sprigs rosemary

2 tablespoons olive oil

salt and freshly ground black pepper

assorted vegetables, peeled and chopped,
to roast

Preheat the oven to 200°C (400°F, Gas Mark 6).

Cut each garlic clove into three slivers. With the point of a small sharp knife, make six to eight incisions in the lamb. Insert the garlic slivers and a small sprig of rosemary into each of the cuts.

Rub the skin of the lamb with 1 tablespoon of the oil. Season with salt and freshly ground black pepper.

Place the lamb in a large baking tin and surround with a selection of peeled and chopped vegetables. Drizzle the vegetables with the remaining oil. Roast the lamb for 65–75 minutes, basting occasionally with the pan juices.

Remove the lamb from the tin, cover with foil and allow to rest for 10 minutes before carving. Keep the vegetables warm until ready to serve.

To make gravy, refer to the instructions on page 144.

Slice the lamb into medium–thick slices, serve with vegetables and accompany with gravy and mint sauce, if desired. If you have someone who is an expert carver, a roast leg of lamb looks magnificent presented at the table on a large platter surrounded by vegetables.

Carrots, potatoes, Jerusalem artichokes, parsnips, swedes, baby brown onions and chunks of sweet potato (garnet yam) are all delicious roasted along with the lamb.

Serves 4–6

roast pears with ginger.

4 ripe pears

2 tablespoons chopped candied ginger
   (in syrup)

2 tablespoons syrup (from ginger jar)

chopped zest of 1 lime

$\frac{1}{2}$ cup lightly packed brown sugar

30 g (1 oz) butter

Preheat the oven to 180°C (350°F, Gas Mark 4).

Halve the pears lengthways, leaving the skin on, and scoop out the cores. Place the pears cut-side up in a baking tin. Top the pears with the candied ginger.

Combine 1 cup of water and the ginger syrup, lime zest and sugar in a small saucepan and bring to the boil. Cool slightly, then pour the syrup over the pears.

Roast, turning and basting occasionally, for 45–50 minutes, or until tender and nicely golden. If the syrup starts to dry up during cooking, add a little hot water to the dish.

Serve pears warm or at room temperature, drizzled with the pan juices and accompanied by a generous spoonful of yoghurt, ice-cream or cream.

Beurre bosc pears are ideal for this dish.

Serves 4

roast pork with crackling.

The best crackling comes from the hindquarters, so choose either a pork
leg or loin to roast. Ask your butcher to score the skin for you.

1 × 1.5 kg (3 lb) piece pork
salt and freshly ground black pepper
3 sprigs rosemary

6 cloves garlic, unpeeled
1 kg (2 lb) potatoes, peeled and
cut into chunks

Preheat the oven to 220°C (425°F, Gas Mark 7).

Pat the pork dry with kitchen paper and rub the scored skin well with salt. Season
with freshly ground pepper.

Place the pork, skin-side up, in a baking tin and tuck the rosemary and garlic underneath. Roast for 20 minutes.

Reduce the heat to 180°C (350°F, Gas Mark 4) and continue to cook for 1 hour.

Add the potatoes to the baking tin and cook, turning occasionally, for a further
1 hour, or until the potatoes are tender inside and crisp on the outside. To test if the
meat is cooked, insert a sharp knife or skewer into the centre – the juice should run
clear. Remove the pork, cut away the crackling and return it to the top shelf of the
oven if it needs further cooking. Cover the meat and potatoes with foil and set aside to
rest for 10 minutes.

To make gravy, refer to the instructions on page 144.

To serve, carve the pork into slices and accompany with potatoes, crackling, gravy
and apple sauce.

*Calculate the cooking time for different pork cuts by allowing 30 minutes for every 500 g (1 lb),
plus an extra 30 minutes.*

Serves 4–6

roast potatoes.

A perfect roast potato is crisp on the outside and soft and fluffy
on the inside.

1 kg (2 lb) floury potatoes   **salt**
2–3 tablespoons olive oil

Preheat the oven to 200°C (400°F, Gas Mark 6).

Peel and cut the potatoes into even-sized pieces. Cook in a large saucepan of boiling salted water for 8–10 minutes, or until just tender. Drain well and return to the saucepan. Shake well in the pan, or use a fork to roughen up the surfaces a bit. (Rough edges help the potatoes to become crisp.)

Pour the oil into a baking tin and place in the hot oven for 5 minutes. Remove, add the potatoes to the tin and stir to coat with the oil. Season well with salt.

Roast on the top shelf of the oven, turning occasionally, for 50–60 minutes, or until crisp and golden. Serve with your favourite roast meat.

Floury potato varieties such as desiree, King Edward, roseval, spunta, kipfler or bintje are best for roasting.

Potatoes absorb less fat and cook faster if placed in a hot baking tin with hot oil.

As a variation, add 3–4 unpeeled garlic cloves and 1 tablespoon of chopped rosemary 10 minutes before the end of the cooking time. Or try chopped bacon stirred into the potatoes 7–10 minutes before the end of the cooking time.

Serves 4–6

salade niçoise.

There really are as many recipes – and rules – for a salade niçoise as there are cooks. It is always a simple and delicious dish, though, and the combination of flavours has travelled well from the south of France to the southern hemisphere. Vary the recipe with ingredients that you have to hand, but here is my basic version.

4 eggs

1 cos (Romaine) lettuce

5 ripe tomatoes, cut into wedges

100 g (3½ oz) small black olives

350 g (11 oz) small new or salad potatoes,
    freshly boiled and halved

250 g (8 oz) green beans, freshly boiled

100 ml (3½ fl oz) good-quality olive oil

2 tablespoons lemon juice

1 teaspoon Dijon mustard

1 × 250 g (8 oz) can tuna in oil, drained

1 teaspoon capers

6–8 anchovy fillets

salt and freshly ground black pepper

Hard-boil the eggs in a saucepan of boiling water for 7 minutes. Set aside until cool, then peel and quarter.

To assemble the salad, trim, wash and dry the lettuce and break the leaves into largish pieces. Combine with the tomatoes, olives, potatoes and beans.

Make a dressing by mixing together the olive oil, lemon juice and mustard.

Lightly dress the salad and transfer to a serving plate. Top with the eggs and the tuna. Sprinkle over the capers and top with the anchovy fillets. Drizzle with a little extra dressing and season well with salt and freshly ground black pepper.

Use good-quality canned tuna. Alternatively, sear four small tuna steaks in a frying pan over high heat for about 2 minutes each side and serve them with the salad.

Serves 4

salt and pepper squid.

600 g (1¼ lb) cleaned and prepared squid
    or calamari tubes

½ cup plain (all-purpose) flour or rice flour

2 tablespoons sea salt

1 tablespoon freshly ground black pepper

1 teaspoon chilli powder

1 medium-sized red chilli, finely chopped

vegetable oil, to fry

Rinse the squid. Cut along each side of the body so it opens out flat. Dry well with kitchen paper. Score the skin with a sharp knife and cut into either 1 cm (½ in) wide strips or 5 cm (2 in) diamonds.

In a shallow dish, combine the flour, sea salt, pepper, chilli powder and chopped chilli. Dip the pieces of squid into the flour mixture and toss to coat. Shake off any excess.

Pour vegetable oil into a large frying pan or wok to a depth of 2 cm (¾ in). Heat the oil to 180°C (350°F) – a cube of bread dropped in the oil should brown in 15 seconds.

Cook the squid in batches in the hot oil for 1–2 minutes, or until golden. Remove with tongs or a slotted spoon and drain on crumpled kitchen paper. Taste and season with a little extra salt and pepper if necessary. This dish should taste salty and spicy.

Serve with lemon or lime wedges.

Replace half the ground black pepper with 2 teaspoons of ground Sichuan peppercorns for an interesting flavour variation.

A pinch of Chinese five-spice powder is good added to the salt and pepper mix.

Peeled uncooked prawns are also good prepared this way.

Serves 4

salt-baked prawns.

This is a simple but very effective way to cook raw prawns – baking them in salt seals the prawns completely so they cook without any juice or flavour escaping. The idea comes from a friend I met at the Sydney Seafood Cooking School.

1 kg (2 lb) coarse rock salt

8 sprigs thyme

4 cloves garlic, skin on

24 medium-sized uncooked prawns (shrimp), shells on

1 bay leaf

lemon wedges, to serve

mayonnaise (see page 192), to serve

Preheat the oven to 220°C (425°F, Gas Mark 7).

Place half the rock salt in a 1 cm (½ in) layer on the base of a small baking tin. Lay half the thyme and half the garlic on the salt and add the prawns. Sprinkle over the remaining thyme and garlic and add the bay leaf, then cover completely with the remaining salt. Sprinkle lightly with a couple of tablespoons of water. Bake for 10–12 minutes.

Crack the salt and remove the prawns – this can be done at the table, if desired.

Serve with lemon wedges and accompany with good-quality mayonnaise.

The salt can be saved and reused to make this dish again.

Serves 4

saltimbocca.

4 × 175 g (6 oz) veal or pork escalopes
salt and freshly ground black pepper
plain (all-purpose) flour, for dusting
4 slices prosciutto or parma ham
8 fresh sage leaves

3 tablespoons olive oil
25 g (1 oz) butter
1 medium ball mozzarella
   (approximately 150 g)
lemon wedges

Using a rolling pin or meat mallet, flatten each escalope to an even thickness of about 5 mm (¼ in), then season with salt and freshly ground black pepper and lightly dust with a little flour. Place a slice of prosciutto or parma ham and 2 sage leaves on each escalope and press down, using a toothpick to secure the ham, if needed.

Heat the oil and butter in a large frying pan over a medium heat. Fry the escalopes in batches for about 2 minutes each side until browned; keep warm while cooking the others.

Preheat the grill to high. With your fingers, break the mozzarella into small pieces and divide between the escalopes, then place under the hot grill for 2 minutes, or until the cheese is slightly melted and just starting to brown.

Serve on hot plates with wedges of lemon. Accompany with buttered baby spinach.

You can flatten and prepare the escalopes – as far as the cooking stage – up to 8 hours ahead and refrigerate them until needed.

To make a simple sauce to go with the saltimbocca, place the frying pan (after removing the escalopes) over a high heat and add 100 ml (3½ fl oz) white wine, stirring to deglaze, and 1 tablespoon chopped parsley, then simmer for a few minutes until reduced and syrupy.

Serves 4

san choy bow.

1 tablespoon peanut oil

1 onion, finely chopped

1 clove garlic, crushed

2 teaspoons grated fresh ginger

600 g (1¼ lb) minced (ground) pork

1 tablespoon soy sauce

2 tablespoons oyster sauce

1 × 220 g (7 oz) can water chestnuts,
   drained and chopped

4 spring onions (scallions), thinly sliced

salt and freshly ground black pepper

250 g (8 oz) bean sprouts

8 iceberg lettuce leaves

Heat the oil in a large frying pan over medium heat. Cook the onion, garlic and ginger, stirring occasionally, for 3–4 minutes, or until the onion is soft. Add the minced pork and cook, breaking up the meat with a fork, for 4–5 minutes, or until the pork is coloured and cooked. Stir in the soy sauce, oyster sauce, water chestnuts and spring onion and cook for a further 3–4 minutes, or until the liquid has reduced. Season to taste with salt and pepper.

Transfer the mixture to a bowl and stir in the bean sprouts. Allow to cool slightly before serving. Place two lettuce leaves on each serving plate and spoon the mixture into the centre of the leaves. Serve immediately.

This recipe is just as good using minced (ground) chicken instead of pork.

Serves 4

satay sauce.

2 tablespoons vegetable oil

1 onion, finely chopped

2 cloves garlic, crushed

1 teaspoon grated fresh ginger

1–2 long red chillies, finely chopped

1 tablespoon brown sugar

½ cup crunchy peanut butter

juice of 1 lime

1 teaspoon Thai fish sauce

2 tablespoons soy sauce

salt and freshly ground black pepper

Heat the oil in a saucepan over medium heat. Add the onion, garlic, ginger and chilli and cook, stirring, for 4–5 minutes, or until the onion is soft. Add the sugar, peanut butter, lime juice, fish sauce, soy sauce and 2–3 tablespoons of water. Simmer gently for 5 minutes, adding a little extra water if needed, to produce a sauce-like consistency. Taste and add a little extra lime juice or fish sauce, if desired. Season to taste with salt and freshly ground pepper.

Store in an airtight container in the refrigerator for up to 1 week.

Add 1 teaspoon of crushed dried chillies, if desired, for extra heat.

Makes about 1 cup

sausage roast.

This delicious recipe comes from my friend and great cook Fiona Beckett.
If you want a supper that calls for minimal effort but is very, very soothing
and comforting, make this.

450 g (14 oz) new or waxy potatoes

2 red (Spanish) onions

4 cloves garlic or a head of 'wet'
   (fresh) garlic

¼ cup olive oil

salt and freshly ground black pepper

6 good-quality lamb and mint or
   lamb and rosemary sausages

Preheat the oven to 200°C (400°F, Gas Mark 6).

Scrub the potatoes clean but don't peel them. Cut into chunky slices about 4–5 cm
(1½–2 in) thick.

Peel and thickly slice the onions and garlic. Place in a medium-sized baking tin with
the potatoes and pour over the oil. Season with salt and pepper, then toss to coat well
with the oil and seasonings.

Roast for 20 minutes. Remove from the oven and turn the vegetables. Lay the
sausages on top of the vegetables, turning them so they get a light coating of oil. Roast
for 20 minutes, then turn the sausages over and cook for a further 15–20 minutes.

I don't think this is a dish that needs gravy, but if you're a gravy addict, feel free.
Serve it with a classic French-style green salad.

Buy good-quality sausages, with a high meat content, from your local butcher.

*This dish can be easily doubled to serve 4–6. Use either one large baking tin or two smaller
tins, swapping their position in the oven halfway through the cooking.*

Serves 2

scones.

3⅓ cups self-raising (self-rising) flour

1 teaspoon baking powder

1 tablespoon caster (superfine) sugar

½ teaspoon salt

60 g (2 oz) unsalted butter, chilled
and diced

1 cup milk

2 teaspoons lemon juice

1 egg, beaten

milk, extra, for brushing

Preheat the oven to 200°C (400°F, Gas Mark 6). Line an oven tray with baking paper.

Sift the flour and baking powder into a large mixing bowl. Stir in the sugar and salt. Add the butter and, using your fingertips, rub the butter into the flour until it resembles fine breadcrumbs.

Mix together the milk and lemon juice – the mixture will curdle slightly. Add the beaten egg and pour into the flour mixture. Mix gently just until a dough forms – be careful not to overwork the dough. Gather into a rough ball shape, turn out onto a lightly floured surface and knead very lightly. The dough should feel slightly wet and sticky.

Flatten out the dough to a thickness of 3 cm (1¼ in) and cut out rounds with a cookie cutter. Place the rounds on the prepared oven tray 2.5 cm (1 in) apart and brush the tops with a little milk. Bake for 10–12 minutes, or until risen and golden.

Remove from the tray and wrap the scones in a clean tea towel to keep them warm and soft. Serve warm with jam, butter or cream.

To make fruit scones, add ½ cup of sultanas and some chopped orange zest.

To make cheese scones, omit the sugar and sift ½ teaspoon of dry mustard with the flour. After rubbing in the butter, stir ¾ cup of grated cheddar into the mixture and proceed with the recipe.

Makes 12

scrambled eggs.

To make perfect scrambled eggs, you need to cook the eggs
very slowly. The best way to achieve this is to cook them in a bowl
placed over a saucepan of simmering water. This method takes longer,
but the result is worth the effort.

6 eggs

1 tablespoon cream

salt and freshly ground black pepper

10 g (¼ oz) butter

Gently whisk the eggs with the cream and a pinch of salt and freshly ground black pepper in a small heatproof mixing bowl.

Place the bowl over a saucepan of gently simmering water, making sure the bottom of the bowl does not touch the water. Cook, turning the mixture occasionally with a large metal spoon, until the egg thickens. As the egg thickens and begins to scramble, add the butter. Season to taste with more salt and freshly ground black pepper. Serve on hot, buttered toast.

Chopped chives or chervil are delicious folded into the mixture just before serving.

Dress up scrambled eggs with some smoked salmon and a glass of bubbly on the side.

Serves 2

seafood chowder.

2 tablespoons olive oil

1 onion, sliced

4 medium-sized potatoes,
   peeled and diced

2 tablespoons plain (all-purpose) flour

1.25 litres (40 fl oz) fish stock or
   vegetable stock

½ cup dry white wine

1 bay leaf

3 sprigs thyme

500 g (1 lb) firm white fish fillets

250 g (8 oz) smoked fish (haddock
   or cod) fillets

500 g (1 lb) medium-sized uncooked prawns
   (shrimp), peeled and deveined

1 cup cream or milk

salt and freshly ground black pepper

2 tablespoons chopped flat-leaf parsley
   or chervil

Heat the oil in a large saucepan, add the onion and potatoes and cook gently, without browning, until the onion is soft and translucent. Sprinkle over the flour and cook, stirring, for 1 minute.

Add the stock, wine, bay leaf and thyme and stir until smooth. Bring to the boil, reduce the heat and simmer for 10–15 minutes, or until the potatoes are soft. Remove the bay leaf and thyme.

Skin the white fish fillets and cut into bite-sized chunks. Break the smoked fish into bite-sized pieces. Add the fish and prawns to the saucepan and simmer for 3–4 minutes, or until the fish is opaque and the prawns have turned pink.

Stir in the cream or milk and heat slowly without bringing to the boil. Season well with salt and freshly ground black pepper. Sprinkle over the parsley or chervil and serve.

Serves 6

shepherd's pie.

2 tablespoons vegetable oil

2 onions, chopped

750 g (1½ lb) minced (ground) lamb

2 tablespoons plain (all-purpose) flour

1 cup beef stock

2 tablespoons tomato paste

2 teaspoons Worcestershire sauce

2 bay leaves

1 teaspoon fresh thyme, fresh marjoram or dried rosemary leaves

salt and freshly ground black pepper

750 g (1½ lb) floury potatoes, peeled

60 g (2 oz) butter

¼ cup milk

20 g (¾ oz) butter, extra

pinch of cayenne pepper

Heat 1 tablespoon of the oil in a frying pan over medium heat and cook the onions for 4–5 minutes, or until soft and golden. Remove and set aside.

Heat the remaining 1 tablespoon of oil in the same frying pan and add the lamb. Cook over medium heat, stirring occasionally, for 7 minutes. Use a fork to break up any lumps. Stir in the flour and cook for 1 minute. Remove from the heat and add the stock, stirring until blended. Return to the heat and bring to the boil, stirring continuously, until thickened. Add the cooked onions, tomato paste, Worcestershire sauce, bay leaves and thyme, marjoram or rosemary. Season to taste with salt and freshly ground black pepper. Set aside to cool.

Meanwhile, cut the potatoes into chunks and cook in a large saucepan of boiling salted water for 15–20 minutes, or until tender. Drain well and mash with the butter and milk until smooth. Season well with salt and freshly ground black pepper.

Preheat the oven to 180°C (350°F, Gas Mark 4).

Transfer the meat mixture to a large ovenproof dish. Spoon over the mashed potato and fluff up with a fork. Dot with the extra butter and sprinkle with the cayenne pepper. Bake for 30–35 minutes, or until golden and bubbling. Serve at the table directly from the dish. Accompany with steamed green beans or spinach.

Serves 4–6

shortbread.

250 g (8 oz) unsalted butter, softened
½ cup caster (superfine) sugar

2 cups plain (all-purpose) flour
½ cup rice flour

Preheat the oven to 150°C (300°F, Gas Mark 2). Line two oven trays with baking paper.

Beat the butter in a bowl with a wooden spoon until soft and smooth. Add the sugar, plain flour and rice flour and work the mixture with the spoon until blended.

Knead the dough lightly on a floured surface to form a firm dough, then chill for 20 minutes.

Divide the dough into two portions and roll out each between two sheets of baking paper to a thickness of 5–7 mm (¼–⅓ in). Cut the dough into shapes with cookie cutters. Place the shapes onto the prepared oven trays and bake for 15–20 minutes, or until pale and dry. Alternatively, roll out each portion of dough to form a circle 18 cm (7 in) in diameter. Mark each circle into wedges with a knife, prick the surface several times with a fork, sprinkle with a little extra sugar and bake for 35–40 minutes, or until pale and dry. Store shortbread in an airtight container for up to 1 week.

Shortbread should be dry with a melt-in-the-mouth texture.
Rice flour gives the shortbread a wonderful grainy texture.
As a variation, add a little grated or finely chopped citrus zest to the dough.

Makes 35–40 biscuits or 2 large rounds

shortcrust pastry.

Shortcrust pastry is easy to make and is suitable for tarts, pies or quiches. Sweet shortcrust is enriched with a little sugar and a beaten egg, which makes it perfect for sweet tarts (see recipe variation below).

2 cups plain (all-purpose) flour
salt

125 g (4 oz) butter, chilled and diced
3–4 tablespoons chilled water

Sift the flour and a pinch of salt into a large bowl. Rub the butter into the flour mixture with your fingertips until it resembles fine breadcrumbs. (As you rub the butter into the flour, lift it up high and let it fall back into the bowl.) Alternatively, pulse the mixture in a food processor until the mixture resembles fine breadcrumbs.

Make a well in the centre, add the chilled water and mix with a flat-bladed knife, using a cutting action rather than a stirring action, until the mixture comes together in beads. Add a little extra water if needed to bring the dough together.

Gather the dough, press gently together into a ball and flatten slightly into a disc. Wrap in plastic wrap and refrigerate for 30 minutes before using.

Homemade shortcrust pastry can be covered in plastic wrap and stored in the fridge for 2–3 days, or frozen for 2–3 months.

To make a sweet shortcrust pastry, add 1 tablespoon of icing (confectioners') sugar to the flour. Add 1 beaten egg yolk and only 2–3 tablespoons of chilled water to the mixture and then follow the basic recipe.

The easiest way to roll out the pastry is to place the ball of dough between two sheets of baking paper and use a large rolling pin. The paper prevents the dough sticking to the surface and makes it easier to handle.

Makes enough for a 20 cm (8 in) pie

singapore-style noodles.

250 g (8 oz) rice vermicelli (cellophane) noodles

2 large red chillies, seeded and roughly chopped

3 cloves garlic, crushed

1 × ½ cm (¼ in) piece fresh ginger, chopped

1 small onion, roughly chopped

¼ cup vegetable oil

2 chicken breasts, thinly sliced

12 uncooked prawns (shrimp), shelled and deveined

1 cup bean sprouts

4 spring onions (scallions), sliced

1 egg, beaten

¼ cup light soy sauce

juice of ½ lemon or lime

salt

Place the noodles in a heatproof bowl and cover with boiling water. Leave to soften for 7 minutes. Drain well and set aside.

Place the chilli, garlic, ginger and onion in a food processor. Use the pulse action to process ingredients to a paste, adding a drizzle of vegetable oil if needed. Alternatively, pound ingredients to a paste in a mortar and pestle.

Heat a wok or large frying pan to hot, then add the vegetable oil, turning to coat the pan. Add the paste and cook, stirring, for 30 seconds – be careful it does not burn.

Add the chicken and stir-fry for 2–3 minutes. Add the prawns and stir-fry for a further minute, or until the chicken is golden and the prawns are cooked. Add the drained noodles and the bean sprouts, spring onions and egg and cook, stirring continuously, for 2 minutes. Pour over the soy sauce and continue to cook and stir until combined and hot. Squeeze over a little lemon or lime juice and season to taste with salt.

Try 250 g (8 oz) of sliced fresh pork fillet in place of the chicken.

Serves 3–4

slow-roasted lamb.

Slow cooking gives you wonderfully succulent and tender meat. Use a medium-sized leg of lamb or get your butcher to bone and roll a large shoulder of lamb.

2 tablespoons vegetable oil

1 medium-sized leg or rolled shoulder
    of lamb

4 rashers bacon or pancetta, chopped

1 onion, chopped

2 cloves garlic, peeled

1 bay leaf

3 sprigs rosemary or thyme

1–1⅓ cups red wine

salt and freshly ground black pepper

Preheat the oven to 200°C (400°F, Gas Mark 6).

Heat the oil in a large casserole dish or deep baking tin over medium heat and brown the lamb on both sides. Remove the lamb, add the bacon and cook, stirring occasionally, for 3 minutes. Add the onion and cook for a further 4–5 minutes, or until tender. Return the lamb to the casserole and add the garlic, bay leaf and rosemary. Pour in the red wine to a depth of about 1 cm (½ in) and bring to the boil.

Cover the casserole with a lid or sheet of foil and place in the oven. Reduce the heat to 160°C (315°F, Gas Mark 2–3) and cook for 4–4½ hours, or until the meat is very tender, turning the lamb and basting occasionally.

Remove the lamb from the dish, cover with foil and allow to rest for 10 minutes before carving.

Skim off any fat from the surface of the pan with a large spoon and remove the garlic, bay leaf and rosemary. If the sauce is a little thin, reduce it over high heat on the stove top. Season to taste with salt and freshly ground black pepper.

Slice the meat and serve with the sauce.

Serves 4–6

slow–roasted pork.

This recipe is from Nigella Lawson's book *Nigella Bites*. 'I do like the sort of cooking that gets on with itself slowly,' she says. Many a Sunday lunch at my home starts with thanks to Nigella.

A point before you start – this dish does take 24 hours to cook, but for most of that time you ignore it completely (and it does make the kitchen smell like something wonderfully delicious is going on).

6 cloves garlic, peeled and chopped	2 tablespoons olive oil
1 × 1 cm (½ in) piece fresh ginger, peeled and chopped	3–4 tablespoons sherry or rice vinegar
	1 × 3–4 kg (6–8 lbs) shoulder pork
2 long red chillies, chopped	2 tablespoons olive oil, extra, to serve

Preheat the oven to 240°C (475°F, Gas Mark 9).

Pound the garlic, ginger, chillies and oil with enough vinegar in a mortar and pestle to form a paste. Alternatively, process the ingredients in a small food processor.

Score the skin of the pork by cutting it in several places with a knife – be careful not to cut all the way through. Rub the chilli paste all over the top of the pork, including deep into the scored skin.

Place the pork, scored-side up, on a roasting rack set over a baking tin. Roast for 30 minutes. Remove from the oven and reduce the heat to 120°C (250°F, Gas Mark ½). Turn the pork over so the scoring is underneath. Bake for 23 hours.

Prior to serving, turn the oven up to the highest setting, turn the pork skin-side up and cook for 30 minutes, or until the crackling is crisp. To serve, slice away the crackling and carve the meat into large pieces.

Serves 6–8

slow-roasted tomatoes.

8 Roma (egg) tomatoes

olive oil

2 teaspoons thyme leaves

salt and freshly ground black pepper

Preheat the oven to 140°C (275°F, Gas Mark 1) and lightly grease an oven tray.

Cut the tomatoes in half lengthways and place, cut-side up, on the prepared oven tray. Drizzle each tomato half lightly with olive oil, then sprinkle evenly with thyme, salt and freshly ground black pepper.

Roast for 1½–2 hours, or until the tomatoes are lightly dried and darkened, but still retain some moisture. Use in salads, as part of sandwich fillings, or tossed through cooked pasta. To store, cover completely with olive oil in a screw-top jar and keep in the refrigerator up to 2 weeks.

Makes 16

spaghetti vongole.

You can prepare the clams (vongole) and make the sauce in the time
it takes to cook the spaghetti.

2 tablespoons olive oil

2 cloves garlic, crushed

1 long red chilli, chopped

200 g (6½ oz) cherry tomatoes, halved

750 g (1½ lb) fresh clams (vongole)

200 g (6½ oz) dried spaghetti

2–3 tablespoons chopped flat-leaf parsley

salt and freshly ground black pepper

1 lemon, quartered, to serve

Put a large saucepan of salted water on to boil.

Pour the oil into a second large saucepan over moderate heat. Add the garlic and chilli and sauté for 2–3 minutes. Add the tomatoes and cook for 1–2 minutes, or until soft. Tip in the clams and stir well. Increase the heat, cover and cook, shaking the pan occasionally, for 5–6 minutes, or until the clams have opened.

Meanwhile, cook the spaghetti in the boiling water until al dente.

Drain the pasta and add it to the saucepan containing the clams. Sprinkle with the parsley and toss the pasta and clams together well. Season to taste with salt and freshly ground black pepper – the juices that clams release when they cook can be salty, so taste first. Serve in large bowls with lemon wedges.

Cleaned mussels may be substituted for the clams.

Serves 2

spaghetti with crab and chilli.

200 g (6½ oz) dried spaghetti

200 g (6½ oz) fresh cooked crab meat,
   white or brown

½ long red chilli, seeded and finely sliced

1 clove garlic, crushed

1 teaspoon grated lemon zest

handful of rocket (arugula), roughly
   chopped

juice of ½ lemon

¼ cup extra-virgin olive oil, plus extra
   to drizzle

sea salt and freshly ground black pepper

2 tablespoons chopped flat-leaf parsley

Bring a large saucepan of salted water to the boil and add the spaghetti. Stir well and boil rapidly for 8 minutes, or until al dente.

Meanwhile, combine the crab, chilli, garlic, lemon zest, rocket, lemon juice and olive oil in a small bowl. Season well with sea salt and freshly ground black pepper.

Drain the cooked spaghetti and return it to the pot. Pour over the crab mixture, add the parsley and stir to combine. Drizzle with a little extra olive oil, if desired. Serve immediately.

Serves 2

spaghetti with garlic, chilli and oil.

This is the simplest and speediest of all pasta dishes. Olive oil is infused with garlic and chilli, which is then stirred into hot pasta. This dish fills the kitchen with the heady aroma of garlic.

400 g (13 oz) dried spaghetti
½ cup olive oil
4 cloves garlic, finely chopped

1–2 large red chillies, seeded and finely chopped
2 tablespoons chopped flat-leaf parsley
salt and freshly ground black pepper

Bring a large saucepan of salted water to the boil and add the spaghetti. Stir well and boil rapidly for 8 minutes, or until the spaghetti is al dente.

Meanwhile, combine the oil, garlic and chilli in a small saucepan. Cook over very low heat for 7–8 minutes to allow the oil to absorb the chilli and garlic flavours. The oil should barely simmer. The garlic should colour slightly, but don't allow it to burn.

Drain the cooked pasta and return it to the large saucepan over moderate heat. Pour over the oil mixture and add the parsley. Toss thoroughly with two forks to coat the pasta with the oil. Season with salt and freshly ground black pepper. Serve immediately.

Allow 100 g (3½ oz) of dried spaghetti per person.

You can vary this dish by using chopped basil or chopped rocket (arugula) in place of the parsley. A squeeze of lemon juice is also delicious.

If you like, serve with freshly grated parmesan.

Serves 4

spaghetti with tomato sauce.

I love the simplicity of this dish – the only cooking required is to boil the spaghetti! You do need good-quality and tasty tomatoes, however, so use vine-ripened varieties, preferably home-grown ones.

500 g (1 lb) tomatoes

2 cloves garlic, very finely chopped

¼ cup shredded basil

⅓ cup extra-virgin olive oil, plus extra, to serve

2 tablespoons balsamic vinegar

salt and freshly ground black pepper

500 g (1 lb) dried spaghetti

freshly grated parmesan, to serve

Though not absolutely necessary, I prefer to peel the tomatoes. To do this, refer to the instructions on page 202.

To make the fresh tomato sauce, halve the tomatoes, remove and discard the seeds and dice the flesh. Place the flesh in a bowl and stir in the garlic, basil, oil and vinegar. Season well with salt and freshly ground black pepper. Allow to stand at room temperature for 1 hour, stirring occasionally.

Bring a large saucepan of salted water to the boil and add the spaghetti. Stir well and boil rapidly until the pasta is al dente.

Drain the cooked pasta and return it to the saucepan. Stir in the sauce. Season to taste with more salt and freshly ground black pepper. Serve spaghetti drizzled with a little extra-virgin olive oil and grated parmesan.

The addition of a little chopped fresh chilli is also delicious.

Serves 4

spaghetti with tuna, rocket and lemon.

This simple dish can be mustered up at a moment's notice and is the perfect pasta for those with not much in the pantry and little time to spare.

250 g (8 oz) dried spaghetti

¼ cup roughly chopped rocket (arugula)

grated zest and juice of 1 lemon

2 tablespoons extra-virgin olive oil, plus extra, to serve

1 clove garlic, chopped

½ long red chilli, chopped (optional)

1 × 200 g (6½ oz) can tuna in oil

salt and freshly ground black pepper

Bring a large saucepan of salted water to the boil and add the spaghetti. Stir well and boil rapidly until the pasta is al dente.

Meanwhile, place the rocket, lemon zest and juice, oil, garlic and chilli in a small bowl. Add the tuna along with its oil. Lightly mash the tuna with a fork, then season well with salt and freshly ground black pepper.

Drain the cooked pasta and return it to the saucepan. Stir in the tuna mixture. Drizzle with a little extra oil and serve immediately.

If you have a jar of capers in the refrigerator, add a tablespoonful to the sauce as a variation.

A crisp green salad is the perfect accompaniment to this pasta dish.

Serves 2

spice cake.

1⅓ cups self-raising (self-rising) flour

seeds from 4 cardamom pods, crushed

½ teaspoon mixed spice

salt

3 large eggs, separated

½ cup caster (superfine) sugar

grated zest of 1 orange

½ cup honey

75 g (2½ oz) butter, melted

⅓ cup strong coffee, freshly made

Preheat the oven to 180°C (350°F, Gas Mark 4). Grease a loaf tin and line the base with baking paper.

Sift the flour, cardamom seeds, mixed spice and a pinch of salt into a bowl.

In a separate bowl, whisk the egg yolks, sugar and zest together for 3–4 minutes, or until pale and fluffy. Add the honey and melted butter and whisk until combined.

Gently fold half the sifted flour into the egg mixture. Lightly stir in the coffee, then fold in the remaining flour.

In a clean, dry bowl, whisk the egg whites with an electric mixer until soft peaks form. Fold the whites through the flour and egg mixture, until combined.

Pour the batter into the prepared loaf tin. Bake for 55–60 minutes, or until golden and firm to the touch. A skewer inserted into the centre should come out clean. Allow to cool in the tin for 10 minutes before turning out onto a wire rack. Serve buttered accompanied with tea or coffee.

Make the cake a day before you want to serve it, as the flavours develop on keeping.

spiced apple sauce.

This sauce is the perfect accompaniment to pork.

2 large cooking apples, peeled, quartered
    and cored
2 tablespoons brown sugar

2 cloves
½ teaspoon mixed spice
pinch of ground ginger

Roughly chop the apples and place into a small saucepan with the sugar, spices and 100 ml (3½ fl oz) of water. Cover and cook over low heat, stirring occasionally, for 30 minutes, or until the apples are soft and broken up. During the cooking, add extra water, if needed, to stop the apples from catching on the bottom of the pan.

Mash with a fork or purée the flesh in a small food processor. Taste and adjust the sweetness and spice to suit your palate.

The flesh of a cooking apple quickly cooks down to a fluffy purée, making it perfect for sauces. Bramley apples are a type of cooking apple. They are now being grown in Tasmania and other cooler-climate locations – look for them at growers' markets.

Makes 1 cup

spiced moroccan chicken.

Yoghurt makes an excellent marinade for chicken – here it is combined with a little spicy harissa.

8 chicken drumsticks

1 tablespoon cornflour (cornstarch)

1 cup plain natural yoghurt

2 tablespoons harissa (see below)

⅓ cup chopped flat-leaf parsley

⅓ cup chopped coriander (cilantro) leaves

juice of 1 lemon

chopped flat-leaf parsley, extra, to serve

1 lemon, quartered, to serve

With a sharp knife make a couple of cuts in the thickest part of each drumstick and place chicken in a ceramic or glass dish.

Combine the cornflour, yoghurt, harissa, herbs and lemon juice in a small bowl. Spread the mixture over the chicken pieces and set aside to marinate for 30 minutes.

Preheat the oven to 190°C (375°F, Gas Mark 5).

Place the chicken in a baking tin and cook, turning occasionally, for 35–40 minutes, or until golden and cooked through. Sprinkle with a little extra parsley, garnish with lemon wedges and serve with a green salad.

Harissa, a spicy paste used in Moroccan cooking, is available from good supermarkets and delicatessens. You can make a simple harissa by soaking 5 dried chillies in a little water for 20 minutes. Drain the chillies and place in a blender with 2 peeled garlic cloves, ¼ cup of olive oil, 1 teaspoon of toasted cumin seeds, 2 teaspoons of toasted coriander seeds and a pinch salt. Blend to a thick paste and store, covered with a little extra oil, in a sealed jar in the refrigerator for up to 2 weeks.

Serves 4

spiced nuts.

350 g (11 oz) unsalted mixed nuts

2 tablespoons olive oil

1 tablespoon brown sugar

2 tablespoons sea salt

¼ teaspoon cayenne pepper

¼ teaspoon ground turmeric

freshly ground black pepper (optional)

Combine all the ingredients in a mixing bowl. Add a little extra cayenne pepper and a grinding of black pepper if you prefer a spicier mix.

Place in a large frying pan and cook, stirring frequently, over moderate heat for 5–7 minutes, or until golden. Taste and season with a little extra salt if desired.

Allow to cool and serve in small bowls as a snack. Spiced nuts make a perfect accompaniment to a drink or two. Once completely cool, store the nuts in an airtight container for up to 1 week.

Make a mixture of your personal favourites. Try macadamias, pecans, cashews and Brazil nuts.
A tablespoon of toasted sesame seeds stirred through the mix makes a delicious addition.

Makes 2 cups

spinach soup.

50 g (1¾ oz) butter

1 onion, roughly chopped

1 leek, sliced

500 g (1 lb) fresh or frozen spinach

3 medium-sized potatoes, peeled and
    roughly chopped

1 bay leaf

1.25 litres (40 fl oz) chicken stock (see
    page 68) or vegetable stock

2 tablespoons cream

pinch of freshly grated nutmeg

salt and freshly ground black pepper

juice of ½ lemon

2 tablespoons chopped chives

Heat the butter over moderate heat in a large saucepan. Add the onion and leek and cook, stirring occasionally, for 4–5 minutes, or until the vegetables are soft but not coloured. Add the spinach and potatoes and cook for 2–3 minutes. Add the bay leaf and stock and bring to the boil. Reduce the heat and simmer for 30 minutes.

Remove from the heat and allow to cool a little. Discard the bay leaf. Purée the soup in batches in a blender or with a hand-held blender until smooth. Stir in the cream and nutmeg, then return the soup to the heat but don't let it boil. Season to taste with salt and freshly ground black pepper and lemon juice. Serve hot or cold, garnished with chives.

I like to accompany this soup with bits of crisp bacon or prosciutto and toast.

Serves 4

sponge cake (genoise).

6 eggs

¾ cup caster (superfine) sugar

1 teaspoon vanilla essence

1 cup plain (all-purpose) flour, sifted

½ cup self-raising (self-rising) flour, sifted

75 g (2½ oz) unsalted butter, melted
    and cooled

1 cup berry jam

1 cup cream

½ teaspoon vanilla extract

icing (confectioners') sugar, to dust

Preheat oven to 180°C (350°F, Gas Mark 4). Grease 2 × 22 cm (8½ in) shallow round cake tins and line the base of each with baking paper.

Combine the eggs, sugar and vanilla in a large heatproof bowl. Place the bowl over a saucepan of gently simmering water, making sure the base of the bowl doesn't touch the water. Beat with an electric mixer for 6–7 minutes, or until pale, thick and doubled in bulk. Remove from the heat and continue to beat for 3 minutes.

Using a large metal spoon, gently fold in the sifted flours, followed by the cooled melted butter. Mix until just combined and there is no trace of white flour.

Spread the mixture evenly into the prepared tins and bake for 25–30 minutes, or until golden and firm to the touch. Leave to cool in the tins for 5 minutes, then turn out onto a wire rack to cool completely.

Spread the jam evenly over one of the cakes. Whip the cream and vanilla until soft peaks form, then spoon or pipe the cream over the jam. Top with the remaining cake. Dust with icing sugar.

It is important to fold in the flour and butter very gently. If you are too vigorous at this stage, you will lose a lot of volume in the egg mixture.

Serves 8

steak.

Choose a good cut of aged meat – either a New York cut, sirloin, T-bone, rump or fillet – about 2.5–3.5 cm (1–1½ in) thick. Allow about 200–250 g (6½–8 oz) per person. Have the butcher trim off the outer layer of fat.

1 × 200–250 g (6½–8 oz) steak | freshly ground black pepper
olive oil, to brush |

Brush one side of the steak with oil and give it a good grinding of black pepper.

Preheat a heavy-based cast-iron frying pan, grill plate or barbecue to very hot.

Sear the steak, oil-side down first, cooking for the desired time (see below). Brush with more oil, give it a good grinding of black pepper, turn the steak over and cook the other side.

Remove from the heat, wrap in foil and allow to rest for 5–10 minutes before serving. Serve with herb butter or mustard and a crisp green salad.

For a rare steak, cook 2–3 minutes each side. For medium, cook 3–4 minutes each side. For well done, cook 3 minutes each side, then turn down the heat and cook for 8–10 minutes, turning once.

To make herb butter, beat 1 chopped clove of garlic and 2 tablespoons of chopped fresh herbs with 100 g (3½ oz) of softened butter until combined. Roll into a log shape, cover with plastic wrap and refrigerate until firm. Cut into slices and serve on top of a hot steak.

Serves 1

steak sandwich.

1 × 150 g (5 oz) rump, chuck, New York cut
    or sirloin steak
olive oil
salt and freshly ground black pepper
1 small baguette, Turkish bread or ciabatta

knob of butter
Dijon mustard
small handful of rocket (arugula)
2 slices ripe tomato

Dry the piece of steak with kitchen paper, then flatten it to a thickness of about 5 mm (¼ in) by hitting it with a rolling pin or mallet, or with your fist.

Heat a heavy grill pan or frying pan to very hot. Brush the steak with a little oil and season well with salt and freshly ground black pepper. Add the steak to the pan and cook for about 1–2 minutes each side – this will give you a medium-done steak. Allow a little more or less cooking time depending on your taste.

Transfer the steak to a plate and let it rest, covered with foil, for about 5 minutes, turning it occasionally to coat it in its own meat juices.

Slice the baguette in half and spread it with a little butter and some Dijon mustard. Place the steak on the bottom half of the bread. Top with a handful of rocket and the slices of tomato. Drizzle with any meat juice from the resting plate and season well with more salt and freshly ground pepper. Top with the remaining bread and serve immediately.

Letting the steak rest after cooking allows the meat to relax, making it tender.

Use your favourite type of bread – I often make a steak sandwich with thick slices of good white Italian-style bread.

Serves 1

sticky date pudding.

175 g (6 oz) pitted dates, chopped

1 teaspoon bicarbonate of soda
(sodium bicarbonate)

60 g (2 oz) unsalted butter, softened

3/4 cup caster (superfine) sugar

2 eggs, lightly beaten

1 1/2 cups self-raising (self-rising) flour

1/2 teaspoon vanilla essence

SAUCE

125 g (4 oz) unsalted butter, cubed

3/4 cup lightly packed brown sugar

200 ml (6 1/2 fl oz) cream

Preheat the oven to 180°C (350°F, Gas Mark 4). Grease an 18 cm (7 in) square cake tin and line the base and sides with baking paper.

Place the dates in a bowl. Add the bicarbonate of soda and pour over 300 ml (9½ fl oz) of boiling water. Set aside.

Beat the softened butter and caster sugar until pale and fluffy. Add the beaten eggs, a bit at a time, beating well after each addition. Sift in the flour. Add the dates and their juice, then the vanilla. Mix well. This will be a wet mixture.

Pour into the prepared tin and bake for 35–45 minutes, or until risen and firm to touch. A skewer inserted in the centre should come out clean.

Meanwhile, make the sauce by placing the butter, brown sugar and cream in a small saucepan. Bring to the boil and simmer for 5 minutes.

Turn the pudding out of the tin and place on a baking tray. Pour one-third of the sauce over the pudding and return it to the oven for 5 minutes, or until golden and bubbling. This gives the pudding a delicious hot caramel topping.

Cut the pudding into squares and serve topped with the remaining sauce, plus cream or ice-cream.

Serves 6–8

strawberry flan.

1 quantity homemade regular shortcrust
    pastry (see page 290), or 1 × 380 g
    (12 oz) packet bought frozen shortcrust
    pastry, thawed
300 ml (9½ fl oz) cream
½ cup plain natural yoghurt

½ cup lightly packed brown sugar
500 g (1 lb) ripe strawberries, hulled and
    halved
2 tablespoons icing (confectioners') sugar
juice of ½ orange
1 teaspoon balsamic vinegar

Prepare the pastry according to the instructions on page 290.

Lightly grease a 21 cm (8½ in) loose-based fluted tart tin. Roll out the pastry between two sheets of baking paper until it is large enough to fit the tart tin. Line the tin with the pastry and trim the edges. Refrigerate for 15 minutes.

Preheat the oven to 200°C (400°F, Gas Mark 6).

Line the pastry case with baking paper. Half-fill the pastry case with pie weights, uncooked dried beans or rice. Bake for 10–15 minutes. Remove the weights and baking paper, return the tin to the oven and cook for a further 10 minutes, or until the pastry is dry and golden. Set aside to cool.

Whip the cream until soft peaks form, then stir in the yoghurt. Spoon the mixture into the tart shell – it should be about three-quarters full. Sprinkle the cream mixture with an even layer of brown sugar. Set aside for 30 minutes.

Meanwhile, place the strawberries in a bowl, sprinkle with the icing sugar and drizzle with the orange juice and balsamic vinegar.

Just before serving, fill the tart with a layer of strawberries.

You can replace the strawberries with any ripe summer fruit. Try a combination of peaches and raspberries, or mango and passionfruit.

Serves 8

strawberry fool.

Nothing could be simpler than this dessert – the perfect fool is just cream, fruit and sugar. Any crushed fruit can make a delicious fool, but soft fruits such as strawberries or raspberries are traditionally used.

250 g (8 oz) strawberries, hulled
2–3 tablespoons icing (confectioners')
  sugar

1 cup cream

Mash the strawberries with the icing sugar until soft and pulpy. (I prefer the slightly lumpy effect obtained by mashing the fruit and the sugar with a fork or potato masher; however, this can just as easily be pulsed in an electric blender.)

Whip the cream until soft peaks form. Stir the cream into the fruit mixture. Taste and add a little extra fruit if desired.

Pile into decorative glasses and chill. Serve accompanied with thin shortbread or wafers.

Although it doesn't dissolve as easily in the fruit, caster (superfine) sugar can be used in place of the icing sugar.

Equal quantities of strawberries and raspberries make a delicious combination.

Try making a fruit fool using the puréed flesh of 2 mangoes, or alternatively the pulp of 6 passionfruit and a squeeze of lime juice.

The addition of a tablespoon or two of plain yoghurt gives an interesting flavour, but you may need to add a little more sugar.

Serves 4

strawberry jam.

1.25 kg (2½ lb) sugar

1.5 kg (3 lb) strawberries, hulled

⅓ cup lemon juice

Preheat the oven to 140°C (275°F, Gas Mark 1).

Place the sugar in an ovenproof dish and warm for 10 minutes. Place clean jam jars in the oven to warm also. Put two saucers into the freezer to chill.

Place the strawberries, lemon juice, warm sugar and ½ cup of water into a large saucepan. Stir over low heat until the sugar has dissolved. Increase the heat and simmer gently for 20 minutes, stirring frequently. Skim off any scum that rises to the surface.

Remove from the heat. Drop 1 teaspoon of jam on one of the chilled saucers and return to the freezer for 1 minute. If the jam forms a skin and wrinkles when pushed with a fingertip, it has reached setting point. If not, continue to cook the mixture, testing every 5 minutes, until the jam reaches setting point. Remove from the heat and allow to stand for 15 minutes before bottling.

Spoon the jam into the warmed jars and allow to cool. Seal, label and date the jars. Store in a cool, dark place for up to 12 months.

Makes 6 cups

stuffed dates.

Plump fresh dates, with their sweet, sticky flesh, are ideal for stuffing. In this recipe, the bitter orange from the marmalade nicely balances out the sweetness of the fruit and chocolate.

12 fresh dates

3 tablespoons orange marmalade

12 whole blanched almonds

110 g (3½ oz) white chocolate

Make a slit in the side of each date and remove the stone.

Carefully spoon about a teaspoon of the marmalade into each date, being careful not to over-fill them. Insert a blanched almond into each slit.

Break the white chocolate into squares and melt it in a heatproof bowl set over a saucepan of hot water, stirring occasionally, until smooth. Remove the bowl from the heat and allow the chocolate to cool slightly. Dip half of each date into the chocolate, then leave to set on a wire rack.

Stuffed dates are delicious served with coffee at the end of dinner.

Makes 12

stuffed peaches.

4 ripe slipstone peaches

8 amaretti biscuits, crushed

30 g (1 oz) butter, chilled and chopped

2 tablespoons demerara sugar or raw sugar, plus extra to sprinkle

2 tablespoons flaked almonds

Preheat the oven to 180°C (350°F, Gas Mark 4). Peel the peaches, if desired, then cut in half and remove the stones.

Roughly combine the crushed biscuits, butter, sugar and flaked almonds.

Place the peach halves close together in a baking tin. Spoon an equal amount of the biscuit mixture into the centre of each peach half. Sprinkle with a little extra sugar.

Bake for 15 minutes, or until the peaches are tender and the biscuit mixture is crisp. Serve with vanilla ice-cream.

Amaretti are little crisp Italian biscuits, flavoured with almond. They are available from most large supermarkets and delicatessens.

Serves 4

summer pudding.

1 kg (2 lb) mixed berries (use a combination
   of raspberries, blackberries,
   blueberries, redcurrants or
   blackcurrants)

⅔ cup caster (superfine) sugar
10 thin slices stale white bread, crusts
   removed

Place the berries, sugar and ¼ cup of water in a saucepan. Bring to a gentle simmer over low heat and cook, stirring to dissolve the sugar, for about 3 minutes, or until the fruit has softened and produced lots of juice. Set aside to cool.

Pour the juice into a flat dish, reserving the fruit.

Cut one slice of bread into a circle small enough to fit the base of a 1.5 litre (48 fl oz) pudding basin, and another large enough to fit the top. Cut the remaining slices into triangles.

Dip both sides of the smaller circle of bread quickly into the juice and place it in the bottom of the basin. Dip both sides of each triangle of bread into the juice, then place around the inside of the basin, overlapping them slightly to make sure there are no gaps. Store any remaining juice in the refrigerator, to serve with the pudding.

Fill the basin with berries and cover with the larger circle of bread, trimming it if necessary. Cover the top of the pudding with plastic wrap and press in a saucer or small plate that just fits inside the rim of the basin. Weigh down the plate with a heavy can or two. Place the basin in a shallow dish to catch any juice that might overflow, and refrigerate for at least 12 hours.

To serve, run a thin knife around the inside of the bowl and invert the pudding onto a serving plate. Cut into wedges and serve accompanied with thick cream and any reserved juice.

Serves 8

sweet chilli sauce.

This versatile sauce goes well with chicken, seafood and meat. Although the recipe contains chillies, sugar is used to take the edge off the heat and give the sauce a pleasant and balanced taste.

³/₄ cup sugar	6 large red chillies, seeded
¹/₂ cup white vinegar	and roughly chopped
1 teaspoon salt	1 tablespoon grated fresh ginger
4 cloves garlic, crushed	1 teaspoon Thai fish sauce

Place the sugar, vinegar, salt and 1 cup of water in a small stainless-steel saucepan. Bring to the boil, stirring to dissolve the sugar, and simmer for 5 minutes.

Add the garlic, chillies and ginger to the saucepan. Simmer over medium heat, stirring frequently, for 15–20 minutes, or until reduced and thickened. Remove from the heat and stir through the fish sauce.

Pulse the mixture in a food processor or blender to produce a sauce with speckles of red chilli. Transfer to a clean, sterilised jar and seal. Serve at room temperature. The sauce can be stored in the refrigerator for up to 1 month.

Using large red chillies, which are milder than small ones, allows you to incorporate enough chilli to achieve a good red-coloured sauce. Add a small red chilli if you prefer the sauce a little hotter.

Makes 1 cup

sweetcorn and chicken soup.

1.75 litres (55 fl oz) chicken stock (see
    page 68) or vegetable stock
3 cobs of corn
1 tablespoon cornflour (cornstarch)
150 ml (4½ fl oz) cream

2 tablespoons dry sherry
2 skinless chicken breasts, finely chopped
salt and freshly ground black pepper
2 tablespoons shredded spring onions
    (scallions)

Bring the stock to the boil in a large saucepan. Add the corn and simmer for 8–10 minutes, or until tender.

Remove the corn from the saucepan, leaving the cooking water in the pan.

Allow the corn to cool enough to handle, then, using a sharp knife, cut the kernels from the cobs.

Place half the kernels back into the saucepan with the reserved cooking liquid. Place the remaining kernels with the cornflour and cream in a food processor and purée until smooth. Transfer to the saucepan and bring to a gentle simmer over medium heat, stirring frequently. Add the sherry and chicken. Stir over medium heat for 5–10 minutes, or until the chicken is cooked. Season to taste with salt and lots of freshly ground black pepper. Serve garnished with the shredded spring onions.

A nice touch is to add a dash of soy sauce to the soup just before serving. It is also good with a drizzle of sesame oil in each bowl.

Serves 4

swiss roll.

4 eggs

½ cup caster (superfine) sugar

1 teaspoon vanilla essence

⅔ cup plain (all-purpose) flour

50 g (1¾ oz) ground almonds (almond meal)

1 teaspoon baking powder

caster (superfine) sugar, extra, to sprinkle

⅓ cup raspberry jam

Preheat the oven to 200°C (400°F, Gas Mark 6). Grease a 20 × 30 cm (8 × 12 in) Swiss roll tin and line the base with baking paper, leaving a little paper overhanging along the two long sides.

Combine the eggs, sugar and vanilla in a large mixing bowl. Whisk with a hand-held electric mixer for 3–4 minutes, or until the mixture is frothy and pale and has increased in volume – the beaters should leave a trail when lifted out of the mixture.

Sift the flour into the bowl and add the ground almonds and baking powder. Using a large metal spoon, gently fold the dry ingredients into the egg mixture until just combined.

Pour the mixture into the prepared tin and tap the tin gently to distribute the batter into the corners. Bake for 10–15 minutes, or until golden and firm to the touch – the cake should have just begun to shrink from the edges of the tin.

Using the overhanging baking paper, turn the cake out onto a piece of baking paper that has been generously sprinkled with caster sugar. Peel off the baking paper from the cooked cake. With the help of the sugared baking paper, roll up the cake from the short end. Let the roll sit for 10 minutes, then unroll it. Trim the edges of the cake and spread evenly with the jam, then re-roll. Transfer to a serving plate.

It is important to fold in the flour and almonds very gently. If you are too vigorous at this stage, you will lose a lot of the volume in the egg mixture.

terrine.

500 g (1 lb) rashers streaky bacon

25 g (³/₄ oz) butter

1 onion, chopped

2 cloves garlic, chopped

750 g (1¹/₂ lb) minced (ground) pork

350 g (11 oz) rindless boned pork belly, finely chopped

250 g (8 oz) chicken livers, finely chopped

100 g (3¹/₂ oz) pistachio nuts

¹/₃ cup brandy

2 tablespoons chopped rosemary

2 tablespoons chopped thyme

2 tablespoons snipped fresh chives

6 juniper berries, crushed

2 teaspoons salt

1¹/₂ teaspoons freshly ground black pepper

Preheat the oven to 170°C (340°F, Gas Mark 3). Lightly grease a 1.5 litre (48 fl oz) terrine or loaf tin. Line the tin horizontally with three quarters of the bacon rashers, overlapping each rasher slightly and leaving 5 cm overhanging the tin.

Melt the butter in a frying pan over low heat. Add the onion and garlic and cook until soft and just coloured. Transfer to a large bowl. Chop the remaining bacon and add it to the onion mixture. Add the remaining ingredients and mix well.

Spoon the mixture into the prepared terrine dish, pushing the mixture down and levelling the top. Fold over the overlapping bacon. Cover the dish with a lid or with foil and place in a deep baking tin. Pour enough boiling water into the baking tin to come halfway up the side of the terrine. Bake for 1½ hours.

Remove the terrine dish from the baking tin and allow to cool.

Meanwhile, cut out a piece of cardboard that fits the inside rim of the dish and cover it with foil. Place it on top of the terrine and place a few unopened cans on top. Weigh down the terrine overnight in the refrigerator.

Turn the terrine out of the dish and thickly slice. Serve with bread and chutney.

Serves 10–12

thai beef salad.

Thai salads are a combination of opposing tastes and textures – crisp salad leaves, soft noodles and a sweet–sour sauce. Use these principles to create your own combinations.

500 g (1 lb) beef fillet or rump

85 g (3 oz) cellophane noodles

1 small cucumber, peeled and diced

250 g (8 oz) mixed salad leaves

DRESSING

2 tablespoons Thai fish sauce

2 tablespoons lime juice

1 tablespoon soy sauce

1 teaspoon vegetable oil

2 small red chillies, seeded
and finely chopped

2 teaspoons soft brown sugar or palm sugar

Cook the beef in a hot frying pan or grill pan for 2–3 minutes each side, or until cooked to your liking. Allow to cool.

Place the cellophane noodles in a heatproof bowl and cover with boiling water. Leave for 6–7 minutes, or until soft. Drain well and cut into 3 cm (1¼ in) lengths.

Place the dressing ingredients in a screw-top jar and shake well to combine.

Slice the beef thinly.

To serve, mix together the cucumber and salad leaves and place on a large platter or in a large bowl. Top with the noodles and slices of beef. Pour over the dressing.

If time permits, brush the beef with a pounded mixture of 2 garlic cloves, 3 coriander roots, a squeeze of lime juice and 2 tablespoons of vegetable oil. Marinate for 20 minutes before cooking.

The beef may be substituted with lamb fillets, chicken fillets or baby squid.

Serves 4

thai green curry paste.

8 long green chillies, seeded and sliced

1 small onion or shallot, roughly chopped

5 cloves garlic, peeled and roughly chopped

1 large handful coriander (cilantro), stems
and leaves

2 stems lemongrass, lower part of stem
crushed and sliced

1 × 5 cm (2 in) piece fresh ginger, peeled
and roughly chopped

3 kaffir lime leaves, shredded

2 teaspoons coriander seeds

1 teaspoon cumin seeds

1 teaspoon sea salt

1 teaspoon freshly ground black pepper

1 tablespoon Thai fish sauce

2–3 tablespoons sunflower or peanut oil

Place the chilli, onion, garlic, coriander stems and leaves, lemongrass, ginger, kaffir lime leaves, coriander seeds, cumin seeds, salt, pepper and fish sauce into a food processor or blender. Add 1 tablespoon of the oil and process. With the machine still running, pour in enough extra oil in a thin stream for the mixture to form a smooth paste. Store, covered with a little extra oil, in a screw-top jar in the refrigerator for up to 1 month.

Makes about 1 cup

thai-style chicken salad.

3 skinless chicken breasts

1 tablespoon peanut oil

salt and freshly ground black pepper

$\frac{1}{3}$ cup raw unsalted peanuts

100 g (3$\frac{1}{2}$ oz) rice vermicelli (cellophane)
    noodles

1 Lebanese cucumber, peeled and diced

250 g (8 oz) mixed salad leaves

1 cup coriander (cilantro) sprigs

DRESSING

2 tablespoons Thai fish sauce

2 tablespoons lime juice

1 tablespoon soy sauce

1 teaspoon peanut oil

2 small red chillies, seeded and finely
    chopped

2 teaspoons brown sugar or palm sugar

Flatten the chicken breasts to a thickness of about 5 mm (¼ in) by hitting them with a rolling pin or mallet, or with your fist.

Heat a large frying pan over high heat. Brush each breast with a little oil and season well with salt and freshly ground black pepper. Place in the pan and cook for 3–4 minutes each side, or until cooked. Remove from the pan and set aside. Add the peanuts to the pan and cook, stirring, until golden. Set aside.

Place the noodles in a heatproof bowl and cover with boiling water. Leave for 6–7 minutes, or until soft. Drain well and cut into 3 cm (1¼ in) lengths.

Place the dressing ingredients in a screw-top jar and shake well to combine.

Slice the chicken into 1 cm (½ in) strips.

To serve, mix together the cucumber, salad leaves, coriander sprigs and noodles and place on a large platter or in a large bowl. Top with the chicken. Pour over the dressing and scatter with the peanuts.

Serves 4

thai-style prawn broth.

1 kg (2 lb) uncooked medium-sized
    prawns (shrimp)
2 stems lemongrass, sliced
2 kaffir lime leaves, finely sliced
2 cloves garlic, chopped
1 teaspoon grated fresh ginger
2 tablespoons chopped coriander
    (cilantro) stems
2 large red chillies, seeded and sliced

1 litre (32 fl oz) fish stock or chicken stock
    (see page 68)
250 g (8 oz) fresh rice noodles
6 spring onions (scallions), sliced
1 tablespoon Thai fish sauce
2–3 tablespoons lime juice
2 cups bean sprouts
salt and freshly ground black pepper
    (optional)
$\frac{1}{3}$ cup fresh coriander (cilantro) leaves

Peel and devein the prawns, leaving the tails intact. Set aside.

Place the prawn heads and shells in a large saucepan with the lemongrass, lime leaves, garlic, ginger, coriander stems and half the chilli. Add the stock and 2 cups of water and bring to the boil. Reduce the heat and simmer for 15 minutes. Strain and discard the solids.

Return the broth to the saucepan and bring to the boil over medium heat. Add the noodles and simmer for 5 minutes, or until soft.

Add the prawns, spring onions, fish sauce, lime juice and the remaining chilli. Cook for 2 minutes, or until the prawns turn pink. Add the bean sprouts.

Taste the broth and add extra fish sauce, lime juice, salt or pepper as desired. Serve immediately, garnished with the coriander leaves.

Serves 4

tiramisu.

3 eggs, separated

⅓ cup caster (superfine) sugar

300 ml (9½ fl oz) mascarpone

1½ cups strong black coffee, at room
    temperature

¼ cup brandy or coffee-flavoured liqueur

16–20 Savoiardi biscuits

100 g (3½ oz) dark chocolate, grated

1 tablespoon cocoa, sifted

Beat the egg yolks and sugar together in a bowl with a hand-held beater or whisk for 3 minutes, or until pale and thick. Gradually fold in the mascarpone.

Using a clean, dry bowl, whisk the egg whites with clean beaters until stiff peaks form. Fold the whites into the mascarpone mixture.

Mix together the coffee and brandy and pour into a flat-bottomed bowl. Using eight of the Savoiardi biscuits, dip each one into the coffee for a few seconds. They will rapidly absorb the coffee, so only a very quick dip is needed. Do not let them become soggy. Line the base of a 1-litre capacity deep ceramic dish with the biscuits – they should sit evenly next to each other. Use a few extra biscuits if your dish is larger.

Cover the biscuits with half the mascarpone mixture. Repeat with a layer of coffee-soaked biscuits and cover with the remaining mascarpone. Cover with plastic wrap and refrigerate for at least 4 hours.

Just before serving, combine the grated chocolate and cocoa and sprinkle over the tiramisu.

Savoiardi or sponge-finger biscuits are dry, light, finger-shaped biscuits. They are available from larger supermarkets and delicatessens.

Tiramisu is also good made in a large glass bowl – a bit like a trifle.

Serves 6

tomato relish.

This relish is deliciously spicy and easy to make. I love it served alongside sausages, cold meats or cheese. A dollop on a cheese sandwich is perfect.

1 kg (2 lb) ripe tomatoes

1 large onion, finely chopped

2 cloves garlic, crushed

2 small red chillies, sliced

1 cup lightly packed brown sugar

1 cup red wine vinegar

$\frac{1}{3}$ cup olive oil

1 teaspoon ground ginger

1 teaspoon ground cumin

1 teaspoon curry powder

salt and freshly ground black pepper

Preheat the oven to 140°C (275°F, Gas Mark 1).

Place clean jam jars in the oven to warm.

Meanwhile, halve the tomatoes and remove the seeds. Roughly chop the tomatoes and place in a saucepan with the remaining ingredients except the salt and pepper. Bring to the boil, reduce the heat and simmer gently, stirring occasionally, for 50–60 minutes, or until the relish is thick, pulpy and jam-like. Season well with salt and freshly ground black pepper.

Pour the relish into warm jam jars and allow to cool. Seal when cold. Store in the fridge for 1 month.

Makes 3 cups

tomato sauce for pasta (pomodoro).

2 tablespoons olive oil

2 onions, chopped

3 cloves garlic, chopped

2 × 400 g (13 oz) cans chopped tomatoes

1 tablespoon sugar

2 tablespoons tomato paste

2 tablespoons finely chopped basil

Heat the oil in a large saucepan over medium heat and sauté the onions and garlic for 5 minutes. Add the tomatoes and sugar and bring to the boil. Reduce the heat and simmer gently, stirring occasionally, for 20 minutes, or until soft and pulpy.

Stir in the tomato paste and basil. Serve as is, or as a purée if you prefer a smoother consistency.

Instead of canned tomatoes you can use 1 kg (2 lb) of peeled, ripe tomatoes.

Serves 4

tomato soup.

Tomato soup is an all-time favourite – worthy of serving as a simple
Sunday-night meal for family, or as a starter at a fine dinner party for friends.

2 tablespoons olive oil

1 onion, chopped

1 carrot, chopped

1 stick celery, chopped

2 cloves garlic, chopped

750 g (1½ lb) ripe tomatoes, quartered

1 × 400 g (13 oz) can chopped tomatoes

1 litre (32 fl oz) chicken stock (see page 68)
     or vegetable stock

salt and freshly ground black pepper

1 tablespoon chopped basil, to garnish

extra-virgin olive oil, to garnish

Heat the oil in a large saucepan. Sauté the onion, carrot, celery and garlic for 5 minutes, then add the fresh tomatoes and cook for 3–4 minutes.

Add the canned tomatoes, stock and 1 cup of water. Bring to the boil, reduce the heat and simmer for 30 minutes.

Remove from the heat and allow to cool a little. Purée the soup in batches in a blender or with a hand-held blender.

Season to taste with salt and freshly ground black pepper.

Serve hot, garnished with chopped basil and a drizzle of extra-virgin olive oil.

Use the best ripe red tomatoes you can find. If the tomatoes lack flavour, add 1 tablespoon of tomato paste.

For a richer version, serve drizzled with a little cream or a dollop of sour cream.

Serves 4

tuna pâté.

2 × 200 g (6½ oz) cans tuna in oil, drained

75 g (2½ oz) butter, softened

125 g (4 oz) cream cheese, softened

juice of 1 lemon

¼ cup snipped fresh chives

2 tablespoons chopped parsley

1 teaspoon Dijon mustard

sea salt and freshly ground black pepper

Place all the ingredients except the salt and pepper in a food processor and, using the pulse action, process the mixture in short bursts until just combined. Season well with sea salt and freshly ground black pepper. Taste and add extra lemon juice, if desired. Serve with crusty bread or crackers.

Makes about 1 cup

upside-down pear cake.

50 g unsalted butter, melted

½ cup raw sugar or demerara sugar

3 large ripe pears, peeled, cored and
   quartered

1½ cups self-raising (self-rising) flour

1 teaspoon ground ginger

salt

1 cup brown sugar

3 eggs, lightly beaten

½ cup milk

175 g unsalted diced butter, extra, softened
   at room temperature

2 tablespoons golden syrup

Preheat the oven to 180°C (350°F, Gas Mark 4). Lightly grease the sides of a 26 cm (10½ in) springform cake tin.

Pour the melted butter into the cake tin and sprinkle over the raw sugar. Arrange the pear quarters, cut-side up, in the base of the cake tin.

Sift the flour, ginger, a pinch of salt and brown sugar into a mixing bowl. Add the eggs, milk, butter and golden syrup and beat with a wooden spoon or electric beater on a low speed until the mixture is combined.

Pour the batter over the pears in the cake tin. Bake for 60 minutes, or until a skewer inserted into the centre of the cake comes out clean. Leave to cool for 15 minutes before turning out onto a wire rack to cool completely.

Halved and cored plums, or peeled, cored and chopped apples, or sliced pineapple rings all make good substitutes for the pears.

Serves 8–10

vanilla bean ice-cream.

2 cups milk

1 vanilla bean

6 egg yolks

125 g (4 oz) caster (superfine) sugar

1 cup cream, lightly whipped

Pour the milk into a small saucepan.

Using a sharp knife, split the vanilla bean in half lengthways. Scrape out the seeds and add the pod and the seeds to the saucepan of milk. Bring the mixture to simmering point over low heat.

In a large mixing bowl, whisk together the egg yolks and sugar for 4–5 minutes, or until the sugar has dissolved and the mixture is thick and pale. Gently whisk the hot milk mixture, including the vanilla bean pod, into the yolk mixture.

Return this mixture to the saucepan and cook over low heat, stirring constantly with a wooden spoon, until the mixture thickens slightly and coats the back of the spoon. Do not allow the mixture to boil or it will curdle. Remove from the heat and strain into a bowl, discarding the bean pod. Set aside to cool.

When cold, whisk in the whipped cream. Churn in an ice-cream machine until firm.

Before serving, soften the ice-cream by placing in the fridge for 15 minutes.

Serves 4–6

vegetarian lasagne.

2 tablespoons olive oil

250 g (8 oz) cherry tomatoes, halved

2 cloves garlic, crushed

3 × 400 g (13 oz) cans crushed tomatoes

salt and freshly ground black pepper

½ cup roughly torn basil leaves

500 g (1 lb) ricotta

2 eggs, lightly beaten

½ cup cream

pinch of ground nutmeg

1 cup coarsely grated parmesan

450 g (14 oz) button mushrooms, sliced

150 g (5 oz) baby English spinach leaves

10–12 sheets dried lasagne

1 cup grated mozzarella

Heat half the oil in a large saucepan over medium heat. Add the cherry tomatoes, garlic and crushed tomatoes and simmer for 30 minutes. Season, add the basil and set aside.

In a bowl, combine the ricotta, eggs, cream, nutmeg and half the parmesan.

Heat the remaining oil in a large saucepan and sauté the mushrooms for 5–6 minutes. Add the spinach and cook for 1–2 minutes, or until the spinach has just softened. Set aside.

Cook the lasagne sheets, two at a time, in a large saucepan of boiling salted water for 30 seconds. Remove and refresh by placing in a bowl of iced water for 2 minutes. Drain well on a clean tea towel.

Preheat the oven to 180°C (350°F, Gas Mark 4). Grease a 25.5 × 18 × 5 cm (10 × 7 × 2 in) ceramic lasagne dish.

Line the dish with a layer of pasta. Cover with half of the tomato sauce and top with half of the mozzarella. Cover with another layer of pasta, then spread over the mushroom mixture and top with half the ricotta mixture. Add another layer of pasta, then the remaining tomato sauce, mozzarella, ricotta and remaining parmesan, seasoning each layer. Bake for 1 hour, or until golden. Leave to rest for 10 minutes before serving.

Serves 6

victoria sponge.

A perfectly made Victoria sponge is a fine thing indeed. This recipe is from British writer Katie Stewart, whose recipes are not only delicious and reliable, but always inspired and generous with information. I return time and time again to her *Times* cookbook (now sadly out of print).

175 g (6 oz) unsalted butter, softened

175 g (6 oz) caster (superfine) sugar

3 large eggs, at room temperature

½ teaspoon vanilla essence

175 g (6 oz) self-raising (self-rising) flour, sifted

3–4 tablespoons fruit jam (apricot, raspberry, strawberry or plum), to fill

icing (confectioners') sugar, to dust

Preheat the oven to 180°C (350°F, Gas Mark 4). Grease 2 × 19 cm (7½ in) shallow round cake tins and line the base of each with baking paper.

In a bowl, beat the butter and sugar with a hand-held electric beater until pale and fluffy – about 8 minutes.

In a separate bowl, beat the eggs and vanilla with a fork. Add the egg mixture to the butter mixture a little at a time, beating well with the electric beater after each addition. Towards the end, if the mixture looks like it is separating, add a little of the flour with the last amount of egg.

Using a large metal spoon, gently fold in half the flour. Fold in the remaining flour until combined – the mixture should drop from the spoon if given a slight shake. Spoon the mixture evenly into the prepared tins and level the tops. Bake for 20–25 minutes, or until golden and springy to the touch. Allow to cool in the tins for 2 minutes, then turn out onto a wire rack to cool completely.

Spread the jam evenly over one of the cakes, then top with the remaining cake. Dust with icing sugar.

vietnamese dipping sauce.

Few tables in southeast Asia are without a little dish of this Vietnamese chilli dipping sauce known as nuoc cham. It is used as a dip for spring rolls and crudités, and to add flavour and heat to noodle and rice dishes. The flavour should be a balance of sweet, sour, salt, chilli and garlic.

¼ cup fish sauce

1 tablespoon white vinegar

2 tablespoons lime juice

2 teaspoons palm sugar or soft brown sugar

2 large red chillies, seeded and thinly sliced

2 cloves garlic, finely chopped

½ small carrot, coarsely grated (optional)

Combine the fish sauce, vinegar, lime juice and 1 tablespoon of water in a small bowl. Add the sugar and stir to dissolve. Add the chillies and garlic. A coarsely grated carrot is often added to give the sauce crunch. Stir well and serve immediately.

As a variation, try adding 1–2 teaspoons of chopped fresh coriander (cilantro) leaves or 1 sliced spring onion (scallion).

Remember, there are no fixed rules with this sauce. Taste as you go and adjust the balance of flavours to suit you.

Nuoc cham is best made just prior to serving. If made ahead, the chilli flavour can often dominate.

Makes ¾ cup

vinaigrette.

A vinaigrette is simply a combination of oil and vinegar, held together with a little Dijon mustard and seasoned with salt and pepper. The classic proportion for a vinaigrette is one part vinegar (or an acidic juice such as lemon juice) to three parts oil.

2 tablespoons vinegar or lemon juice	½ cup olive oil
1 teaspoon Dijon mustard	salt and freshly ground black pepper

Place the vinegar or lemon juice, mustard and olive oil in a screw-top jar. Season well with salt and freshly ground black pepper. Put the lid on the jar and shake well to combine. The vinaigrette will keep for 4–5 days in the fridge.

Vary the types of oil and vinegar you use. When choosing the oil and vinegar, remember they should complement each other. The rich texture and fruity taste of extra-virgin olive oil is well balanced by balsamic vinegar, whereas nut oils are good teamed with fruit vinegars. Chilli- or herb-flavoured oils are balanced by the use of wine vinegars or lemon juice.

The oil and vinegar will separate on standing, so store in a screw-top jar and shake well just before adding to a salad.

Use crushed garlic, chopped fresh chilli or chopped fresh herbs to add variety to the vinaigrette.

Makes ½ cup

watermelon and lime granita.

A granita is a frozen grainy water ice made from lightly sweetened fruit syrup. It's delicious on a hot summer's day.

½ cup sugar

2 cups puréed watermelon flesh

2 tablespoons lime juice

Combine the sugar and ½ cup of water in a small saucepan. Bring to the boil over medium heat, stirring to dissolve the sugar. Allow to cool.

Combine the watermelon purée and the lime juice with the cool syrup. Pour into a shallow container, cover and freeze for 1 hour, or until the purée around the edge of the tray is frozen. Break up the crystals with a fork using a scraping action. Return to the freezer and repeat the scraping procedure every 45 minutes, or until you have a glistening mass of smooth ice crystals. This can take 2−3 hours.

Ideally the granita should be eaten at once, but it may be poured into a storage container, covered with greaseproof paper and returned to the freezer. To serve, soften the mixture in the fridge for 10−15 minutes, then stir again with a fork to break up the ice crystals. Serve within 1−2 days, in tall glasses with long spoons.

If you have stored the granita overnight, you will need to soften, scrape with a fork and refreeze it again before serving.

To achieve the perfect granita, there is no substitute for the fork technique.

Serves 4

yoghurt cheese.

This is a simple soft cheese with a lovely creamy texture – a little like cream cheese – which can be easily made at home. Yoghurt gives it a nice tang.

1 litre (32 fl oz) plain natural yoghurt | **1 teaspoon salt**

Line a sieve or colander with a large square of damp muslin. Stir the salt into the yoghurt and pour the yoghurt into the lined sieve. Tie the muslin with string to form a bag, then hang the yoghurt from a shelf in the refrigerator, placing a bowl underneath to catch the draining liquid. Leave for 24–48 hours.

Remove from the refrigerator and roll the cheese into walnut-sized balls. Store in the refrigerator and eat within a couple of days.

Adding herbs to the finished cheese is a delicious variation. Stir in 1–2 tablespoons of chives, basil or parsley and some extra salt or pepper if needed.

Yoghurt cheese is delicious served alongside fresh or poached fruit. Leave out the salt from the original mixture and serve sweetened with a little sugar or honey.

To store the cheese for a week or so, transfer the balls to a screw-top jar and pour over enough olive oil to cover. You can add a sprig of rosemary, some chopped herbs or 1 crushed clove of garlic to the jar to flavour the cheese, if desired.

Makes 8–10 balls

yoghurt cream.

I make this simple dessert more than any other – the results are delicious and the effort is minimal. It can be served either as an accompaniment to fruit (both fresh and cooked), or as part of a topping for fresh fruit. It is best made at least 3 hours in advance to allow the sugar to 'melt'.

300 ml (9½ fl oz) cream
100 ml (3½ fl oz) plain natural yoghurt

½ cup lightly packed brown sugar

Pour the cream into a medium-sized bowl and beat with a whisk or hand-held electric mixer until it forms soft peaks. Stir through the yoghurt. Transfer to a 3-cup-capacity deep dish (the cream should be at least 5 cm (2 in) deep) and smooth the surface.

Sprinkle the top with an even layer of brown sugar, covering the yoghurt cream completely – this may take a little extra sugar, depending on the size of the dish.

Place in the refrigerator for 3–4 hours. You will end up with a softly set yoghurt and cream mixture with a runny 'caramel' topping.

Yoghurt cream is delicious served with grilled peaches.

I make a 'cheat's fruit brûlée' by putting a layer of fruit (berries or freshly sliced mango work well) in the base of the dish before adding the yoghurt cream and brown sugar.

The cream is also delicious flavoured with a little vanilla.

yorkshire puddings.

Traditionally served with roast beef, Yorkshire pudding
is a speciality from the north of England.

2 cups plain (all-purpose) flour

½ teaspoon salt

3 eggs, lightly beaten

2 cups milk

oil, dripping or lard

Sift the flour and salt into a mixing bowl. Make a well in the centre and add the beaten eggs. Mix with a wooden spoon and gradually add the milk, beating until smooth.

Leave the batter to rest for at least 1 hour.

Preheat the oven to 220°C (425°F, Gas Mark 7).

Use individual Yorkshire pudding tins or muffin tins. Put ½ teaspoon of oil, dripping or lard into each individual tin. Place in the oven for 5 minutes, or until the fat is very hot and smoking.

Pour the batter evenly into the tins, return to the oven and cook on the top shelf for 15–20 minutes, or until risen and golden. Don't be tempted to open the oven before they're ready, otherwise they will collapse.

Resting the batter is crucial. It allows the starch in the flour to swell, which bursts when it hits the hot oil, giving a light texture.

For perfect timing when cooking a roast, allow the meat to cook and then remove from the oven. Increase the heat and cook the puddings while the meat is resting.

You can make one large Yorkshire pudding in a roasting tin, if you like. In this case, spoon 2 tablespoons of oil, dripping or lard into the tin to heat. Pour in the batter and cook for 35–40 minutes, or until risen and golden.

Makes 12

zabaglione.

Zabaglione is an Italian-style custard made with egg yolks, sugar and marsala.
It is usually eaten warm from small glasses and is delicious accompanied with thin,
sweet biscuits, sponge fingers or sprinkled with crumbled amaretti biscuits.

4 eggs	**grated zest of ½ lemon**
⅓ cup caster (superfine) sugar	**100 ml (3½ fl oz) marsala**

Place the eggs, sugar and lemon zest in a bowl. Whisk by hand (if you are feeling strong) or with a hand-held electric beater until pale and frothy.

Place the bowl over a saucepan half-filled with hot water – make sure the bowl doesn't touch the water. Place the saucepan over low heat. Slowly whisk in the marsala, then continue to whisk for a further 5 minutes, or until the mixture is warm, frothy, mousse-like and doubled in volume. Be careful that the mixture doesn't boil or it will curdle and the eggs will start to scramble. If it is becoming too hot, remove from the heat for a moment and continue to whisk until it cools slightly.

Serve warm in small glasses.

Marsala is a sweet fortified wine made in Sicily. It is traditional to use marsala for zabaglione, but a sweet dessert wine can be used instead.

Zabaglione is delicious poured over sliced ripe strawberries, berries or peaches.

Zabaglione can also be chilled for several hours and served cold.

Serves 4

conversions.

All cup and spoon measurements are level.

I use 60 g (2 oz, grade 3) eggs.

All recipes were tested using a regular convection oven. If you are using a fan-forced oven, set your oven temperature to approximately 20°C (70°F) lower than is recommended in the recipe.

Cup conversions

1 cup uncooked arborio rice = 220 g (7 oz)
1 cup uncooked basmati/long-grain rice = 200 g (6 ½ oz)
1 cup sugar = 250 g (8 oz)
1 cup brown sugar = 185 g (6 oz)
1 cup caster (superfine) sugar = 250 g (8 oz)
1 cup icing (confectioners') sugar = 250 g (8 oz)
1 cup fresh breadcrumbs = 80 g (2 ½ oz)
1 cup plain or self-raising (self-rising) flour = 150g (5 oz)
1 cup cornflour (cornstarch) = 150 g (5 oz)
1 cup grated cheddar = 125 g (4 oz)
1 cup grated mozzarella = 150 g (5 oz)
1 cup grated parmesan = 100 g (3 ½ oz)

Liquid conversions

metric	imperial	standard cups
30 ml	1 fl oz	2 tablespoons
60 ml	2 fl oz	¼ cup
80 ml	2¾ fl oz	⅓ cup
125 ml	4 fl oz	½ cup
185 ml	6 fl oz	¾ cup
250 ml	8 fl oz	1 cup

Dry measurements

metric	imperial
15 g	½ oz
30 g	1 oz
45 g	1 ½ oz
55 g	2 oz
125 g	4 oz
150 g	5 oz
200 g	6½ oz
225 g	7 oz
250 g	8 oz
500 g	1 lb
1 kg	2 lb

Oven temperatures

Celcius	Fahrenheit	Gas Mark
120°C very slow	250°F	1
150°C slow	300°F	2
160°C warm	315°F	2–3
180°C moderate	350°F	4
190°C moderately hot	375°F	5
200°C moderately hot	400°F	6
220°C hot	425°F	7
230°C very hot	450°F	8
240°C very hot	475°F	9

index.

affogato 2

almond bread 4

anzac biscuits 5

apples

    apple and cinnamon teacake 6

    apple pie 7

    apple tart 8

    baked apples 16

    braised pork chops with apple 38

    rhubarb and apple crumble 258

    spiced apple sauce 303

apricot jam 10

apricot turnovers 11

asian-style coleslaw 93

asparagus 12

    asparagus risotto 14

aubergine *see* eggplant

bacon, leek and barley soup 15

baked apples 16

baked custard 18

baked eggs 20

baked ricotta 21

banana bread 22

banana smoothie 24

bang bang chicken 25

barbecue sauce 26

batter, beer 30

beef

    beef casserole 29

    beef and mushroom pie 28

    bolognese sauce 36

    hamburgers 150

    roast beef fillet 264

    steak 310

    steak sandwich 312

    thai beef salad 330

beer batter 30

beetroot, roast 265

berry friands 128

bircher muesli 31

biscotti 32

biscuits

    anzac biscuits 5

    biscotti 32

    cheese biscuits 50

    chocolate chip cookies 76

    chocolate cookies 77

    gingerbread biscuits 140

    orange biscuits 208

    peanut biscuits 224

    shortbread 288

    see also slices

blueberry muffins 200

boiled eggs 34

bolognese sauce 36

braised pork chops with apple 38

brandy butter 39

brandy crème anglaise 100

bread

    banana bread 22

    bread 40

    bruschetta 44

    damper 110

    focaccia 122

    garlic bread 135

    rosemary focaccia 122

    see also toast

bread and butter pudding 42

bread sauce 43

brownies

    chocolate 72

    orange and macadamia brownies 72

bruschetta 44

butter

    brandy butter 39

    garlic butter 135

    herb butter 310

    maître d'hôtel butter 182

caesar salad 46

cakes

    apple and cinnamon teacake 6

    carrot cake 47

    chocolate cake 74

    chocolate cake (flourless) 75

    chocolate peanut butter cake 83

    cupcakes 104

    friands 128

    fruit cake 132

    ginger cake 139

    lamingtons 164

    lemon cake 168

    madeleines 180

    orange cupcakes 104

    orange poppy seed cake 210

    orange semolina cake 211

    spice cake 302

    sponge cake (genoise) 309

    syrup cake 139

    swiss roll 327

    upside-down pear cake 341

    victoria sponge 346

capsicum, roast 266

carrot cake 47

carrot salad 48

casseroles

    beef casserole 29

    chicken casserole with peas and pancetta 56

    chicken pot roast 66

cheese

    baked ricotta 21

    cheese biscuits 50

    cheese and chive dumplings 112

    cheese scones 284

    cheese soufflés 52

    feta, cheddar and chive muffins 115

    macaroni cheese 179

    yoghurt cheese 351

cheesecake 54

cherries, poached 234

chicken

    bang bang chicken 25

    chicken cacciatore 55

    chicken casserole with peas and pancetta 56

    chicken curry 57

    chicken, lemon and rocket risotto 58

    chicken liver pâté 60

    chicken noodle soup 62

    chicken pie 64

    chicken pot roast 66

    chicken stock 68

    chinese-style braised chicken 71

    lemon chicken 169

    portuguese chicken 228

    roast chicken 268

    spiced moroccan chicken 304

    sweetcorn and chicken soup 326

    thai-style chicken salad 332

chilli

    chilli oil 69

    chilli sauce 70

    piri piri sauce 228

    spaghetti with crab and chilli 296

spaghetti with garlic, chilli and oil 298

sweet chilli sauce 324

chinese-style braised chicken 71

chocolate

chocolate brownies 72

chocolate cake 74

chocolate cake (flourless) 75

chocolate chip cookies 76

chocolate cookies 77

chocolate fondant puddings 78

chocolate ganache 79

chocolate icing 82

chocolate macaroons 79

chocolate mousse 80

chocolate muffins 82

chocolate peanut butter cake 83

chocolate puddings 84

chocolate sauce 85

chocolate truffles 86

cocoa 91

hot chocolate 156

mocha 198

orange and macadamia brownies 72

tiramisu 334

christmas pudding 88

chutneys and relishes

mango chutney 184

onion marmalade 206

tomato relish 336

cinnamon toast 90

cocktail sauce 248

cocoa 91

coconut fish curry 92

coffee

affogato 2

mocha 198

tiramisu 334

coleslaw 93

asian-style coleslaw 93

conversions 357

cordial

orange cordial 209

raspberry cordial 253

corn

corn on the cob 94

creamed corn 99

sweetcorn and chicken soup 326

corned beef (silverside) 96

coulis

mango coulis 254

raspberry coulis 254

couscous 97

couscous salad 97

cranberry sauce 98

cream cheese icing 47

cream, yoghurt 351

creamed corn 99

crème anglaise 100

crème brûlée 102

crêpes with lemon and sugar 103

crumble, rhubarb and apple 258

cupcakes 104

orange cupcakes 104

curd

lemon curd 170

orange curd 170

passionfruit curd 170

curries

chicken curry 57

coconut fish curry 92

curry powder 106

indian-style lamb curry 158

thai green curry paste 331

custard 108

baked custard 18

crème anglaise 100
crème brûlée 102
portuguese custard tarts 243
zabaglione 354

damper 110
dates
sticky date pudding 313
stuffed dates 318
dipping sauce 127
vietnamese dipping sauce 248
dips
eggplant dip 113
guacamole 148
hummus 157
dressings
mayonnaise 192
mustard dressing 142
mustard mayonnaise 96
salsa verde 237
vinaigrette 349
drinks
banana smoothie 24
cocoa 91
hot chocolate 156
lemonade 178
mocha 198
orange cordial 209
raspberry cordial 253
tea, pot of 244
dumplings 112
cheese and chive dumplings 112

eggplant dip 113
eggplant parmigiana 114
eggs
baked eggs 20
boiled eggs 34

poached eggs 235
scrambled eggs 285

feta, cheddar and chive muffins 115
fish
coconut fish curry 92
fish cakes 116
fish lasagne 117
fish pie 118
fish roasted in paper 119
gravlax 142
kedgeree 160
poached salmon with salsa verde 237
salade niçoise 276
spaghetti with tuna, rocket and lemon 301
tuna pâté 340
flaky pastry 120
flan, strawberry 314
focaccia 122
rosemary focaccia 122
fool, strawberry 315
freeform blueberry pie 124
french toast 126
fresh vietnamese spring rolls 127
friands 128
berry friands 128
fried rice 130
frittata 131
frosting see icing and frosting
fruit cake 132
fruit scones 284
fruit tart 134

garlic bread 135
garlic butter 135
garlic prawns 136
gazpacho 138
ginger cake 139

gingerbread biscuits 140
granita, watermelon and lime 350
granola 141
gravlax 142
gravy 144
greek salad 145
gremolata 162
grilled peaches 146
guacamole 148

hamburgers 150
harissa 304
hazelnut slice 151
herb butter 310
herb omelette 152
hokey-pokey ice-cream 154
hollandaise sauce 153
honeycomb 154
hot chocolate 156
hummus 157

ice-cream
    affogato 2
    hokey-pokey ice-cream 154
    lemon ice-cream 174
    orange and cardamom ice-cream 214
    passionfruit ice-cream 214
    raspberry sundae 256
    vanilla bean 342
icing and frosting
    chocolate ganache 79
    chocolate icing 82
    cream cheese icing 47
    lemon icing (frosting) 104
    lemon topping 167
    strawberry icing 104
indian-style lamb curry 158

jams
    apricot jam 10
    strawberry jam 316
jelly 159

kedgeree 160

laksa 161
lamb
    indian-style lamb curry 158
    lamb shanks 162
    roast leg of lamb 270
    shepherd's pie 287
    slow-roasted lamb 292
lamingtons 164
lasagne 166
    fish lasagne 117
    vegetarian lasagne 344
lemon
    chicken, lemon and rocket risotto 58
    lemon bars 167
    lemon cake 168
    lemon chicken 169
    lemon curd 170
    lemon delicious pudding 172
    lemon ice-cream 174
    lemon icing (frosting) 104
    lemon posset 176
    lemon tart 177
    lemon topping 167
lemonade 178
lime and watermelon granita 350

macaroni cheese 179
madeleines 180
maître d'hôtel butter 182
mango chutney 184
mango coulis 254

mango sorbet 185

marinated olives 186

marinated pork fillets 188

marmalade

    citrus marmalade 189

    onion marmalade 206

mashed potato 190

mayonnaise 192

    mustard mayonnaise 96

meatballs 193

meatloaf 194

meringues 195

    chocolate macaroons 79

    pavlova 220

minestrone 196

mocha 198

mousse, chocolate 80

muesli, bircher 31

muffins

    basic recipe 200

    blueberry muffins 200

    chocolate muffins 82

    feta, cheddar and chive muffins 115

    pecan muffins 200

mushroom and beef pie 28

mussels 204

    mussel broth 202

mustard dressing 142

mustard mayonnaise 96

nectarine sorbet 185

noodles

    bang bang chicken 25

    chicken noodle soup 62

    laksa 161

    singapore-style noodles 291

nuts, spiced 306

oil, chilli 69

olives, marinated 186

omelette, herb 152

onion marmalade 206

oranges

    marmalade 189

    orange biscuits 208

    orange and cardamom ice-cream 214

    orange cordial 209

    orange cupcakes 104

    orange curd 170

    orange and macadamia brownies 72

    orange poppy seed cake 210

    orange semolina cake 211

pancakes 212

pannacotta 213

passionfruit curd 170

passionfruit ice-cream 214

passionfruit syllabub 216

pasta

    bolognese sauce 36

    fish lasagne 117

    fresh pasta 217

    lasagne 166

    macaroni cheese 179

    pasta with zucchini 218

    spaghetti with crab and chilli 296

    spaghetti with garlic, chilli and oil 298

    spaghetti with tomato sauce 300

    spaghetti with tuna, rocket and lemon 301

    spaghetti vongole 295

    tomato sauce for pasta (pomodoro) 338

    vegetarian lasagne 344

pastry

    flaky pastry 120

    shortcrust pastry 290

shortcrust pastry (sweet) 290
pâté
    chicken liver pâté 60
    tuna pâté 340
pavlova 220
pea soup 221
peaches
    grilled peaches 146
    peach pie 222
    peach sorbet 185
    stuffed peaches 320
peanuts
    chocolate peanut butter cake 83
    peanut biscuits 224
pears
    poached pears 236
    roast pears with ginger 272
    upside-down pear cake 341
pecan muffins 200
pecan pie 226
pesto 227
pies
    apple pie 7
    beef and mushroom pie 28
    chicken pie 64
    fish pie 118
    freeform blueberry pie 124
    peach pie 222
    pecan pie 226
    shepherd's pie 287
piri piri sauce 228
pizza
    pizza base 229
    pizza bianca 230
    pizza margherita 232
    tomato pizza sauce 232
poached cherries 234
poached eggs 235

poached pears 236
poached salmon with salsa verde 237
polenta 238
pommes anna 239
pork
    braised pork chops with apple 38
    marinated pork fillets 188
    pork satays 240
    roast pork with crackling 274
    san choy bow 280
    slow-roasted pork 293
    terrine 328
porridge 242
portuguese chicken 228
portuguese custard tarts 243
pot of tea 244
potatoes
    mashed potato 190
    pommes anna 239
    potato gratin 246
    potato salad 247
    roast potatoes 275
    shepherd's pie 287
prawns
    garlic prawns 136
    prawn cocktail 248
    prawn toasts 249
    salt-baked prawns 278
    thai-style prawn broth 333
puddings
    bread and butter pudding 42
    chocolate fondant puddings 78
    chocolate puddings 84
    christmas pudding 88
    lemon delicious pudding 172
    lemon posset 176
    pannacotta 213
    rice pudding 260

sticky date pudding 313
summer pudding 322
tiramisu 334
pumpkin soup 250

quiche lorraine 252

raspberry cordial 253
raspberry coulis 254
raspberry sorbet 185
raspberry sundae 256
ratatouille 257
relish *see* chutneys and relishes
rhubarb and apple crumble 258
rice
fried rice 130
kedgeree 160
perfect fluffy rice 259
rice pudding 260
risotto 261
asparagus risotto 14
chicken, lemon and rocket risotto 58
risotto with sausage and red wine 262
roast beef fillet 264
roast beetroot 265
roast capsicum 266
roast chicken 268
roast leg of lamb 270
roast pears with ginger 272
roast pork with crackling 274
roast potatoes 275
rosemary focaccia 122

salads
asian-style coleslaw 93
caesar salad 46
carrot salad 48
coleslaw 93

couscous salad 97
greek salad 145
potato salad 247
salade niçoise 276
thai beef salad 330
thai-style chicken salad 332
salmon
gravlax 142
poached salmon with salsa verde 237
salsa verde 237
salt, seasoned 34
salt-baked prawns 278
salt and pepper squid 277
saltimbocca 279
san choy bow 280
sandwich, steak 312
satay sauce 282
satays, pork 240
sauces, savoury
barbecue sauce 26
bolognese sauce 36
bread sauce 43
chilli sauce 70
cocktail sauce 248
cranberry sauce 98
dipping sauce 127
gravy 144
hollandaise sauce 153
piri piri sauce 228
salsa verde 237
satay sauce 282
sweet chilli sauce 324
tomato pizza sauce 232
tomato sauce 300
tomato sauce for pasta (pomodoro)
338
vietnamese dipping sauce 348
see also dressings

sauces, sweet
    chocolate sauce 85
    raspberry coulis 254
    spiced apple sauce 303
sausages
    risotto with sausage and red wine 262
    sausage roast 283
scones 284
    cheese scones 284
    fruit scones 284
scrambled eggs 285
seafood
    garlic prawns 136
    mussel broth 202
    mussels 204
    prawn cocktail 248
    prawn toasts 249
    salt and pepper squid 277
    salt-baked prawns 278
    seafood chowder 286
    spaghetti with crab and chilli 296
    spaghetti vongole 295
    thai-style prawn broth 333
seasoned salt 34
shepherd's pie 287
shortbread 288
shortcrust pastry 290
silverside (corned beef) 96
singapore-style noodles 291
slices
    chocolate brownies 72
    hazelnut slice 151
    lemon bars 167
    orange and macadamia brownies 72
slow-roasted lamb 292
slow-roasted pork 293
slow-roasted tomatoes 294
smoothie, banana 24

sorbet
    mango sorbet 185
    nectarine sorbet 185
    peach sorbet 185
    raspberry sorbet 185
    strawberry sorbet 185
soufflé, cheese 52
soups
    bacon, leek and barley soup 15
    chicken noodle soup 62
    gazpacho 138
    minestrone 196
    mussel broth 202
    pea soup 221
    pumpkin soup 250
    seafood chowder 286
    spinach soup 308
    sweetcorn and chicken soup 326
    thai-style prawn broth 333
    tomato soup 339
spaghetti with crab and chilli 296
spaghetti with garlic, chilli and oil 298
spaghetti with tomato sauce 300
spaghetti with tuna, rocket and lemon 301
spaghetti vongole 295
spice cake 302
spiced apple sauce 303
spiced moroccan chicken 304
spiced nuts 306
spinach soup 308
sponge cake (genoise) 309
spring rolls, fresh vietnamese 127
steak 310
steak sandwich 312
sticky date pudding 313
stock, chicken 68
strawberry flan 314
strawberry fool 315

strawberry icing 104

strawberry jam 316

strawberry sorbet 185

stuffed dates 318

stuffed peaches 320

summer pudding 322

sundae, raspberry 256

sweet chilli sauce 324

sweetcorn *see* corn

swiss roll 327

syllabub, passionfruit 216

syrup cake 139

tarts

    apple tart 8

    fruit tart 134

    lemon tart 177

    portuguese custard tarts 243

    strawberry flan 314

tea, pot of 244

terrine 328

thai beef salad 330

thai green curry paste 331

thai-style chicken salad 332

thai-style prawn broth 333

tiramisu 334

toast

    cinnamon toast 90

    french toast 126

    prawn toasts 249

tomatoes

    gazpacho 138

slow-roasted tomatoes 294

tomato pizza sauce 232

tomato relish 326

tomato sauce 300

tomato sauce for pasta (pomodoro) 338

tomato soup 339

truffles, chocolate 86

tuna

    salade niçoise 276

    spaghetti with tuna, rocket and lemon 301

    tuna pâté 340

turnovers, apricot 11

upside-down pear cake 341

vanilla bean ice-cream 342

vegetarian lasagne 344

victoria sponge 346

vietnamese dipping sauce 348

vinaigrette 349

watermelon and lime granita 350

yoghurt

    lemon ice-cream 174

    spiced moroccan chicken 304

    yoghurt cheese 351

    yoghurt cream 352

yorkshire puddings 353

zaatar 34

zabaglione 354

Acknowledgements

Firstly I want to express my thanks to the editorial team at *The Weekend Australian* for carefully checking my words every week.

Big hugs and gratitude to the wonderful Julie Gibbs, a gorgeous, brave, optimistic and supportive soul, and the best publisher one could ever wish for. Also huge thanks to all the friendly Penguins in the Sydney office, both past and present, who have made sense of my mutterings, scribblings and frantic emails.

I want to send three cheers to Andre Martin for his patience, talent and great pictures. Hugs to my big-hearted friend Mary Harris for letting me raid her treasure trove of props and good things in kitchen cupboards.

I want to thank the generous and talented writers and cooks who have not only let me use their recipes, but have treated me with their friendship, knowledge, advice, gossip and an occasional glass of red wine – thank you Maggie Beer, Katie Stewart, Nigella Lawson, Fiona Beckett, Anna Del Conte, Lorna Wing, Jill Dupleix, Diana Wilson, Angela Boggiano, Nigel Slater and Terry Durack.

Thanks also to all my loyal readers for taking the time to send me your comments and emails.

To Francis Maietta, as always, for his support, humour, friendship, wisdom and love.